Paul Huggard

SINGING THE BLUES
The Long Walk Back
to Happiness on Hill 16
1974–2011

Halleluaj Press

About the author

Paul Huggard was born in 1965. He fell in love with The Dubs at the age of nine and they have been a constant in his life ever since. He is at his happiest and saddest standing on Hill 16. It all depends on what is happening on the field below. His main passions in life are sport and music. He was a secondary school teacher in Dublin for 19 years before leaving to follow his dreams. As well as writing, Paul now works as an educational tutor and mentor. He lives in Co. Carlow with his wife Jane and their son Samuel. This is his first book.

For more information visit **www.paulhuggard.com**

Dedicated to:
Mick Holden
(1955–2007)

First published in 2011 by
Halleluaj Press
Kilbride
Co. Carlow
Ireland

ISBN: 978-0-9566615-1-7
Cover/book design and layout: Guilder Design (www.guilderdesign.com)
Printed by: Opus Print Ltd.

Contents

Acknowledgements

I would like to thank everyone who has played a part in the creation of this book. In particular to Maurice Grehan, Eddie O'Neill and Niall O'Laoghaire for their enthusiasm, encouragement and attention to detail. It meant more to me than you will ever know.

Thanks also to Christopher Sweeney for his editing and advice; you pointed me in the right direction when I was in danger of losing my way.

Special thanks must go to Bernard Brogan Senior, Liam Gaskin and Therese Lynch for their kindness and invaluable help.

A big thank you to Duff and his lucky underpants (and to Michelle for buying them), Maurice, P.O., Niall and my brother John, as well as the supporting cast, for their friendship down through the years and for allowing me to tell my story.

Thanks to Pauline for all the weather advice, hot dinners, cups of tea and a bed for the night.

Thanks to all of those who have played their part in the Dublin Gaelic Football odyssey: players, management, backroom staff, clubs, suits and fans. Not to mention the other 30 counties and Meath. Without you there would be no story to tell.

I would also like to record my gratitude to the Hedigan family for all the pints and their permission for the photograph on the back cover.

And last but not least, Jane and Samuel for all their love, faith and patience. I couldn't have done it without you.

Foreword

The narrative of Dublin football over the last 37 years has never been dull. The seventies was a wonderful time to be a player with all the success and glamour that surrounded the Dublin team. In many ways that time has defined everything that has happened since. Subsequent Dublin teams have found themselves being measured against the deeds of what was done back then. It hasn't made their job any easier.

But the seventies weren't just about what happened on the field of play. The Hill was brought back to life by Heffo's Army and its tale has run parallel to events on the field ever since. As a result the Hill and the stands that tower above it have their own stories to tell.

Singing the Blues is a unique perspective on the Dublin story, a fan's view of the matches and the moments that have defined Dublin football over an extremely testing period. It brings back to life the thrills and the tension of Dublin's gladiatorial clashes with the other giants of Gaelic football. It will take you back to your own experiences, the good memories as well as the heart-breaking ones. It is an account of the people, managers, players and fans, who have played their part in the Dublin experience.

As well as delving into the past, it also traces the transition of the current squad from the turmoil of their devastating defeat to Kerry in 2009 through to their incredible All-Ireland success against the same opponents in 2011. In doing so it captures perfectly the excitement of that amazing day from the other side of the fence.

Singing the Blues will also be enjoyed by the rest of Ireland. If you like the thought of Dubliners feeling a bit of pain then there's plenty in this for you! The title says it all. Being a Dublin fan hasn't been easy, but it is days like this year's All-Ireland win that make it all worthwhile.

Singing the Blues is an entertaining and informative take on the high and lows of what has become an enduring story.

Bernard Brogan Senior

Chapter One

Aftermath

Sunday 18 September 2011

All-Ireland Senior Football Championship Final:
Dublin versus Kerry

The pub, like most other pubs in the general proximity of Croke Park, was heaving. The atmosphere on that late Sunday afternoon could best be described as moist, with pints, sweat and tears being swilled around. The noise, well the noise was indescribable, with shouting, cheering, singing and roaring being heard in equal measures. To anyone who walked in and for some reason had no idea what had just happened in Dublin that day, it must have been scary. Complete strangers were hugging, grown men were crying, people wore a look that hinted at some great glory. Kind of like a happy thousand yard stare. What had happened to cause this noise, this chaos, this outpouring of joy? We'd won. Simple as that. We'd been waiting 16 years for this day. Sam was finally home.

Chapter Two

The End Of The World

Monday 3 August 2009

All-Ireland Senior Football Championship Quarter-Final
Dublin versus Kerry

A goal behind after 36 seconds, this was always going to be a long afternoon. In truth, I felt like leaving for home there and then but I don't leave matches early. I always stay to the bitter end, even on the bad days. I felt sick to the pit of my stomach knowing that something awful was about to unfold before my very eyes. If I had been watching the game at home I would have been peeping out from behind the sofa but there is no hiding place on Hill 16. Fifteen minutes later and Kerry are out of sight, light years ahead of us on so many levels, they've being doing this to us for years now, leading us on a merry dance that leaves us chasing the ghosts of the seventies. Afterwards Pat Gilroy referred to his players in those early minutes as "startled earwigs". Whatever the hell that meant; it was a memorable phrase that has come to define Dublin's latest collapse.

At the beginning of the game we had been full of hope, beat Kerry and we were destined for our first All-Ireland final appearance since 1995. Pat Gilroy was the man to lead us there, a former player with an All-Ireland winner's medal in his pocket; he knew what it would take to return us to our former glory. Another in a long line of Dublin managers who had attempted to lay the ghost of the seventies, a time when Dublin were kings. He had gambled on staying loyal to the team who had capitulated against Tyrone a year earlier and it seemed to be working. Off the back of a training camp in La Manga and a fighting Leinster final win against Kildare the players seemed to be in a good place. In contrast Kerry were still licking the wounds of another All-Ireland final loss to Tyrone, their patchy form leaving even their loyal brethren reading the last rites. It felt like Dublin's time had finally come. We haven't had a better opportunity to beat Kerry in thirty-one years. Today was going to be the day.

Fourteen points down at half-time, and the Hill actually booed the team off.

The first time I had ever heard that happen in 27 years of attending Dublin games, a sign of the times when failure is no longer tolerated. It takes a lot for the Hill to turn on its heroes. Booing players who give their all for no financial reward doesn't come easy, a collective abandonment of a team that had given us five Leinster titles, but this fresh capitulation was a bridge too far for even the most committed Dub. Some soul-searching helped us realise the error of our ways during the break and we cheered the players back on. All year Pat Gilroy had been calm and collected, but now he lost it, telling his players that the performance was unacceptable, that they had let themselves down. Pride was the only thing left to fight for. But Kerry wouldn't even allow us that, as they win the second half as well.

Afterwards, as we shuffle out onto Clonliffe Road we meet the smug faces amongst the throng of triumphant Kerry supporters. It's one of the reasons I always head for the sea of blue that is the Hill, segregation has its advantages. I prefer to mourn in the comfort of my own home. But there is no getting away from these Kerry fans as we head up towards the canal on our way to Hedigans, a famous old pub that featured in James Joyce's Ulysses.

Kerry do smug better than any other county in Ireland. They expect to win and don't seem all that surprised when it happens. They don't even seem to enjoy it very much, just another day at the office, nothing to get over excited about. Beating the Dubs is nothing new. Twelve times the sides have met since 1975 with Kerry winning nine to Dublin's two with one drawn game. One of the Kerry players even saw fit to bounce the ball on his head in the closing stages. Rubbing our noses in it. We can only keep our heads down and walk on as we try to ignore the delight that threatens to break out all round us. I'd like it better if they would smile; it's not against the law to be happy when you win. It just seems such a travesty to waste winning on people who seem to take so little pleasure from it. Maybe they just hold onto their joy until they get home, or it could be that winning on a regular basis dulls the soul. Maybe The Sawdoctors were right. To win just once might be better after all.

It's time to get out of here and start the post-mortem. Beaten again, and by our old arch rivals Kerry. We haven't beaten the Kingdom in a championship match since the epic encounter in 1977. Even if that year's semi-final was one of the greatest games of all time, we seem to be paying a high price for it. Today was meant to be the day that the curse was lifted, but after such a demoralising collapse it feels like that day will never come. Beaten by a massive 17 points and it could have been worse: having kicked the daylights out of us in the first period, Kerry waltzed through the second half saving their energy for 'bigger' games ahead, leaving us to pick through the wreckage.

In truth the game was over after 36 seconds. That was all it took Kerry to cut through the Dublin defence and score a killer goal; 'Gooch' Cooper rolling the ball into an empty net in front of the massed ranks of shocked Dublin fans on the Hill. The first goal that Dublin had conceded all summer, and the last. Mike McCarthy had taken the ball at full tilt 25 yards from goal before transferring the ball to Cooper. Dublin's defence had parted like the Red Sea. The awful memory of David Beggy's crucial goal for Meath in the classic 1991 encounter came to mind as I watched Cooper wheel away in delight. Sport has a habit of dragging you back to the past. Never the future. Always the past.

All week we had listened to various media pundits writing this Kerry team off. No matter how hard you try, it gets in on you, raises the expectations. Dublin had been installed as overwhelming favourites off the back of their Leinster final win over an improving Kildare side, a game that had revealed a new steel to this Dublin team, as Ger Brennan's sending off forced his 14 colleagues to dig deep to see the Lilywhites off in a stirring encounter. Many of the older guard, Whelan, Griffin, Cullen, had stood tall in a gripping last 10 minutes. It seemed that Pat Gilroy, Dublin's rookie manager, had changed the complexion of a team that too often doubted itself when the going got tough. But now we knew that beating Kildare had been a false dawn. It had taken Kerry only 36 seconds to expose our soft underbelly.

Should have seen it coming I suppose.

Kerry had played the role of underdog to perfection in the days leading up to the massacre. Pat Spillane wrote off their chances the minute the draw came out; the game was afoot. Dublin's year? According to the media every year is meant to be Dublin's year, but on the Hill we knew better than to get ahead of ourselves. We knew that Kerry would relish a shot at the Dubs in Croker. What better way to reignite the hunger of a team that had sleepwalked through the qualifiers?

To make matters worse this was the second time in 12 months that this had happened. A year earlier Tyrone had appeared on the quarter-final horizon in frighteningly similar circumstances: former champions in need of reassurance. Who better to give them the lift they needed than the good old Dubs? And we duly obliged: 3-14 to 1-08. Another hammering, the feeling of desolation was similar to today's.

In some ways a heavy defeat is a little easier to take than the nail biting one point loss that empties the soul of all hope. A trouncing allows you to digest the outcome at a relatively early stage of the proceedings leaving the rest of the afternoon to work on your mental state before the time to leave the ground comes round. By the time you are walking out the gates you are already moving on, better to start the healing as early as possible. But today was not like that; another thumping following on so soon from the Tyrone nightmare was too much even for the well-adjusted to digest with any sense of balance.

It was the end of the road for this group of players; that much was clear. New faces would have to be brought in or we were heading for the wilderness again. Had Gilroy learned anything from this? His decision to stand by the team he had inherited from Pillar Caffrey was an understandable one. The players deserved another chance. But instead of kicking on, Gilroy had been repaid with another collapse of monumental proportions, something had to change and fast. Wandering out of the Hill there wasn't even the odd "there's always next year" to be heard. A low murmur filled the air as a crowd lost in introspection headed for home. Even the cider boys seemed shocked and stunned.

The trouble had started with the quarter-final draw, it always does. With the exception of Westmeath in 2006 and Derry in 2007, we have faced Kerry or Tyrone in the other five quarter-finals we have competed in since 2004. Beaten each time by the eventual champions, we have become a stepping-stone for the two heavyweights of the modern game. I was waiting for the draw this year when my wife Jane asked me what I was watching, "Waiting for Dublin to draw Kerry," I replied. The person drawing the second ball even had the audacity to utter "Ah. The big one!" Sure enough, my worst fears were confirmed. All as grimly predictable as the thrashing we eventually got.

Hedigans at last, an oasis of misery in a desert of disappointment, not much solace to be found here today, apart from the relief that only beer can bring, bar men rush frantically from customer to customer, trying to feed the pain as fast as they can. Only the odd Kerry man lightens the mood. Blue shirted warriors look deep into their pints, not knowing what to say, not knowing where to begin the inquest. We've been here so many times before that it's starting to feel like home. I look around the room; it looks like a scene from 'One Flew over the Cuckoo's Nest' as the bewildered try to take it all in… it didn't make any sense. Seventeen Fucking Points. Nineteen seventy-eight all over again.

I sit back and look at Duff, taking comfort in a pint of Guinness. We've been making the annual pilgrimage to Hill 16 since the early nineties. I met Duff through a mutual friend and once I found out that he was a Dub our friendship was cemented. Up until then I had been going to Dublin games alone. Duff looks a little older than he did a couple of hours earlier, 47 going on 60, the lines on his furrowed brow etched that little bit deeper.

Right now I can't see beyond today, need to let the disappointment run through my system before I can even think of letting it go. It will sit there for days, reminding me of what might have been, first thing in the morning, last thing at night, something precious gone. I needed to find a way out, that's what friends are for. Ger will know what to do. As a former teacher and Waterford hurling fan he has the experience and the sense of humour I am looking for, sees the beauty in a broken heart. I had tried my best to commiserate with him following the humbling of his hurling heroes in the 2008 All-Ireland final, but all to no avail. It's impossible to heal another man's sporting pain, for weeks he was unable to speak about it, never wanting to go to another game again, before gradually the fog lifted as a new season dawned. His only friend during those lonely winter months had been his cynicism, it was his way of dealing with the emptiness that comes with the end of the world, that and the realisation that nothing as bad could ever happen again.

But then half the fun of sport is talking about where it all went wrong; in some ways it can even feel better than a win. Men use sport to unload their weary minds. This is where we can speak about our feelings. A man's sporting ties say a lot about his approach to life. Most like to be on the winning side, but there is a lot of succour to found in losing; it allows the pain to come out. After a few well-earned pints we shake ourselves down and before long we were reminiscing about some of the great losses we have suffered over the years. Badges of honour. The good days forgotten as we looked deep within. As the night closed in our minds turned to the months ahead as we tried to place today in our pantheon of all-time great defeats. We've moved on before, no reason why we can't do it again. The victories seem to slip away all too soon after the initial ecstasy has gone. It's the defeats that linger, make the good days worthwhile. Without them we would have no reason to live for the good times. Our top 10 list of losses takes some beating, makes for miserable reading. But sometimes pleasure lurks in the most mysterious of places.

That's another problem with Kerry, they do post-mortems better than anyone. A winter without Sam gives them the opportunity to look deep within, to question their very existence. If they lose, they hold onto their loss, they own it, and they clothe it in the poetic rhetoric of defeat. They seem to enjoy losing more than winning. Losing brings out a graciousness that lies hidden on the good days. When they win they seem to want to fight the world. When they lose they hang their troubles out on the washing line and stare at them all winter, make sense of what went wrong and come out all guns blazing in the new season. No opponent is more dangerous than a Kerry footballer with a ferocious thirst for redemption in his heart. As for us, we never seem to learn from our mistakes, greeting each new season with renewed optimism regardless of the facts. We're a different breed. We sweep our problems under the carpet, hoping that they'll mysteriously disappear. Up in Dublin we seem to like making the same mistakes over and over again.

Chapter Three

Out Of The Blue

Sunday 22 September 1974

All-Ireland Senior Football Championship Final
Dublin versus Galway

It was during the bleak early seventies that I fell in love with the Dubs. There wasn't much fun to be had in a country run by police and priests. We lived in Lucan, one of the new middle class suburbs springing up in west Dublin. In GAA terms, I came from the wrong side of the tracks, a Protestant who attended a rugby-playing, fee paying secondary school. So, no All-Ireland medals for me then. But my Dad was instrumental in introducing me to Gaelic football, although as he entered his late sixties he no longer went to any matches. Our family loved its sport; we gathered around the telly as one and watched whatever was going: football, hurling, soccer, racing, show-jumping, tennis, boxing and cricket. We didn't discriminate; there was no such thing as a foreign game in our house.

I learned the value of safety in numbers when it came to viewing big sporting occasions and that sport was not for the faint-hearted. Watching the Dutch being beaten by West Germany in the 1974 World Cup final demonstrated that the good guys don't always win, very few fairy tales come true. A valuable lesson for a Dublin fan.

But it wasn't all bad news as a lanky Republic of Ireland striker called Don Givens took us to places we had never been with successive hat-tricks against the U.S.S.R. and Turkey. Such magical days seemed to be in direct contrast to everyday life, anything seemed possible. The summer of 1974 would be the ultimate demonstration of the healing power of sport for me as the Dublin football team played a huge part in bringing a struggling city back to life.

Cork were the reigning All-Ireland football champions that summer as Dublin started out as no-hopers. Since their last success in 1963, Dublin had been cast adrift in the GAA doldrums. I was nine years-old. Nine was young in those days as you were allowed to grow up in your own time; all was sweetness, light and innocence in the life of your average Dublin young fella. Ireland may have been stuck in a never-ending recession but it didn't seem to matter. We had plenty of other things to make us happy.

Sport gave us hope. And I was clued-in enough to know when something out of the ordinary was happening. I listened very carefully to what my Dad and two older brothers were saying. I was busy trying to be a man. Anything that could help me towards that goal was taken on board. Apparently, something was stirring in the world of Dublin football. To tell you the truth, until then, I hadn't even been aware that Dublin had a football team and now here they were in with a chance of winning something called the All-Ireland.

My Dad was full of wonderful sporting insights. He was a typical father of that generation, unsure how to connect with us, he loved us but he just couldn't figure out how to break out of the straight jacket he was in. Being a bank manager probably hadn't helped. It was left to Mum, a wonderful woman, to give us the affection we needed. It was sport that brought out my father's caring side and allowed us to share his world. I remember when he crept into our room one night to tell us that Ali had beaten Smoking Joe Frazier, news too big to wait until morning. It was a time when big news was really big news, it travelled so slowly then. The whole country would sit down together to watch the evening bulletin, to watch events in Ireland and the wider world: Nixon leaving the White House, Bloody Sunday, Watergate, the Dublin and Monaghan Bombings. Events that left a mark on all of us.

Events in Dalymount Park seemed almost as exciting as those in America as Liam Brady did for those pesky Soviets on a glorious autumnal Wednesday afternoon, our contribution to the Cold War. But not even my father had seen this Dublin team coming. It seemed that their wily manager, a man called Kevin Heffernan had caught everyone on the hop. Even the players seemed surprised by their sudden change in fortune. But it was only when Dublin upset Cork in the semi-final that the world sat up and began to take notice. Excitement gripped the city as we looked forward to the third Sunday in September. The rest of the country buried their heads in their hands and feared the worst.

Only Galway stood between the Dubs and history. I may have been young and innocent but I was still old enough to know when a bandwagon was starting to roll and I was determined to be on it. Jumping on a bandwagon is part of the Irish DNA. We just hop on, no questions asked. And so it was with the Dubs back in September 1974. I booked my place in front of the TV and waited for the big day. I could tell my father was fascinated with this Heffernan fellow. He liked someone who went their own way. Heffo was certainly something different, carried himself with a confidence that suggested anything was possible. It helped that he resembled a student revolutionary, his anorak and slacks fitting nicely with his wispy hairstyle. Heffo was cool in a seventies sort of way, a bit of a character, a leader of men. We had the likes of Busby and Shankly to look up to across the water, but now it seemed that we had a sporting Messiah of our very own. Heffo and I had something in common, with both of us reared far from the world of the GAA. His father was more hunting and shooting than Gaelic football and it was only when his family moved to Marino that the young Kevin came into contact with the game that would define his life. His playing days for St. Vincent's and Dublin are the stuff of legend, culminating in an All-Ireland final victory over Derry, but it was the 1955 loss to Kerry that he carried in his heart as he started out as Dublin manager in 1974. Heffernan's day job in the ESB may have contributed to providing Dublin with the electricity it needed, but what he was about to do was to give the city a power surge that it would never forget. Such was the tide of support building up behind the Dublin team that I began to feel a little bit of sympathy for Galway. I was always a sucker for an underdog.

As I sat in front of the TV on the day of the final any compassion I felt was quickly forgotten. Galway were far from being harmless fodder for the city masses and an early Michael Rooney goal for the Tribesmen shocked us to our core. But Dublin kept their cool and picked off a number of valuable points to stay in the hunt even though they trailed at half-time. Midway through the second half, disaster struck. Galway were awarded a penalty. Time stood still as Liam Salmons placed the ball down. Apparently Salmons had never missed a penalty. The Dublin goalkeeper Paddy Cullen was wandering along his goal-line like a man waiting anxiously for a CIE bus to turn up. Salmon hit the ball at a nice height, allowing Dublin's goalkeeper to dance to his left to push the ball away: "He's saved it! He's saved it! Oh Paddy Cullen!" roared the disembodied voice of RTÉ commentator Michael

O'Hehir in celebration. Michael celebrated everything that happened on a football field. Even a plastic bag blowing across the pitch would enthral Michael as if it had some part to play in the unfolding story. This was his world, the place where he came alive. His voice danced across the grass that was being graced by the gods he was born to describe. A voice that made you feel as if you knew each of the players personally, always poetic, never pretentious, always straightforward; he called a spade a spade and a shemozzle a shemozzle. He wanted the players to do well and he wanted great games, willing the players on to great deeds. He was a dramatist, a wizard of the spoken word and he had a talent for making even the most pedestrian match sound epic. He introduced us to the Dublin players in 1974 and kept us up to speed with their progress through a wondrous decade of Gaelic football. I missed him when he was gone.

Michael was right. It was a stunning save. And pandemonium ensued as the blue and navy crêpe paper hats bounced up and down on the Canal End terrace behind the goal. As well as our own Shankly, we now had our very own Pat Jennings. Galway hearts were broken and Dublin hearts swelled with pride. "Another point by Jimmy Keaveney; the man who came back." Jimmy was Dublin's sharp shooter, a rotund figure who had been enticed out of retirement by Heffo, the final piece in the jigsaw. The last few minutes passed in a sky blue blur as Dublin knocked over the points that guaranteed that the Sam Maguire trophy was destined to return to the capital city for the first time since 1963. O'Hehir summed it all up with: "The Jacks are back and the way they are playing now, the Galway backs are jacked."

I remember the Hill pouring onto the end line in the last few minutes as they waited to acclaim their heroes at the final whistle, anxious stewards doing their best to hold back the happy hordes. Martin Sludden, the referee at the centre of the 2010 Leinster final debacle between Meath and Louth, could have learnt a lot from his counterpart in the 1974 decider. With the Galway keeper lining up a kick out, the yellow shirted official took off for the centre of the pitch with a sprint before turning towards the tunnel. His final act of the day came with a flurry of his arms as he blew the whistle with his back to the play as the ball sailed towards centre field. He was immediately surrounded by a number of Garda officers. It was textbook stuff. He wasn't the only one to make it home safely that day. After 11 long years Sam was back in the capital.

The 1974 success was a hugely significant boost for a city that was on its knees. Memories of the bombings and the terrible loss of life earlier that year were still fresh in our minds. My father was in town that day, but thankfully he left for home just before the bombs went off. We were never more relieved to see him walking back in through the front gate of our Lucan home. The city was badly in need of some heroes. People were proud to be from Dublin again; they pushed their chests out and felt good. They had found a new identity as part of Heffo's army. At long last it finally felt as if they mattered.

I was no different, the sheer excitement of seeing Dublin captain Seán Doherty lift the Sam Maguire has stayed with me to this day. I was never the same again. From now on I was a Dub. Minutes later I was out in my back garden replaying the game. I was Brian Mullins, my brothers were Galway, and Dad was Michael O'Hehir. Mum was making the tea.

That a wonderful Kerry team should arrive on the scene a year later was an act of God; two great teams going toe to toe in a never-to-be forgotten era. Nineteen seventy-four was no one off; this story was only just beginning. It could be argued that the Dublin-Kerry rivalry saved the seventies. They allowed us to enjoy ourselves, gave the decade a beauty that it probably didn't deserve. The stage was set up for a shoot-out that would swing one way and then the other before Dublin's older team finally ran out of steam, but not before they had given us more memories than we knew what to do with, leaving us to spend the next thirty years desperately trying to recapture the glory days.

It is interesting to hear the players talking about the mantra that Heffo drummed into them before the '74 final: One Opportunity. They proved that was not the case, but in sport you never know. One day, one game can change the course of history. That day in September 1974 was such a day. Heffernan, who knew that they couldn't afford to let it pass them by, had a sixth sense that allowed him to drive his players on. Paddy Cullen's penalty save soon passed into legend. Paddy was one of us. He lived right beside my school. I walked past his house everyday on my way home. I could only dream of meeting my English soccer heroes, but these guys lived amongst us, and they had achieved all this.

As for me, that one afternoon had me hooked for life.

Chapter Four

What's Another Year?

Sunday 13 June 2010

Leinster Senior Football Championship Quarter-Final
Dublin versus Wexford

I was working in Berlin when the 2010 National League got underway. I thought I had a dodgy internet connection when I saw the opening result, a win against Kerry in Killarney. Nothing for Kerry to worry about, only a league game after all. But for Dublin's fledgling squad it was a big deal, our first win on Kingdom soil since 1982. News of the Gilroy revolution was spreading as far as Germany with Dublin's manager ripping it up and starting again. Big names were gone, their careers ended by the Kerry debacle, to be replaced by fresh faces of youth. In October Dublin's boss took his new look team to Corduff in Monaghan for a challenge match. The type of night when nothing else matters except trying to convince your manager that you are worth persevering with. Both sides tore into each other as if their lives depended on it. Apparently the capitulation against Kerry was addressed. Pints were had. The battle lines were drawn. Winning on the road was set down as a marker. Things would be different from now on.

Despite the distance from the German capital to Parnell Park I managed to follow Dublin's progress with an increasing sense of incredulity as the weeks passed. The Kerry win wasn't just a one-off and all-in-all they were doing quite well. But that's the thing about the National League, there's always an element of doubt, it's hard to know how seriously each team is taking the whole thing. But at least we were winning and that was something.

I live in Carlow these days, a Dub in exile, so my journeys to the home of football take a lot longer than they used to. But when the first match day of a new summer rolls around I am more than ready. Time and distance doesn't dampen my spirit. If anything it has added to the anticipation. So once again I free my wrinkled blue tee-shirts from their winter hibernation for their first iron of the year. I am a bit of a sucker for Carroll's, the souvenir shop that flogs everything Irish. Deciding what tee-shirt to wear is a big moment. I have never been one for the replica shirt. I prefer to be different, looking for that little bit of class that only a Carroll's tee-shirt can bring. There are some ground rules, it has to be blue and it has to have the word 'Dublin' on it. Anything else on the Hill just wouldn't be acceptable. I wave goodbye to my wife Jane before climbing into the car. My baby son Samuel stares at me from his seat in the back, asking himself what new adventure today will bring. I'll be dropping him off at a friend's along the way. He might not know it yet but he is losing his father to football for the day.

Samuel's entry into the world was a long drawn out affair. He had been due to arrive in the twenty-four hours prior to the previous year's opening championship outing against Meath. I watched on television as Dublin scraped home by two points. Two weeks later he still hadn't appeared meaning that I missed the Westmeath game. With a mouth-watering Leinster final against an improving Kildare side next up, I was wondering if Samuel was hell-bent on scuppering my footballing summer. Thankfully he arrived with a week to spare and I was free to make the annual pilgrimage to Croke Park to see Dublin record their fifth successive Leinster title. In the hours before we put Samuel in the car to drive him home from the hospital some culchie smart-arse texted me. The message was short but it cut right through my soul: "That'll be the only Sam you'll be bringing home this year!" There's always one.

I can feel a sense of early summer coursing through my veins as I drive out the gate; football has that effect. The brighter evenings signal a return to summer, that and the anticipation of another season watching the Dubs chasing All-Ireland glory. We've hardly seen the sun in two years, but to be fair the weather has been looking up a wee bit this year. There were two whole days last week when it didn't rain. When it comes to warm summer days and Dublin football it pays to be an optimist.

Those of us who stand on Hill 16 tend to hope more than we believe, without hope we would have nothing. Sam hasn't been seen in the capital since 1995, the glorious seventies a distant memory at this stage. The rest of the country sees us as arrogant and yet we are nothing of the sort. What have we got to be arrogant about? Fifteen long years. Believe me, the tribe that gathers on Hill 16 each summer has long since lost any sense of superiority that existed back in the golden age of the seventies when the best Dublin team of all time captured the hearts and minds of a city, as well as three All-Ireland titles in four years. Nowadays their legacy hangs like an albatross around the necks of the current squad, every move set against the backdrop of past deeds. One All-Ireland would sweep away the weight of expectation that weighs them down. But right now the third Sunday in September seems to be as further away as ever.

Better to take it one game at a time. Wexford will be no pushovers. We wouldn't want to lose the run of ourselves in early June, that's the press boys' job, the *Evening Herald* hacks salivating over the thoughts of a Dublin team going all the way, twelve page pull-outs and extra sales. My mind drifts back to last August, green and gold jerseys trampling all over our broken dreams. I try my best to push the 'Gooch' Cooper out of my mind before Samuel brings me back to reality. He needs a bottle before we get to the babysitter.

The sight of exiled Dubs standing at the bus stop in Castledermot whets my appetite; the first time I saw one I thought he was lost. And then it dawned on me. The poor fecker was actually living deep in the heart of Kildare. Refugees of the Tiger years, forced further and further from the city in search of affordable homes, the traditional migration towards the east reversed as Dubs settled into their new surroundings. The terms 'blow in' and 'dulchie' (a coming together of Dub and culchie) became more commonplace as our country brethren voiced their disapproval. We were welcome to visit but staying was a whole different matter altogether. Suddenly the shoe was on the other foot. But it wasn't all bad news, with the plantation of Meath almost complete.

Thankfully the early planters were there to show the newcomers the ropes, I should know, my brother was one of them. John now finds himself living in Enfield. The thought of having to visit him so deep in enemy territory turned my stomach at first, but you know what, it feels more like a suburb of Dublin every day as sky-blue jerseys, the requisite attire of the exiled Dub, mix with even stronger northside accents to create a home from home. The quiet infiltration of Dubs into the Royal county had gone almost unnoticed until one morning the natives climbed out of their beds to find that the feckers were everywhere. It was no longer safe to go to the pub. The local GAA clubs were infested with Jackeen whipper-snappers learning to give as good as they got. The next generation of Dubs will be made of sterner stuff, tougher, more battle-hardened and street wise. And all because they grew up in Meath.

As for my own exile to the sticks, it is the happy price I've paid for falling for Jane, a fun loving Carlow girl. Living in the country allows us to have our cats and dogs as well as the sense of space I craved for as I entered my forties. Life in the Dublin suburbs had become a little jaded with too much time spent sitting in endless traffic jams on the way to another lifeless shopping centre. Either that or I was having a mid-life crisis. Better to have it in the countryside I thought. It wasn't like I was moving to the other side of the world; I would only be an hour's drive from my favourite city. It wasn't all plain sailing though. When Jane asked me what it would take for me to move down from Dublin I thought long and hard before answering "Sky Sports." A week later it was installed.

On the Moone by-pass, I am mulling over the changes on the Dublin team. We will be taking to the field against Wexford with five debutants and a couple of others with very little experience of championship football. The full-back line has been totally revamped with Rory O'Carroll coming in at full-back, alongside Michael Fitzsimons and Philly McMahon. Cian O'Sullivan comes in at centre-half back, another new name that will test the experts on the Hill. Calling a player by the wrong name is an embarrassing mistake and we'll need to study the programme closely today. For years now the names have been rolling off our tongues, but today is different, the kind of day when you need to have your homework done. Either that or keep your mouth shut. I'll take it easy; get to know the new guys before I lay my cards on the table. My only worry is my friend P.O., Antrim man and Sonny Knowles lookalike, who has the annoying habit of asking out loud: "Who's that guy?" It's bad enough that he is parading his own ignorance without showing us up as well; his northern twang ricocheting off the sharper Dublin accents that surround us. His untimely enquiry is usually met with a stony silence as we try to pretend we haven't heard the question, leaving Duff to shuffle through the programme as he tries desperately to find the Dublin team. Duff always buys the programme. He's one of the few. Apparently Dublin fans don't buy programmes, yet another culchie conspiracy theory. But it's all to no avail, we have been snared, as some stranger puts us straight. The tone of his voice is mocking, puts us in our place.

New faces and new tactics; Gilroy has taken the lessons to be learnt from last year to heart. Ever the pragmatist rumour has it that he commissioned an in-depth study of what went wrong against Kerry. The answer must have been everything. The solution is that we are going to model ourselves on Tyrone. In a revolutionary move players will be picked in their specialist positions, no more square pegs in round holes; the main aim being to tighten up the defensive side of our game. With this in mind Dublin have been pulling bodies back behind the ball and tackling with a new-found intensity. Being competitive is the name of the game, meaning swagger will be a thing of the past.

Gilroy has been at pains to dampen down the usual hype that attends Dublin's entry into the championship, emphasising that this year is going to be a 'work in progress'. I get the feeling we might be hearing this term a lot over the next few months. Still anything is better than a bunch of startled earwigs.

I like Pat, he seems like a sensible kind of bloke. I like his low key approach, he seems to have a life outside of football, an astute businessman who goes home to his family at the end of the day. Football is kept in proportion. Such an approach allows him to step back and breath, to see the bigger picture. The Dublin job has consumed many of his predecessors, left them battered and broken. Pat seems to know where he wants this team to go, getting there is the problem. The jury is still out on whether we need a sixth Leinster title in a row. Some feel that a trip through the back door might harden the younger players up. I'm not so sure, Dublin sides are all about momentum, more 'all or nothing' than 'work in progress', especially a young team that needs to build its confidence. We have to be careful what we wish for. Armagh in Crossmaglen on a wind swept Saturday evening isn't my idea of fun. This season requires Gilroy to be braver than any Dublin manager has been for years. He has to stick to his young guns, come hell or high water, he cannot afford to turn to the old guard at the first hint of trouble.

As I moved towards Naas my sense of excitement intensified as my thoughts turned to my favourite place in the whole wide world. It feels like I'm coming home each time I set foot on the hallowed concrete of Hill 16. It's where my heart beats; it's where I feel most Irish. As a southern Protestant the Hill would not be seen as my natural habitat; indeed my Methodist mother worried about my father allowing me to attend games on a Sunday, the day of rest. But she soon relented once she saw the enjoyment my visits to Croke Park brought me. Still I'm not in bad company, apparently Sam Maguire kicked with his left foot as well.

If ever a bunch of people needed collective counselling then it is the faithful hordes on the Hill. It's a passionate place, but passion comes with a price. The last few years haven't been easy. A lot of us look older now. Take Duff for example. He aged about five years during one particularly traumatic game against Kildare, years that he has never been able to claw back.

Dubs on Hill 16 come in all shapes and sizes. A band of brothers made up of wonderful characters.

In the last few years **Late Dub** (sometimes referred to as **Beer belly Dub**) has come to the fore, his final pint is the one before his last, leading to a number of games being delayed. This has driven our country folk demented, given them yet another stick to beat us with. Somewhat ironically late Dub is always the first to complain when Dublin start slowly, probably the consequence of their warm-up routine being thrown out the window due to the delay.

Dulchie Dub is a product of the Tiger years, but with house prices falling in the capital they may become a relic of our recent past as they return to their natural habitat. I fit neatly into this category. I'm still working on the beer belly.

Working Class Dub was popular in the seventies but there are signs that he is making a comeback as the recession takes hold, proud of his roots and mad as hell. He is a close cousin of angry Dub who is angry with the world, you name it, and he can get angry about it.

Serious Dub subscribes to the Shankly way of thinking. Football isn't a matter of life and death, it's far more important than that. The first "You Fuckin' Eejit" of the season is never far away. These guys moan their way through the afternoon, their pessimism knows no bounds, meaning that they are often happier when things go wrong. Take them into a world where Dublin win and they would be nothing. It can be a little weird being surrounded by thousands of taxi drivers.

Not So Funny Dub is a different creature altogether. Although they may seem slightly funny at first, you soon realise that the tumbleweed is never far away. Any signs of encouragement are to be avoided, laugh and you will regret it for the rest of the afternoon as they regale you with their full repertoire. Stuck between a rock and a hard place, it's enough to send me running back into the welcoming arms of the Jack Dee brigade.

Lady GAA GAA Dub is all make-up and slapstick. These girls bring a bit of the X-factor to the Hill, something that's always needed in such a testosterone-driven environment. The Jackies as they like to be called wear the newest Dublin shirt, chatter into their mobiles nonstop, hardly ever look at the game and spend the whole afternoon holding a smoking cigarette under P.O.'s nose. One day six of them slid past us, as they squeezed through each of the girls uttered a polite "Sorry… Tanks". Teaching colleague and self-confessed Kildare man Ciaran was last in line, a man with a sense of humour that has always been drier than a camel's arse in a sand storm. He took one final lingering look at the last ass disappearing into a deep blue sea before uttering "There go the WAGS".

Teenage Dub comes in various guises, polite, painful, arrogant or withdrawn depending on their mood. They don't do happy unless they're pissed and then they are just annoying. Some of them carry off the moody look of an Afghani dope smuggler so well that I find myself looking to see where their camel is parked.

Laid Back Dub takes it all in his stride. For them an afternoon on the Hill is to be enjoyed rather than endured. Laid Back Dub is the guy you want to be standing beside when the going gets tough. They are usually built like a brick shithouse and exude an inner calm that comes with being comfortable with your place in the world. Whatever will be will be.

Musical Dub is the one with the bodhrán.

Drunken Dub and **Dopey Dub** go hand in hand. One has the potential to beat the shit out of you if you are unfortunate enough to catch his eye, the other will probably give you a chemically enhanced hug if you stray too near. Both of these are usually found in the opium den that exists behind the Railway goal, a part of the Hill that nobody in their right mind would go.

Another friend of ours Maurice got his coordinates wrong one day and led us into its midst. Let's just say it won't be happening again.

Optimistic Dub hasn't been seen since the seventies.

There are loads of women on the Hill. They tend to be the sensible ones. Someone has to be.

The Hill is our home. Not surprisingly, the other 31 counties have a different view. Some rival supporters don't like to admit it but many of them view us with a certain degree of wonder and envy. For others the Hill is an evil place, full of pint drinking, cocaine snorting, pot-bellied heroin addicts who can't keep time. It's not as if the GAA can do without Dublin, with crowds closer to 80,000 being the norm once the blue bandwagon starts rolling in earnest. But still the wider GAA family bitches and moans about all the negatives that the Dubs bring to the game. There aren't any. It's not like we win anything anyway.

It's time to pick up P.O. A former teacher and colleague, a real friend who has been a constant in my life for over thirty years now, just like the Dublin football team. P.O.'s unusual, an outsider who likes Dublin. Despite his northern roots he has adopted the Dubs as his second team. He's a scientist, likes to break a game down, until he's examined every last bit of it. In the last few years he has tended to sit in the stands, but today we have enticed him back to stand amongst the great unwashed. He doesn't like the view from the Hill, thinks you can see nothing from there. But it's not about the view, it's about the people. Duff will be with us. I have made it back from Berlin with a week to spare. I felt refreshed, more than ready for whatever the day would bring. Little did I know that the Dubs were about to unleash a whole season's worth of emotion on us in one crazy afternoon.

The number of Dublin shirts at the bus stops multiplies dramatically as we pass through Lucan and Palmerstown, the new suburban breeding grounds. I predict a Dublin win by six points. P.O. is not so sure. Two years earlier Dublin had destroyed Wexford in a one-sided Leinster final. But any team with Matty Forde is dangerous. Wexford will be no pushovers. Without the likes of Ciarán Whelan, Shane Ryan and Jason Sherlock the Dublin team has lost its central spine. In addition Alan Brogan, Mossy Quinn and Bryan

Cullen find themselves warming the bench as Gilroy goes for broke. But there is still a fair amount of experience for the younger players to fall back on should the going get tough with Stephen Cluxton in goal and Barry Cahill, Ross McConnell, Conal Keaney and Bernard Brogan set to start. One of my favourites, David Henry has been appointed captain. Henry, a permanent fixture in the full-back line in recent years, starts in the half-forward line as Gilroy turns the attack into defence. Maybe square pegs aren't a thing of the past after all.

As usual the Sunday papers are heaping the pressure on Dublin's young guns. Often such a level of expectation proves to be too much too soon. Take young Diarmuid Connolly, an extremely talented footballer, but after being painted as the next saviour of Dublin football he sunk without trace in his first season, before showing signs that he was coming to terms with what was expected of him the following year. But still he has much to prove. It remains to be seen whether he will play a part in Pat's revolution.

We drive up alongside Heuston station before turning onto the quays and heading towards Phibsborough. P.O. is still talking as we get out of the car, he never stops, not even to draw breath. We have arrived at Duff's. Duff is Samuel's godfather, a man of honour and good values. He doesn't ask for much in life: his only vice is a few pints of Guinness, a cigarette and a trip to the Golden Chip after the pub. I unload my overnight bag and push the wing mirrors of the car in for safe-keeping before ringing the door bell. Duff's mum Pauline opens the door, great to see her again after a long winter. Like her son, Pauline is an avid follower of the Dubs' fortunes. The only difference is that she does it from the relative comfort of her armchair from which she kicks every ball. Pauline knows her football, laughs at the psychotic nature of recent Dublin teams. She's seen it all before, nothing surprises her. She would have got on well with my father. Pauline is also our weather girl. As we tuck into lunch, she anxiously surveys the skies before regaling us with her rarely wrong forecast. We say our goodbyes as we step out the front door into another season. Three men, one poncho, the outlook doesn't look good.

Above us the skies carry a sense of foreboding; the poncho will be out in force today. We wander past Hedigans before heading down the canal. My heart misses a beat as I catch my first site of the coliseum in the distance, cloaked in a grey mist as the conversation turns to the state of the Irish economy. No point in going there, better to stick to the football. The canal is quieter than usual, the cider drinkers driven underground by the threat of the deluge to come or maybe they just can't afford it anymore.

I stop to look at the merchandising stalls on the way up to Quinn's. Nothing new today, the usual hats, scarves and rosettes. I cast a derisory eye at the straw hats on display, relics of the past, we might as well bring their crêpe paper cousins back. Unlike their straw counterparts they had a certain style to them, as if they were the uniform of an invading army with 'Up the Dubs' stamped across the front, the first drops of rain unleashed a dye that trickled down the wearer's face, all part of the seventies experience. As the modern sky threatens to unleash its fury I buy the new century's equivalent of the crêpe hat, a poncho. They may look ridiculous but they work. All the blue ones are gone, forcing me to settle for a white one. Any port in a storm; just as well Kildare have already bitten the dust.

Four hours after I left Carlow I finally set foot on the Hill. Forty-nine thousand turn up in the end; the hard-core, not bad for a Leinster quarter-final. Still a significant drop from the sixty thousand that would have been expected over the last few years, with people picking and choosing their games more carefully now, mindful of the pennies. Meath and Laois are also here today. Pockets of green shirts are dotted around the Hill, huddled together for protection, "Hill 16 is Dublin only" is sung with a menace that we reserve for Meath. By the time Dublin take to the field they're gone.

As if to welcome us to a new season the heavens finally open, down below things aren't much better, as Dublin produce possibly the worst 35 minutes of football I have had the misery to witness. The policy of massing bodies behind the ball is playing into Wexford's hands, leaving us light up front, as well as giving the Wexford half-back line free rein to do as they please. It seems that tactics have overtaken common sense. Dublin seem rigid, players afraid to push forward in support of a forward line starved of first-half possession. The Hill is restless, angry as Dublin score only two points to trail by six.

For the second time in a row a Dublin team is booed off at half-time in a championship match. I am in shock. Surely we couldn't get any worse. Only

P.O. is talking, trying to make some sense of it all, we just stand in silence, waiting for the end to come. I try to convince myself that things will get better, that Wexford will tire, and that we are attacking into the Hill in the second-half, another reason to be cheerful. Instead things get even worse. Dublin's first point in twenty-four minutes fails to kick-start a comeback. If anything the frustration grows as passes go astray, players solo into trouble and sure enough, with just twenty minutes left we are seven points behind.

At least I am safe on the Hill, cut off from the Wexford fans getting more excited by the minute. Beep. Beep. A text message from another former teaching colleague sitting in the Hogan Stand, Andrew, a Wexford man, a rugby man through-and-through, I wonder what the hell he is doing here. Raining on my parade that's what, maybe I am not that safe after all.

It is proving too much for some. Kerry was bad enough, but losing to Wexford would be a new low. A considerable number of Dublin fans leave; anger mixed with a painful realisation of how far this Dublin team has fallen. I have never understood what makes a person leave early, after all anything can happen. Nine times out of ten it won't, but that one in ten is worth waiting for. As if to prove the doubters wrong the tide begins to turn, slowly at first, as the fear of winning grips the Wexford team. Their keeper is trying to eat up valuable seconds, wasting time that he doesn't need to waste, driving an already frustrated Hill to distraction.

And without any warning, Dublin suddenly wake up with a flurry of points. We cheer half-heartedly, saving our breath for the qualifiers, as a Paul Flynn point begins the fight back, our first score in a very long time. Alan Brogan kicks a quick second and we begin to sit up and take notice when his younger brother Bernard pops over a third quick-fire point following a goal mouth scramble. The Hill is beginning to hum.

Gilroy is emptying the bench in a desperate attempt to save his job. Eoghan O'Gara, I look him up in the programme before P.O. can ask, is leading the charge. I like the look of O'Gara, aggressive, no-nonsense, not frightened to take people on, bursting through tackles and creating mayhem where before there had been calm. The Wexford backline, so comfortable all afternoon, is suddenly being overrun.

And then Denis Bastick goes and gets himself sent-off: back to square one. But before we can settle back into our manic depressive state Bernard Brogan lifts the mood as he fires past Anthony Masterson in the Wexford goal. A goal is always a moment to be savoured on the Hill. Suddenly we are level and although Wexford hit back to go ahead again, a couple of points from Conal Keaney put us in front for the first time. In 11 crazy minutes the game had been turned on its head. The sun even comes out as if to celebrate. Ponchos off, sunscreen on. Even P.O. is quiet as he tries to work out what the hell has just happened.

But the drama isn't over yet. Dublin are reduced to thirteen when Ger Brennan receives a second yellow. Ger is Dublin's bad boy, always a good bet to have an early bath. Worse is to come when Matty Forde levels matters with just seconds remaining. Despite their unexpected collapse, Wexford are refusing to die, happier to be coming from behind, the natural order restored. I have a terrible feeling in the pit of my stomach. Are Wexford going to snatch a famous victory from the jaws of defeat?

As soon as the referee blows for extra time, I know that Dublin will win. Wexford are out on their feet, all their energy spent, whatever momentum they have is gone. Back to their full complement of fifteen, a bizarre rule, the Dubs waste little time in making the game safe as Mossy Quinn's shot comes back off the Canal End goalpost before dropping into the grateful hands of Bernard Brogan who smashes the ball home. We celebrate as if he has scored the winning goal in an All-Ireland final. Game over, Dublin run out comfortable winners by 2-16 to 0-15.

As we make our way back up towards the car, relief gives way to doubt. Dublin had been blessed. Gilroy had been forced to call in the cavalry, older players who were supposed to be making way for a new team. There were a few pluses, Bernard Brogan's match-winning performance as well as Eoghan O'Gara and Michael Dara MacAuley, whose work rate and ball winning ability, as well as his clever use of possession, mark him out as one to watch, someone for us to hang our hopes on. The full-back line had kept us in the game. Apart from that there is little to be said. Dublin had looked flat and uninspired for much of the afternoon, having set out to defend against a team they should have been taking the game to, and it was only when Gilroy threw caution to the wind that the game opened up. I wonder about the people who had left early.

We say goodbye to Duff and head for home. I switch on the radio to catch the other scores, but P.O.'s voice drowns out the post-match analysis as he gives me his version of the game. He talks for what seems like hours before I drop him off in Lucan. His final verdict hangs in the car like a stale air freshener for ages afterwards. There is no getting away from it, he is right of course, Dublin were shite.

Chapter Five

Thy Kingdom Come

Sunday 28 September 1975

All-Ireland Senior Football Championship Final
Dublin versus Kerry

As the 1975 All-Ireland final came into view I was still confined to the relative safety of my armchair. My father had more than a bit of the health and safety officer about him. Even a year later, he forbid me from attending Home Farm's friendly game against Manchester United. He still felt that I was too young to be allowed to mix with the type of 'blaggards' that frequented such events. And apparently the Hill was full of them. Heffo's Army were a scary bunch, better viewed from a distance, preferably from the relative safety of about twelve miles away.

As for me, I was fascinated by life on the Hill, particularly the fashion sense. Doc Martens, crêpe paper hats and jeans that stopped well above the ankle were the uniform of the day. The crêpe paper hat was typically Irish, it served no particular purpose, looked ridiculous, but for some reason it worked. In the days before the arrival of the skinhead, the Dubs wore their hair long. To me the Hill looked like freedom itself; inhabited by thousands of Luke Kelly clones, jammed in together, swaying to and fro, singing their songs, having the time of their lives. But I knew Dad was right, I wasn't ready just yet. I'm not sure if I even knew where Croke Park was back then.

Having come from nowhere to triumph the previous September, Dublin were overwhelming favourites to retain their All-Ireland title. They were now regarded as the dominant force in Gaelic football. Gaelic is like that, one afternoon can change the world. Great teams suddenly find themselves cast adrift as the power they have taken for granted for years suddenly deserts them. Great teams become more fearful with every passing year, feeling the aches and pains that old age brings, as they sense that the end is not far away. They may have prepared well, taken nothing for granted, done everything right, and still it's not enough. Something deep inside is gone and doubt has replaced hope in the back of the mind. Where once there was innocent bravery, now there is only fear. Defending a lead, holding on to what you've got, becomes more important than building one. Often it goes unnoticed until it's too late, arriving on the day when it's least expected, bringing their story to an end.

In the other changing room young pretenders lie in wait, hungry, fearless, and ready to ambush their more fancied rivals.

In 1975 Dublin were the new boys on the chopping block – invincible, but no longer invisible – and danger was looming over the horizon. Something was stirring in the Kingdom of Kerry, where a young coach by the name of Mick O'Dwyer was putting together a brand new team that would do great deeds. Kerry may as well have cloned Heffo. O'Dwyer was cut from the same cloth, a motivator, a deep thinker as well as a lover of good football, except when it was played by the Dubs. O'Dwyer wanted two things more than any other, the first was Sam, and the second, beating Dublin, would be the icing on the cake.

In the meantime, Dublin got on with their business, hot favourites to beat Kerry in the final. There didn't seem to be a lot to be worried about, but every silver lining has a cloud. Dublin were leaking goals at an alarming rate, ten in the championship so far. Kerry had arrived in the final almost unnoticed. But that's the way Kerry like it; they love to be written off. It stirs something within them, a sense of historic pride that they carry with them everywhere they go.

I should know. My family has the Kingdom in its blood, and when it came to football, Dad was a Kerry supporter. I could see a twinkle in his eye as the big day approached. He knew Kerry had a real chance – a year earlier Dublin had been in Kerry's position – now they were out in the open. An early John Egan goal settled the Kerry nerves, and Dublin found themselves playing catch-up all day long, struggling to pay the interest on Kerry's first twenty minutes of domination. What I remember most of all is the awful tackle that laid out Kerry's Mickey O'Sullivan. His mazy run and its terrible end are best summed up by Michael O'Hehir: "And here come Kerry again... Mickey O'Sullivan going racing through... Alan Larkin in front of him... He's past Alan Larkin... Paddy Reilly's after him... Georgie Wilson's after him... Everybody's after him" – when suddenly he meets the full force of Seán

Doherty's elbow – "He's well and truly looked after now, he's down." Poor auld Mickey was carted off to hospital. It showed us the other side of Doherty, the no bullshit merchant, ruthless when he needed to be. At the final whistle it was the Kerry men who raised their arms in triumph. I felt like the Hill, stunned. As for Dad, he had the air of a man who had seen this coming.

In the days that followed the city tried to work out what had gone wrong. The most popular theory was over confidence, but anyone who knew Kevin Heffernan would have known that was unlikely. He had suffered at the hands of Kerry in the past. Others blamed the absence of Bobby Doyle from the starting line-up as well as the withdrawal of a penalty to Dublin after it had been given. Whatever the reason, there can be little argument that Dublin were clearly second best. No excuses; it was just as well because this Dublin team didn't do excuses. When they looked in the mirror they were honest enough to recognise what had to change. Beaten was beaten, it didn't matter how it had happened. Now it was time to put the record straight.

Chapter Six

The Sweet Smell Of Revenge

Sunday 26 of September 1976

**All-Ireland Senior Football Championship Final
Dublin versus Kerry**

Waiting for a year is never easy, but the dark winter months fuel the hurt, feed the thirst for revenge, as necessary as the winning score that will bring redemption. Dublin would not be found wanting. They dusted themselves down and turned their minds to plotting their revenge, starting with a win over Kerry in front of 25,000 in the National League. This encounter had all the edge and intensity of a championship match. Despite Dublin collecting their first National League title in eighteen years, with a hard fought win over Derry, Heffernan was far from satisfied. For the ghost of '75 to be laid to rest, Heffo wanted another All-Ireland. Most of all he wanted one that included a Kerry scalp and only then would he rest easy.

Changes were afoot in the Dublin camp. Tony Hanahoe was appointed captain. Pat O'Neill, Tommy Drumm and Kevin Moran were drafted into a half-back line that had taken the blame for the avalanche of goals that had been conceded in the previous campaign. O'Neill brought a studiousness to the backline with every interception and pass undertaken with the painstaking precision of a forensic examination. Like any great player Drumm always seemed to have time on his hands as well as the uncanny ability to be in the right place at the right time. Moran played with a freedom that only youth can bring. Dublin's fresh impetus was on show as they beat Meath in the Leinster final but in reality they had a penalty miss by Meath's young star Colm O'Rourke to thank for their victory. After beating Galway in a dour semi, Dublin were back in another final, happy to see that their opponents were the reigning champions. The stage was set for the mother of all showdowns. Jackeen versus culchie was capturing the imagination of the country. The build-up was tense; even Dad wasn't his usual self.

The tone was set in the first minute of the game. Kevin Moran took a pass from Brian Mullins in midfield and advanced deep into enemy territory, his flowing locks doing their best to keep up with him; he then played a one-two with Bernard Brogan before shooting narrowly wide. The ball whistled past the post with Paudie O'Mahony rooted to the spot in the Kerry goal. Moran probably should have scored; he could have taken a few more paces before shooting. But it didn't really matter as the new boy in town had thrown down the gauntlet. It was a statement of intent: Dublin would not be caught on the hop this time.

Moran later claimed that he had been told to do it. That says it all about Kevin Heffernan; he recognised the value of an early psychological blow. He wanted Dublin to lay down a marker and he knew that the fearless Moran was the man to do it. Moran's youthful exuberance meant that he didn't question his leader, didn't worry about the gaping hole he would leave at the back. He did what he was told and came within a whisker of perfection. It didn't matter that the ball went wide, what mattered was that Dublin were on their way and that Kerry were on the back foot. Self-belief flooded through the blue shirts, and Dublin went on to score three goals in a famous victory. John McCarthy, the pickpocket who unlocked the tightest of defences' at the most crucial times, scored the first goal with a typical effort close in, to give Dublin the breathing space they needed and, in a reversal of roles from the previous September, it was Kerry's turn to chase the game.

After half-time, Jimmy Keaveney slotted home a perfect penalty. Penalties are notoriously difficult to score in Gaelic football, but Jimmy was special: the big man had no fear -perfect technique and concentration. Baby steps as he shuffled towards the ball. BANG – GOAL. He would have made a great sniper. Brian Mullins scored the clincher. Mullins was the rock on which many opponents foundered. With Kerry threatening to haul Dublin in, the St Vincent's man took Anton O'Toole's pass and turned cleverly before sliding the ball past Charlie Nelligan to cap a marvellous Dublin performance. As usual O'Toole played his part to perfection, quietly working away in the background, combining a languid skill with a fierce work ethic, a lethal combination on any sporting stage. As well as the stars of the show, this Dublin team had its fair share of unsung heroes, the likes of Gay O'Driscoll who never stopped running, always to be found in the thick of the action. This day was as much theirs as the boys who put the ball in the back of the net. The September sun shone, and Dublin had their All-Ireland title back. As usual, Michael O'Hehir summed it all up with a flourish: "3 goals and 8 points for Dublin, 10 points for Kerry, and the Jacks are well and truly back." The stage was now set for the greatest game of them all.

Chapter Seven

The Greatest Game

Sunday 18 August 1977

All-Ireland Senior Football Championship Semi-Final
Dublin versus Kerry

But first the Dubs had to deal with a shock to their very core. Heffo was gone. In October Kevin Heffernan announced that he was stepping down as manager, citing the pressures of work, as well as the demands that managing Dublin brought. He had wanted to go after 1974 with his three year plan completed in one, but had been dissuaded by Dublin County Board Chairman Jimmy Gray. This time he was not for turning. No time was wasted as Tony Hanahoe was appointed player manager with Donal Colfer and Lorcan Redmond, key men in Dublin's return to glory, agreeing to stay on as selectors.

As Heffo's general on the field, Hanahoe had always put the needs of the team before his own, a trait that meant his move into management was a seamless one, his ability to see the bigger picture allied with his studious and single minded approach allowed him to maintain a good relationship with his colleagues, whilst maintaining the discipline that is key to any successful team. Despite the loss of their charismatic leader the transition proved to be relatively smooth meaning that Dublin were in good shape as the 1977 championship season kicked off. Any threat of over-confidence was knocked on the head when they surrendered their National League title to Kerry in June. Perhaps Dublin's new player-manager knew exactly what he was doing when he dragged a late shot wide to deprive Dublin of victory.

The next time the sides met the stakes were much higher, with a place in the All-Ireland final up for grabs. Over 59,000 turned up for the latest instalment of what was becoming a gripping saga. This was a game that had everything: great skill, superb scores, jaw dropping intensity, hurried mistakes, unbelievable tension, gripping drama and an explosion at the end that surpassed all that had gone before.

Michael O'Hehir was not found wanting, his wonderful description matching the gripping drama unfolding on the field of play. Michael had a no nonsense approach to how the game should be played, that was obvious when he described Kerry making a mess of an early chance to put the first score of the game on the board: "They tried a fiddling arrangement." Seconds later, Jimmy Keaveney was flat on his back in front of the Kerry goal, a Bobby Doyle pass had put him through for the perfect opportunity but Dublin's Pele had fluffed his lines. "Oh Jimmy! Oh Jimmy! Oh Jimmy!" The surprise in O'Hehir's voice said it all; it wasn't like Jimmy to miss when he could see the whites of the goalkeeper's eyes. But such a frantic start was in keeping with what was to come. Just like the 1975 final it was Kerry who came out of the traps first courtesy of an early goal from Sean Walsh. Dublin managed to stay in touch but with half-time approaching they trailed by five points. It wasn't looking good. But two late points gave Dublin heart going into the break. Kerry's lead had been cut to three: 1-6 to 0-6. The pace of the game had been relentless. Even the spectators needed a half-time rest.

At the start of the second-half, Kevin Moran reprised the opening moments of the previous year's final with another inspirational run towards the Hill 16 goal. His finish was disappointing, a tame effort straight into the waiting hands of Charlie Nelligan. But once again he had lifted Dublin spirits and a Dublin goal was coming. It duly arrived when Tommy Drumm played a one-two with Bobby Doyle out on the Cusack Stand sideline before knocking a high ball in towards the Kerry goal. John McCarthy fisted it on to Tony Hanahoe who had the ball knocked out of his hand by Tim Kennelly, only for the breaking ball to fall conveniently into the hands of the in rushing McCarthy who fisted the ball home. The Hill erupted. The gods had smiled on us. Dublin suddenly had belief where there had been none and the sides were level after only two minutes of the second-half. But Kerry rallied to hit the front again. It was such a wonderful contest that O'Hehir felt moved to proclaim "Twenty-nine minutes of this left. Hallelujah."

Dublin clawed their way back to the mountain top to lead for the first time in the game: 1-10 to 1-09. Kerry levelled. Bobby Doyle fired Dublin back into the lead with twelve minutes left: 1-11 to 1-10. Once again Kerry hit back immediately: 1-11 to 1-11. Mikey Sheehy fired them ahead and John Egan added another point: Kerry 1-13 Dublin 1-11. Ten minutes to go. Kerry were flowing downstream, playing irresistible football with Dublin looking out on their feet. There seemed to be no way back.

But the best was yet to come. Brian Mullins kicked a line ball into Anton O'Toole from in front of the Hogan Stand and Anton dropped the ball in towards the Kerry goal. Fate played a hand when a Kerry player reached desperately to try and intercept but only succeeded in deflecting the ball away from a better placed colleague. Instead, the ball fell into the path of Tony Hanahoe, he fed David Hickey, the boy next door, who hammered the ball home. "It's a goal", cried O'Hehir. Unbelievably, Dublin were ahead again: 2-11 to 1-13 with six minutes left. But six minutes might as well have been a lifetime, so much was happening so quickly. The tension was increasing by the minute, the pace unrelenting as both teams threw themselves into the final act.

Ogie Moran lined up a free from halfway and arrowed the ball towards the Dublin square. The whole ground held its breath as Dublin's full-back Seán Doherty rose into the air and plucked the ball out of the heavens, he collided with Kevin Moran on the way down but managed to retain possession as he hit the ground before fighting his way back to his feet and clearing the ball up field. What happened next is best left to O'Hehir as Dublin swept from one end of the field to the other at blistering pace. "What a save by Seán Doherty... Bobby Doyle ... The tension and anxiety of the whole lot of them ... This is David Hickey coming away now... This is Tony Hanahoe... In now to Bernard Brogan... He's in front of goal... He can't miss... He hasn't. Bernard Brogan drilling for oil... He drilled for a goal there and drilled right into the back of the net!" Oil was the new gold, but in O'Hehir's world it was equated with a place in the All-Ireland final, the currency by which his heroes realised their worth. Dublin's third goal left them 3-11 to 1-13 ahead, Kerry were gone, there was no coming back from that. Hanahoe added another point to leave the final score: 3-12 to 1-13. O'Hehir described it as the "Resurrection of Dublin."

Was it the greatest game of all time? It felt like it at the time and it still does today. That is not to do disservice to all the other great games that have been played over the years. The fact that Dublin won is one of the main reasons we look back so fondly on that day. Kerry played worse on other days and ran out easy winners, but that's sport, it doesn't always work out the way you want it to. Kerry could have done no more; they had asked Dublin all the questions that needed to be asked. But it wasn't to be. This was meant to be Dublin's day. The reason it was so special was because both teams played so well, with so many of the actors on the stage choosing this day to give their best performance. It must have been a hell of a job to pick a man of the match.

Dublin went on to wrap up their third All-Ireland in four years with a 5-12 to 3-6 win over Armagh. But following the excitement of the semi-final, the final proved to be a bit of an anti-climax. It was one of those games were the outcome was never in doubt, one of those days when the Dublin forward line purred. Bobby Doyle and Bernard Brogan were like a couple of lads on a night out, wreaking havoc wherever they went, dancing past the bouncers at the nightclub door. Although Armagh hit the back of their opponents net three times they had no answer as a rampant Dublin recorded the biggest ever total for a winning team in an All-Ireland final, with Jimmy Keaveney breaking the individual scoring record in the final with 2-6. Jimmy had more than a bit of the rascal in him, the kind of guy who looked like he would be more at home in the pub but here he was breaking records in the twilight of his career, scoring goals that any Brazilian would have been proud of. Not to be outdone Paddy Cullen saved another penalty towards the end. With his second All-Ireland final save from the spot Paddy was fast becoming the high king of penalty saves, always the extrovert, the maker of stories he would enjoy telling when he retired. It was the first time since the 1920s that Dublin had managed to retain the All-Ireland. It also meant that the classic semi-final had not been in vain.

Chapter Eight

The Beginning Of The End

Sunday 24 September 1978

All-Ireland Senior Football Championship Final
Dublin versus Kerry

By 1978 Kevin Heffernan was back as manager and Dublin and Kerry were back in the All-Ireland final. Heffo's hunger had returned, even if some of the players resented his decision to throw himself back into the mix. The country held its breath and wondered what this year's encounter would throw up. Dublin began as if they were going to blow Kerry away, their football in the first 23 minutes was possibly the best that they had ever played, but the killer goal wouldn't come, despite a lead of six points to one. Dublin were so dominant that their full-back line had pushed up in an attempt to get involved in the rout, with Kerry's forwards forced back in search of some meaningful ball. Huge empty spaces lay in behind the Dublin defence as the metropolitans piled forward. The Kingdom was on the brink of collapse when Bobby Doyle was whistled up for over carrying – the first in a number of baffling decisions by Kildare referee Seamus Aldridge – a man who from that day on has had a special place in Dublin hearts. Kerry took full advantage with a sweeping move that allowed Pat Spillane to put John Egan in the clear. Egan duly flicked the ball over the advancing Paddy Cullen to put Kerry back in the game. Within minutes Kerry were level.

With half-time approaching the game was on a knife-edge when Aldridge struck again. Earlier on, he had missed the aftermath of a clash between Ger Power and Paddy Cullen. This time Paddy had no such luck as he came out to field the ball towards the end line. As Power backed into him again, Paddy gestured to Aldridge for a free. Aldridge gave a free all right but incredibly he awarded it to Kerry. Instead of heading for home Paddy stood complaining. Robbie Kelleher handed the ball to Mikey Sheehy, big mistake; Mikey looked up to see a big open goal to his left as he placed the ball down, he looked up once more and chipped it into the empty net. Paddy arrived back just after the ball, wrapping himself around the goalpost in the process. Perhaps Con Houlihan summed it up best the next day in the *Evening Press*:

"Poor Paddy was like a fireman arriving back to find the station ablaze." Incredibly, the half-time scoreboard read 2-3 to Kerry and 0-7 to Dublin.

Despite the shocking turn of events all was not lost. But whatever chance a shell shocked Dublin had was blown away a minute into the second-half by Eoin Liston's opening goal of the day. His second arrived soon afterwards, a beauty that left Michael O'Hehir to describe poor Paddy Cullen as "Stranded without an oar, without a boat." And it wasn't just Paddy that was all at sea. Liston added a fifth goal as Dublin fell apart, an army in retreat with Kevin Moran hobbling around with a serious hamstring injury to go with his bloody bandaged head, in what was destined to be his final game for Dublin before he headed back to Manchester to continue his blossoming soccer career. That was nothing compared to Brian Mullins was struggling with a damaged Achilles tendon, a cracked rib and double vision.

Fingers were pointed at the age of the Dublin team in the days that followed as supporters and pundits tried to make sense of a collapse that no one saw coming. Others felt that Dublin's early dominance had lured them into a trap, Kerry's cuteness feared as much as their footballing brilliance. Many pointed an accusing finger at Seamus Aldridge, many still do.

By the beginning of the 1979 championship it was clear that this great Dublin team was in decline. Seán Doherty, Gay O'Driscoll, Robbie Kelleher and Kevin Moran were all gone from the starting line up and to make matters worse, Jimmy Keaveney was ruled out of the rest of the championship, following his was sending-off in the Leinster final against Offaly. At the time it didn't seem to matter all that much with 13 minutes left and Jimmy long gone, Dublin trailed by 9 points to 4. But still this extraordinary team refused to lie down and die, in front of over 52,000 they pulled themselves up off the floor to rage against the dying of the light. As referee Pat Collins looked at his watch, Brian Mullins gained possession and moved the ball onto Anton O'Toole who gave it back to Mullins, Brian found Bernard Brogan who rounded two Offaly defenders before firing an unstoppable shot past Martin Furlong. Seconds later the final whistle went. Dublin had prevailed by 1-8 to 9 points. Offaly's time would come but not before they had their card marked by a Dublin team who refused to give up when all seemed lost. A legendary day, a day when they could have thrown in the towel, but despite weary legs and heavy hearts, they still found the will to win. The same qualities were on display when they edged out Roscommon in a tight semi-final.

The build up to the final had the feel of a wake. Deep in our hearts we knew that this was the end, they had done well to get this far, and so it proved, this aging Dublin team was no match for a Kerry team that was moving effortlessly up through the gears. Even the sending-off of Kerry's Páidí Ó Sé early in the second-half failed to ignite a one sided game, with Mikey Sheehy's penalty fourteen minutes from time finally putting us out of our misery, there were to be no heroics from Paddy Cullen this time: Kerry 3-13 Dublin 1-8.

At the end The Hill rose to applaud their heroes, this was a day to celebrate the deeds of a group of men who will live long in the memory. The colour that the Dubs of the seventies brought to the game made for a potent mix, both on and off the field, the likes of which may never be seen again. They left us with great moments and great goals. They also left us The Hill. The famous terrace at the Railway End had become a ghost town before Heffo's Army returned it to its former glories. No matter what happened from then on, one thing was sure, the Dublin football team would never be deserted by its loyal followers again. When I find myself standing on Hill 16 now, I see the people who were there in the seventies as well as the rest of us who are there because of the seventies.

Following six All-Ireland finals in a row Dublin went into hibernation, allowing a city that had been enthralled to pause for breath, leaving a more youthful Kerry side to go in search of what would prove to be an elusive five in a row. But all was not lost. With Kevin Heffernan growing restless for more glory, we wouldn't have to wait long for a return to the rare auld times. Only this time I was determined to be there in person.

Chapter Nine

Where Do We Go To From Here?

Sunday 27 June 2010

Leinster Senior Football Championship Semi-Final
Dublin versus Meath

Dublin and Meath don't like each other. It's as simple as that. The Meath-Dublin rivalry of the eighties and nineties replaced the Kerry-Dublin one of the seventies. For us, beating Meath is always considered a good day's work. They may have lost some of their nastiness in recent years, but back in their heyday they were a ruthless bunch of outlaws who did whatever it took to win. With their smiling and affable manager Sean Boylan, the acceptable face of that philosophy. It was hard to dislike Boylan, he always treated us with respect and spoke from the heart. On the opposite end of the scale was their full-back, Mick Lyons, Dublin's most wanted man. Lyons would run up to the Hill and pump his chest out and look directly into our eyes. As a statement of intent it was raw and threatening, throwing down the gauntlet in no uncertain terms. With Lyons, no quarter was given or asked. Opposing players were safer when they had the ball; at least the ref was looking at them. The Royals had come close to unseating Dublin in Leinster during the seventies, but it was during the eighties that the rivalry moved up a gear.

By 1991 Meath had gained the upper hand following their breakthrough win over a tired Dublin team five years earlier. The good news was that we wouldn't have to endure the tension that a sixth successive Dublin-Meath provincial final would bring; the bad news was that we were to meet in the first round. The winners would have a Leinster title in the bag, and the losers would have nothing to do for the rest of the summer.

I was on the Hill for the first three games. The first game was as nerve-racking as all the others that had gone before. As usual with Meath, no quarter was given or asked, every loose ball as fiercely contested as if the final outcome depended on it. With a minute left on the clock, Dublin led by a point, but a minute is a long time in a Dublin-Meath match, and so it proved as P.J. Gillic launched the ball towards the Dublin goal in front of

Hill 16. We watched its trajectory with a growing sense of dread. Goalkeeper John O'Leary tore from his goal and launched himself at the dropping ball, only to miss it completely. As the ball bounced, we held our breath. I prepared myself for the worst, certain it was going to end up in the Dublin net. We were out. The ball bounced over the bar. The sides were level. We were back in. All in the space of a few crazy seconds. The final whistle brought forth mixed emotions, we had lived to fight another day, but the overwhelming feeling was one of regret. Having squandered a five point half-time lead, we felt our chance was gone.

I spent the month of June getting up early and heading into town to queue for tickets outside the Dublin County Board offices. Long lines stretched down the street with rumour and counter-rumour the order of the day. It wasn't just about getting in, it was about being on the Hill. Those who had already received their tickets couldn't resist a bit of mischief: "There's very few left now," they'd say, "The Hill tickets are all gone." I pretended not to hear them, hoped that they were taking the piss. Each day my prayers were answered, I would look to the sky and thank God, before returning home clutching my precious Hill ticket with a ferocious pride.

The second game was a replica of the first: controlled mayhem. The Hill felt like a cocoon, blue shirted strangers telling me not to lose heart when Dublin went behind. I was content to see the Meath supporters before and after, but during the game I needed to be with my own tribe. My days in the Canal End were well and truly over. I looked at the green and gold flags waving as the Meath team entered the field of play and thanked my lucky stars that I was where I was.

For some reason the Hill seemed quieter than usual, pensive and preoccupied. Some young Meath fans in the Cusack Stand decided to taunt us with our silence. Their squeaky voices daring us to respond. Within seconds, 13,000 voices boomed out in aggressive defiance, the awesome power of the Hill unleashed as "C'mon You Boys in Blue" swept down in waves onto the pitch below. I looked across at the faces of the guilty few being admonished by some wise old Meath heads, better to let sleeping dogs lie. It was Meath's turn to lead at half-time, but Dublin rallied in a gripping second-half and it took a late Brian Stafford free to pull Meath level. For the second game in a row Dublin should have wrapped it up in the dying seconds. Vinny Murphy had a great chance to punch the winning point, but for some reason he decided to go for goal and Michael McQuillan saved his effort in front of a disbelieving Hill. Even extra time failed to separate the sides and it ended 1-11 to 1-11. Veteran Barney Rock had kicked eight valuable points. Jack Sheedy's goal in extra-time was crucial in hauling Dublin back into a game that was slipping away. It had been another lesson in keeping the faith. So, it was back into the city to queue again in the early morning light. If you wanted a ticket badly enough you got your arse out of bed.

I was starting to get worried. I had booked my holidays back in May. If the sides couldn't sort out their differences on Sunday, June 23rd, I was in real danger of missing the fourth instalment of what was becoming a never-ending saga. The sides were so well matched it was difficult to see what could possibly separate them. On the third day, Dublin rose again and had the upper hand until Gerry McEntee came on to bolster the Meath midfield. Every passing minute seemed to bring a freshness of intent; neither side was prepared to back down. Tired minds and tired limbs drew on seemingly inexhaustible supplies of character and energy and an ever-greater familiarity was breeding an ever-nastier contempt. At one point Dublin's number 12 was guilty of a foul worthy of a booking and play was stopped as the ref set about hunting him down. He proceeded to turn each Dublin player around in an attempt to find the perpetrator. Like us, he knew the number he was looking for. All of this was taking place on the halfway line. What made the incident all the more enjoyable was that the player in question was standing on the goal line beside John O'Leary in front of Hill 16, having withdrawn deep behind his own lines in the hope of evading capture, the last man that the referee would get to. Each time another player showed his number to an increasingly desperate man in black, the Hill cheered in defiance. By about the eighth player, the referee finally admitted defeat and gave up. Another small victory in what was becoming a war without end.

The battle on the sidelines was equally enthralling. Paddy Cullen, the publican, battling it out with Sean Boylan, the herbalist. Paddy saw it as a shoot out, but Boylan was the more wily one, kept his cards close to his chest, revelled in the chess game that was unfolding. At one point Boylan wandered down in front of the Hill to pass on instructions to one of his disciples. The Hill bristled with indignation, he was entering our patch, but it was hard to dislike the Meath manager, he always spoke well of the Dubs, welcomed the challenge. But that didn't stop him doing what it took to win. We watched as he walked his usual quirky walk along the end line, captivated by his bravery. We were silent, taking it all in when one voice spoke for us all. "Fuck off ya witch doctor."

At the final whistle the sides were level again. Meath looked well placed to win in extra time, but just as in the previous encounter a Dublin goal altered the picture dramatically. This time it was left to Paul Clarke to do the necessary. Paul Curran's late point meant yet another replay: Dublin 1-14 Meath 2-11. It was Meath's turn to have the regrets. My nightmare had come true.

By the time of the fourth encounter, I would be in Barcelona, left to rely on one phone call to my father to find out the fate of my beloved Dubs. By now, the importance of the game was resonating far beyond the borders of the two counties involved. It had even reached Catalonia. It didn't take a genius to see that the rest of the country was up for Meath. Anyone but the Dubs. I did my best to keep myself occupied in the Catalan sunshine but nothing could take my mind off what was happening back in Croker. Eventually the time came when I was sure that the game had run its course. Maybe I would make the fifth instalment. My father answered almost immediately. I wondered if it was a good sign that he had been hovering near the phone, trying to identify a clue as to the outcome in the tone and resonance of his voice. He didn't waste any time, no point in prolonging the agony. He spoke in the businesslike manner befitting a former bank manager: Dublin had lost, Meath had won.

I asked Dad what had happened, I needed to know the gut-wrenching details. How your team is beaten is as important as the beating itself, but he was having none of it, it would be better if I watched it when I got back. I knew then that something awful had happened. I walked around in a daze for the rest of the night and had a few beers to numb the pain. I thought of the lads back in Hedigans. At least they had been there. But I had the added guilt of being absent when my team and my mates needed me the most.

I watched the game when I came home. Those fateful last few minutes are etched on my soul, they say such events are character-building but I don't think that this particular experience has ever stood to me. It just left a huge gaping hole in my heart that no amount of victories over Meath in the years that followed could ever fill. Even today, I turn away when I see the build-up to the Kevin Foley goal beginning to take shape whenever it's rerun on TV. I'm tired of urging the Dublin defenders to pull him down. Eleven fucking passes. Seán Doherty would have put an end to it there and then. Eleven too many. Level again. The Hill in a state of bewilderment.

Fifteen minutes earlier, Dublin had led by six points and Meath were on their knees. But Brian Stafford pinched a goal and fate smiled on them when Keith Barr drove a penalty wide with eight minutes left. If he had knocked it over the bar Dublin would have led by four. Just like Vinny Murphy in game two, Barr had missed a glorious opportunity to put another nail in the Meath coffin. But Keith owed nobody any apologies, the Dublin players must have felt that it was virtually impossible to shake this Meath side off, hence his decision to go for the knockout blow. It should also be pointed out that the kick should have been retaken as Barr had had the dubious company of Mick Lyons in his run up to take the penalty. Keith was always one of my favourite players, relentless in his pursuit of victory; he had stepped up to the plate when the kick was awarded. On another day he would have been a hero. But Foley's goal meant that the lead so painstakingly built up over the course of the afternoon was suddenly gone; blown away in an instant. Extra-time beckoned. But Meath smelled blood. John O'Leary's kick-out was gobbled up by Liam Hayes who thundered towards the Dublin goal. Hayes passed to P.J. Gillic who found David Beggy all alone; Beggy belted the ball over the bar to put Meath ahead. And still the gods were not finished with us as Jack Sheedy's long-range free drifted wide and that was that.

Paddy Cullen had been right all along. It had ended in a glorious shoot out, except that none of us had expected the sheriff to be gunned down. For a month the Irish sporting world was dominated by Dublin and Meath, what had been a local rivalry up until then began to stir the national interest and by July it was front page news. Eamon Dunphy wrote a piece eulogising the spirit and bravery shown by both sets of players in *The Sunday Independent*, with his praise being heart-felt and thoroughly deserved at the end of one of Ireland's greatest ever sporting sagas.

Games between these two sides rarely had the glamour or touch of class that characterised the Dublin-Kerry rivalry but they were just as gripping to watch. They were a different kind of spectacle, all about physical intensity, in-your-face savagery tempered with a strange respect, a brutal rawness mixed with an unforgiving will to win, containing remarkable skill and poise under the most intense pressure. There was little time to dwell on the ball, little time to look up and pick your pass. But somehow amongst the mayhem, there were players who could make a difference, who found precious time to do brilliant things. Even neutrals found themselves drawn to the awful beauty of the passion play that was unfolding that summer. The players became household names, giants who stalked the land in search of ultimate victory.

In the end the difference between the two sides came down to experience. Meath knew how to win, how to profit from adversity. Time and again, they picked themselves up off the canvas to get the job done. But the epic had exhausted them. Left to stumble towards another All-Ireland final, they were eventually ambushed by a fresher Down side. By the third Sunday in September, mentally and physically drained, Boylan's men were but a tired shadow of their former selves. It was a small consolation, I suppose, Meath might have beaten us but at least we had the considerable pleasure of knowing that we had played our part in their eventual downfall.

In recent years games between the two counties have lessened in intensity, it no longer seems to matter as much, partly due to the alternative route through the qualifiers, which means that losing to Meath is no longer the end of the summer. Last year's clash was disappointing, with Dublin running out more comfortable winners than the two point gap suggested. As a result the build up to today's game has been low key, with most pundits tipping Dublin. But which Dublin will turn up?

And still it was Meath, their name enough to stir the bitter memories of the past, the thought of defeat enough to turn my stomach inside out. A few pints were needed to calm the nerves, so I headed up to Duff's on the Saturday night. We ended up discussing Gilroy long into the night, still unsure of the latest former player to try to bring back the glory days. His tenure had begun with the kind of victories that get the Hill on your side, beating Meath and a resurgent Kildare had ticked all the right boxes, but the collapse against Kerry emptied his bank account of everything that had gone before. He talked a good game, kept his cards close to his chest, called a spade a spade. There would be no hiding place this year, the Hill growing impatient, anxious to see some progress. Wexford had been a new low, evidence that Dublin football was in terminal decline. Tomorrow will tell us a lot, but we need to see the bigger picture, if blooding players meant losing to Meath then so be it. It was a sacrifice worth making. The short-term fixes of recent years hadn't brought the team any nearer to what was becoming an increasingly elusive All-Ireland. Ultimately that is Pat's dilemma, short term pain for long term gain.

The support is split. Many feel that Pat isn't up to the job, a surprise choice for manager. Not a big enough name, not charismatic enough. The usual suspects were bandied about, Mick O'Dwyer and Joe Kernan, outsiders. The manner of Gilroy's appointment didn't help, as he slipped into the job without the usual fanfare, as if nobody else wanted the job. At least Pat is a Dub, the one thing he has going for him. His playing career was another bone of contention, sure he had an All-Ireland medal but for much of his Dublin career he had been a peripheral figure, always struggling to nail down a starting place, nothing pretty about his game. He was a worker, someone who did the hard yards so that others could shine, not a bad trait in a manager. The Dublin County Board had a habit of turning to former players to fill the void, but usually they were bigger names. Condemned by many before he started, Gilroy showed a steely determination in those early months, said the right things, and kept his true thoughts to himself and still it wasn't enough. But I was sick of the bullshit; we needed a football manager, not a mouthpiece for the media. I liked Pat's style, was confident that he would do a good job. Following the Wexford game I was no longer so sure.

By the time we reached the Hill the next day, the idea that defeat to Meath could ever be a good thing had been forgotten. The sight of Meath jerseys on the way to the ground was enough to get the blood boiling, the ghosts of '91 taunting us as we made our way down Clonliffe Road towards the row of barriers that lead to the Hill. Times have changed. It had been nine long years since the Royals last tasted success against Dublin. No time is ever a good time to lose to Meath. They have a way of making us pay. I think back to 1986 and 1996, two times when Meath broke the Dublin stranglehold to dominate for years to come. Today has that feel about it.

Duff had his man bag searched on the way in. I don't know what he carries in there, water, cigarettes, a spare pair of Dublin jocks. I don't ask. P.O. is already on the Hill, awaiting our arrival, chattering away to himself. I could feel Duff's nervousness, matches against Meath bring out the worst in him, as he anxiously dragged on a cigarette. He has a habit of punching me on the back just prior to the throw in. Today those punches carry the added intensity that comes with Meath. We like our superstitions, favourite hats, scarves, and treasured jerseys, whatever it takes to make us feel better about our chances of bringing Sam home. It's not unknown for Duff to go a whole summer without washing his jersey, anything to keep a winning run going. One year I decided to let my hair grow for as long as Dublin remained in the championship, knowing that the chance of me ending up as a hippie come September were pretty slim. It has rarely worked. This year we are seeing how we do without any superstitions. Even if it doesn't change a thing at least Duff will smell a bit better. But that doesn't stop him hitting me on the back. I guess old habits die hard.

There is a brooding intensity on the Hill when Meath are the enemy. Meath versus Dublin takes us to reservoirs of hate that we rarely visit in our everyday lives. For 70 minutes we forget who we are. Teachers, shop assistants, bankers, lorry drivers, candlestick makers or hardened criminals, it doesn't seem to matter. You can feel the rawness in the air. It's as if a mist drifts across the ground, only lifting when the battle is done and the crowd has headed for home. On days like this Croke Park is a place of passion, a place where people, men and women, boys and girls, young and old, come to worship, to feel alive, to feel that it's all worthwhile. They suspend the juices of their imagination and give themselves over to their heroes. This is the real thing.

Sometimes we get to release our inner joy and some days, the bad days, we get to visit the dark places of the soul. No pretence. No hidden agendas. Here we are as close to our real selves as we can get. Here we are true to our spirit. Some days the rawness frightens us. Makes us question who we really are. Within minutes we have become the most basic of creatures, letting loose the demons that lie trapped below, that lie dormant in our everyday lives, looking for a voice, a way out.

Right now too much pressure is being bottled up and it has to come out somewhere. Hill 16 is as good a place as any. It's at its best on the day of a big match. There's a buzz that isn't there on the other days when the stakes aren't as high. For a couple of hours on a Sunday afternoon we become one. For many males sport is our emotional safety valve, the stage upon which we shed our tears. Chances are that the sadness is often to do with something else. It's strange the things that come out in the wash.

Hill 16 philosophy is worth the admission fee alone. If you say anything remotely personal on the Hill, you need to be aware that it's entering the public domain. And there's nowhere more public than Hill 16. The game unfolding down below is another matter all together, running parallel to the afternoon unfolding on the Hill. You can't have one without the other. Only recently Niall, a proud Baldoyle man, moaned that you never get to relax watching this Dublin team. We had just blown a 14 point lead against Mayo in the league when a big burly skinhead turned to him and said in a disbelieving tone "Surely you don't come here for the relaxation."

Dublin versus Meath usually comes down to the survival of the fittest. Sometimes it just comes down to luck. We both like to feel that we are the superior race. Two tribes going to war with every ball fought for as if our lives depend on it. The Hill thinks and feels as one, a guttural roar coming together with what's happening on the pitch. No let-up. A Meath goal at the Railway End inevitably results in a defiant look towards the Hill, as players and supporters relish the hurt they have inflicted. We stand defiant, pretending that we haven't noticed, while to our right contorted faces push down the terrace in an attempt to reap vengeance.

As Dublin take to the field, we scream our approval. Meath follow, the 15 horsemen of the apocalypse, and the primal roar that greets the Royals is drowned out by the outpouring of disapproval that emanates from Hill 16. Both noises come from the very pit of the stomach. We refuse to acknowledge the Meath support, to admit to their presence would be to show weakness.

We watch the Dublin team going through their paces in the warm up. Gilroy strolls amongst them, tall and purposeful, passing on last minute words of encouragement, tinkering with the routine where he sees fit. Pat always looks serious and menacing, his shaved head adding to the 'don't mess with me' message that he seems to be perfecting as he grows into the job. He's cut the cord between the players and the Hill. They no longer tap into our energy, staying focused on the task ahead. His predecessor saw it differently, with the team marching down towards us with their chests pushed out in a brazen show of pride, making us feel wanted. Now we don't know what to think.

Prayers are said. "C'mon You Boys In Blue. C'mon You Boys In Blue. C'mon You Boys. C'mon You Boys In Blue" Hands clap and out-stretched arms reach for the sky in unison. The hypnotic rhythm of the bodhráns gives some order to the mayhem. Even the fear disappears as we sing our national anthem and for a few precious moments, both sides feel as one. But once the preliminaries are over, we settle back into our respective corners. Adrenalin pumping through our veins as the final roar takes on a murderous intent as the referee lifts the ball to the sky.

Slowly he lets it go. Letting it float through the air. It's the last bit of peace it will get for the time being. "The ball is in and the game is on'"

Dublin start well. Bryan Cullen's fisted point directly in front of us puts Dublin two points to the good. The boys in blue are vibrant and purposeful. I am feeling good, drinking it in. Rumour has it that the players stayed at home last night. Prior to the Wexford game they stayed in a hotel. Apparently it worked in the league but following the trauma against Wexford, the idea has been ditched. Such inside knowledge is a valuable currency on the Hill. Then disaster strikes. Barry Cahill is soloing up the field when he is controversially pulled up for over-carrying. Meath move the ball quickly to Stephen Bray who cuts inside to score the opening goal. Dublin pull themselves together to score the next three points, only for Meath to hit back with three of their own to leave the sides level at half-time. The break gives us time to gather our thoughts. P.O. is confident, nothing for Dublin to worry about. Duff is quiet. There are four of us today, the full compliment. Niall has returned having missed the outing against Wexford, another regular.

Meath were now attacking into the Hill. Five minutes in, Cian Ward bangs in Meath's second goal. The intake of breath on the Hill reflects the seriousness of the situation. With Meath growing in confidence, we needed to strike back immediately. Suddenly a blue shirt is through on goal, we hold our breath and pray; the outcome balances on what happens next. Paul Flynn's rasping shot hits the inside of the upright, before flashing across the goal and going wide on the far side. The gods have spoken.

Three more Meath goals follow. The final ignominy comes when two Dublin players go for a high ball, leaving Brian Farrell all alone in acres of space and he takes full advantage to hammer the final nail in the Dublin coffin with another cool finish: 5-9 to 0-13. Yet another hammering to go with those handed out by Tyrone and Kerry. Is there no end to our misery?

No room for excuses this time around, except for the referee that is. He's destined for the full Maurice treatment. Maurice, another member of our band of brothers, has an after match ritual whereby he tears any referee deemed to have done Dublin a wrong out of the programme and sets his photograph on fire. Three of Meath's goals looked questionable. But our problems run deeper than a few dodgy decisions. Defeat is always a possibility against Meath, but this? Dublin have conceded five goals in a provincial championship game for the first time in eighty-one years, a third thumping in three years. The only way is up. Dublin's backline had fallen apart in the second-half, the whole defensive system creaked as Meath turned up the heat. After the success of getting twelve men behind the ball in the league it seems that Gilroy has lost faith in those principles and reverted to type. It wasn't good enough against Tyrone or Kerry and now it has been exposed by Meath. The road back promises to be a very long one.

The press are going to love this; lots of raw meat to pick at. Thousands of green shirted smiling faces meet us as we leave the ground, they'd be crazy not to enjoy this one. As Hill 16 pours out into the real world the mumble of discontent turns to a torrent as the full realisation of the magnitude of today's defeat sinks in. People shake their heads and look to the heavens. Anger is in the air. In the crush, I can hear people calling for Gilroy's head, the easy fix. He needs to be given the rest of the season to at least try and pick up the pieces. Days like this are part of sport, the ones when everything goes wrong; it's how you react to it that counts.

As we wander up the back streets towards the canal we bump into a Meath father and his teenage son. Dad is minding his own business. He knows what it is to be a winner in enemy territory: keep the head down, one foot in front of the other and get home in one piece. But blessed are the young for they know not how to hide the inner joy that comes with the spoils of victory, free of the baggage that we carry. The kid smiles at us and I smile back, no point in being a bad loser. I find myself congratulating them, admitting it will be a long time before this Dublin team will win another Leinster. The boy innocently asks me when Dublin last won the All-Ireland. Nineteen ninety-five. He wasn't even born. Sickened, I decide against the pub post-mortem, say my goodbyes to the lads and jump in the car. I switch on some loud music and head for Carlow.

As I drive home I find myself breaking out in a cold sweat, twitching, rubbing my head. Being beaten by Meath does that to you. So it's into the qualifiers we go, where wounded animals like Cork and Armagh lurk. The draw will be crucial, we need a soft landing after the horrors of today, a home tie to calm the nerves. Many wanted it to be this way. Now that they have got their wish, I wonder if it seems quite so appealing.

I see Pat Gilroy interviewed later. He manages to sound philosophical, no mention of any startled earwigs. He says all the right things and admits that today wasn't good enough. Pat is one of those guys who treats defeat the same as victory. I haven't seen him smile yet and he's almost two years into the job, preferring to present a calm exterior in public. He's been let down by the players today, some of the defending was abject, some of the problems of his own making, he needs to decide where to go from here. He promises to work hard to put things right and heads off. I get the feeling that he is heading straight for the training ground.

Jane asks how we got on as I grumpily make my way through the front door. She has other things she would rather be doing than pondering the existential struggles of the Dublin football team. But even Jane knows that a degree of understanding is needed right now. Losing to Meath is never easy. I mention the qualifiers. If Dublin get their act together Saturdays will disappear from the family agenda for the next few weeks. Samuel will lose his father, Jane her husband. The draw is kind, Tipperary at home. Somewhat surprisingly the game will be played in Croke Park, not exactly what the back door boys had in mind. Gilroy has two weeks to sort out what is becoming a sorry mess. Right now Tipperary are the least of his worries.

Chapter Ten

The Twelve Apostles

Sunday 18 September 1983

All-Ireland Senior Football Championship Final
Dublin versus Galway

Dublin arrived in the 1983 Leinster final against the reigning All-Ireland champions as massive underdogs. Kevin Heffernan was desperate to break the Offaly stranglehold but he also knew that his Dublin side was anything but the finished article. Beating a team that was chasing a third provincial crown in a row was a tall order, they had crushed Dublin a year earlier and there was little to suggest it would be any different this time around. The potential was there: the likes of Ciaran Duff, affectionately known as Dully by the Dublin support, and Barney Rock were developing nicely, but there remained much work to be done as Heffernan faced into the opening encounter of the summer against an improving Meath side.

Having said that it was always dangerous to underestimate the drive of a man who had stuck around after the glory days of the seventies had faded. Heffo was up to his old tricks, mixing youth with experience: it had worked in '74, why not again? In a move that brought back memories of Keaveney's return nine years earlier, Anton O'Toole was coaxed out of retirement to fill the full-forward berth. The spine of the team was further strengthened by the return of Brian Mullins following a horrific car crash; what Dublin's midfield general had lost in mobility he more than made up for with sheer guts and determination. With captain Tommy Drumm at centre-half back Dublin had more than enough leaders on the field. Young players like Joe McNally brought a fresh innocence and energy to proceedings as Dublin opened their campaign. Nobody could have anticipated the heights the team would reach over the next few months following an uninspiring opening day draw with Meath.

In contrast the second game was a real thriller as Meath revealed the never say die qualities that would stand them in good stead in the years ahead. But this was destined to be Dublin's day. Having blown an eight point lead, they reasserted themselves in extra-time to run out winners by 3-9 to 0-16. Two goals from sharp shooter Barney Rock were enough to see Dublin into the next round. Barney was the new Keaveney, deadly from the placed ball, born with an eye for goal. His shocking red hair stood out but it didn't seem to make it any easier for defenders to track his runs into the areas that mattered. His first goal revealed his class, a stunning shot into the top corner. The Hill had a new hero, although credit must also go to Paddy Cullen's successor in the Dublin goal. It seemed that John O'Leary had caught Paddy's penalty fever with a save that proved just as crucial in ensuring a Dublin victory.

I watched the highlights on television and marvelled at the mayhem on the Hill following Barney's punched goal in extra-time. The ball had sailed up into the air, the faces on the terrace suspended in animation as they followed its flight before Barney fisted it home, skin and hair flying as the yahoos danced with delight at the thought of a return to the good times. But there was still a long way to go, starting with Louth in the semi-final. I waited impatiently for the result as I watched the RTÉ News on a typically lazy Sunday evening. Dublin had run out easy winners by 1-12 to 0-3. The score sounded impressive, but Dublin's display had been disappointing. It seemed that Offaly had little to worry about, rumour has it that they eased up in training in anticipation of greater challenges to come.

Leinster final day: I turned on the radio on and waited for the drama to unfold. At first the commentator seemed confused. There was a third Dublin man at midfield, John Caffrey the outlaw that was defying rigid GAA logic. But this was Heffo, he did things his own way, had his own thoughts on how the game should be played, changed his tactics to suit the day that was in it. Two goals before half-time from Caffrey and McNally stunned the Offaly men who were left scratching their heads, wondering what to do about the wandering minstrel in the middle of the park. The second goal scorer McNally was another product of the Heffernan way of thinking, picking players for particular roles, having been converted from goalkeeper to free-scoring corner-forward. The pieces of the jigsaw were falling nicely into place. Not even the wonderful Matt Connor's late goal could prevent a famous Dublin win. I vowed that I would be there for the All-Ireland semi-final against Cork. News of Cork's late winning goal against Kerry in the Munster final was greeted with joy in the capital. We were in with a real chance now; although Cork would be no pushovers anything was better than facing Kerry.

Sunday 21 August 1983 was a red-letter day, I had waited for this day since that first time I had watched the Dubs nine years earlier. I was on my way to Croke Park, my first time to see Dublin in the flesh. I had convinced one of my old primary school pals to go with me, he knew the way. My eyes wide open as I spotted the ground in the distance, a great slab of concrete reaching for the sky, standing tall above the rabbit warren of terraced houses that surrounded it. Kids were out in the streets kicking ball. This was football country. I was drinking it all in, listening to the banter, enjoying the incredible characters all around us, the squeaky voices of the Cork crowd mixing with the hardness of the Dublin accents. The Hill was far too scary to contemplate, so we paid in at the Canal End. I stood for what seemed like hours, as I waited for the game to start, staring at the Hill. I couldn't take my eyes off it, a haze of blue in the distance, swaying as it filled to the brim. It seemed to move together, a seething mass of bubbling Dubs. I knew it wouldn't be long before I was there myself. The ground was exactly as I had imagined it, it felt like I had been there before; it looked just the same as it had on television.

Anton O'Toole's early goal gave Dublin an unexpected cushion of four points. It was obvious that Michael O'Hehir was glad to see the Dubs back: "Jim Ronayne into Anton O'Toole... O'Toole shaking off one man... going through... a shot and a goal. The Hill has gone mad and the man that made them mad was Anton O'Toole." It was the first goal I could remember Anton scoring, he had always played the provider in his heyday, but this goal proved to be as crucial as anything he had done before. It took a while for Cork to wake up but when they did they took control with two first-half goals from the predatory Dinny Allen with the Cork fans on the Canal End starting to find their voice. The pensive mood on the Hill was duly noted by O'Hehir who referred to "The jury on the Hill awaiting the next action." But with O'Toole and Mullins using all of their experience, Dublin were far from finished. With the score standing at Dublin 1-6 Cork 2-6 the stage was set for a gripping second-half.

No matter how hard Dublin tried, they just couldn't get any closer to Cork as the minutes ticked by. I prayed for a goal, for time to standstill, but all to no avail. I obviously wasn't on God's frequency. He was hardly expecting to hear from a Protestant in Croke Park. With only 12 minutes remaining, Cork's lead had risen to a daunting 5. Even the most ardent devotee couldn't have seen how Dublin were going to avoid the heartache of a semi-final defeat as the game entered its last 10 minutes, the excited chatter of the Cork fans in total contrast to the sense of emptiness I felt as the game moved towards its inevitable end.

But still Dublin would not give up and two quick points cut the deficit to three. I looked at my watch again – five to go – a goal would be enough to save Dublin and bring the game to a replay, but as the game entered injury-time it looked less and less likely. The Cork defence were in total control, Jimmy Kerrigan had done an excellent job on Dublin's danger man, Barney Rock; poor Barney had hardly had a kick all day. But great players only need one opportunity. Even Michael O'Hehir hadn't given up hope when he uttered the prophetic words: "Can Dublin do to Cork what Cork did to Kerry?" swiftly followed by: "We're in the dying minute of the game now... Ciaran Duff... Brian Mullins out to the wing and this is Ray Hazley... a cross in front of the goal and... a goal." The Lord had finally spoken as a breath taking move had ripped Cork's defiance asunder. He must have known I was here after all.

The outbreak of pandemonium on the Canal End matched the bedlam on the Hill. I was too busy jumping up and down to notice. I had never known a moment like it; it was as if time had stopped ticking. I felt lighter as the weight of the previous 69 minutes lifted off my shoulders and all the pressure inside my head was gone in an instant. We were level. Barney had come to the rescue. O'Hehir's words were drowned out as the whole of Dublin erupted; relief and delight rolling into one crazy outpouring of uncontainable joy. The Hill a blur of blue rhapsody: Cork 2-11 Dublin 2-11 and the final whistle went almost immediately. Somehow we had lived to fight another day.

The replay was confirmed for Páirc Uí Chaoimh. Bad news for me, there was no way my Dad would let me go. Good news for Kevin Heffernan who was relishing the thoughts of a trip south. He could feel Cork's overconfidence, knew that they thought the job was done. The game wasn't even live on television. I had lived in Cork for the first few years of my life, before we moved to Dublin when Dad retired in 1972. I was itching to make the journey but when my brother John declined my offer of a trip to our old hunting ground I had to be satisfied with another afternoon by the radio. Having tasted the atmosphere the previous Sunday that was easier said than done.

In one of the great migrations in Irish history thousands of Dubs descended on Leeside. When they got there they set up home on Hill 17 at the Blackrock end of the ground. Once again Dublin started brightly with Dully's exquisite point 29 seconds in, but this time there was no let up. The Dublin players were fired up, the hesitancy of the first game forgotten as they added a goal after three minutes, Brian Mullins smacking home a penalty. The pace was relentless, the excitement at fever pitch, blue shirts everywhere as Cork tried to come to terms with what was happening to them. By half-time the lead had jumped to five. Mullins was at his imperious best, leading from the front in possibly his best display in the blue shirt. He was singled out for a physical battering but after every knock, he simply got on with driving Dublin forward in wave after wave of attacks. Every time Cork seemed to be clawing their way back into contention a rampant Dublin hit them with a sucker punch, with further goals from Dully, Rock and McNally backing up their capital swagger. McNally's side-footed finish brought the Dublin hordes pouring onto the pitch in celebration, shirtless teeny boppers and tanned beer bellied torsos bouncing in celebration of a famous win. I had to make do with a dance around our back garden. My memories of the highlights are still dominated by Ciaran Duff's pronunciation of the word "Definitely." This was Dublinese at its very best. Dully broke it into three: "Def - in, with a massive emphasis on the, -ITELY". My mouth hung open as he said it again and again. He just wouldn't stop. As well as seeing Dublin back in the final, I had the added bonus of learning a new language.

I had to be at the final. Thankfully, I didn't need a ticket. The 1983 final is remembered for many reasons: one of them being that it was the last non-ticket All-Ireland. Seventy-one thousand nine hundred and eighty-eight people paid in and many more were lifted over the turnstiles. The old ground was dangerously overcrowded and thousands of latecomers were trapped in a crush outside before being turned away. How no one was killed was a miracle as Hill 16 swayed dangerously throughout. However, John and I were relatively comfortable up at the back of the Canal End, having made it to the ground early, our only irritation the swirling wind and rain sweeping in over our heads.

If the win over Cork had shown Dublin at their swashbuckling best, the final brought out very different qualities. This was a day for trench warfare, as the awful weather dominated from start to finish, a typical autumn day, the kind that swept the leaves from the trees and turned them into sludge before they hit the ground. Galway were struggling to kick the ball any distance as they faced into what amounted to a gale, getting out of their own half was an achievement in itself. The battle raged as players struggled to execute even the simplest of manoeuvres, frustration and desire resulting in vicious intent. Hand-to-hand combat was breaking out over every scrap of possession, Dublin getting nervier by the minute as they laboured to make use of the wind at their backs, even more so when Galway bagged the first point of the day.

It was nine long minutes before Barney Rock registered Dublin's first point with a long range free. You could almost feel the relief on the Hill. Twelve minutes in we got the break we needed. With Joe McNally lying on the ground injured, Kevin Heffernan saw fit to jog across the pitch towards his stricken forward. Galway goalkeeper Padraic Coyne either didn't see Heffo or decided to ignore him. External bodies were normal traffic on a GAA pitch, all part of the unfolding drama. Coyne's misplaced kick-out went straight into the hands of the grateful Barney Rock, who lobbed the ball back over the keeper from forty yards for the opening goal of the game, a magnificent piece of opportunism, typical Rock. As usual Michael O'Hehir was keeping track of developments: "Joe McNally being attended to as the game goes on... Barney Rock... it's a goal... a goal for Dublin... Padraic couldn't get back and shades of Paddy Cullen and an All-Ireland final against Kerry a few years ago but this one was taken legitimately." It was nice of Michael to mention that bit at the end. Seamus Aldridge: guilty as charged. At first nobody was sure what had happened. I looked to my brother as younger siblings do, searching for an answer. None was forthcoming. John was just as confused as everybody else, conversations between strangers breaking out all around as we tried to make sense of what we had just seen. I remember thinking that Antrim referee John Gough had stopped play, but the green flag was raised at the far end of the ground and the goal stood. Five minutes later Jim Ronayne kicked a wonderful over the shoulder point to stretch the Dublin lead to 1-2 to 0-1, every score something to hold onto for the second-half to come, Dublin taking on the characteristics of a squirrel collecting precious nuts for the winter. Within minutes Ciaran Duff added to the Dublin total with another placed ball, the ball taking on the trajectory of an incoming missile as it fizzed over the bar as it caught on the wind. With 20 minutes gone driving rain swept in across the ground, but we didn't care as another Barney rock free stretched the lead to 6. The Hill was rocking. I thought of Dad at home, curled up beside the fire, enjoying the unfolding drama. An umbrella, shopping bags, whatever was available was used as supporters tried to keep themselves dry. It was so bad that Michael O'Hehir felt compelled to comment, "Heaven help the Hill" as the skies opened. Michael cared about the Hill, gave it human qualities that made it seem a friendlier place. Somehow Galway sneaked another point to cut the deficit.

And then the game did what it had been threatening to do for the last 27 minutes, explode. The first major flashpoint occurred when Brian Mullins lashed out at Brian Talty, leaving the referee with no choice but to point towards the sideline. Mullins certainly didn't owe anyone any apologies as he trudged disconsolately off the pitch. However, on this day of all days, he had let his side down. It would fall to others to lead the team home.

Three minutes later two more players were headed for an early bath. The second Dublin player to be sent-off was Ray Hazley. Years later when Duff was on holiday in Italy he met an Irish guy in a bar. He asked Duff how the Dubs were doing these days. The conversation turned to the 1983 final. He asked Duff if he could remember the three Dubs sent off that day. "Mullins." "Yep." "Ciaran Duff." (He was unlikely to forget his namesake.) "Correct." and "Ray Hazley?" Three out of three. It was only then that the stranger revealed his identity. He was none other than the man himself. Ray Hazley on tour! Of the three to make the lonely walk to the line, Ray was probably the most unfortunate having become embroiled in a bout of fisticuffs with Tomás Tierney in front of the Hogan Stand towards the end of a hectic first-half.

Being down to 13 didn't seem to bother P.J. Buckley who banged over an incredible long range free, another rocket, to increase the Dublin lead to 1-5 to 0-2 at half-time. As the rain abated a rainbow appeared at the back of the Hill. I couldn't help thinking that the Sam Maguire lay at the end of it. As we shook the rain off we were oblivious to the pandemonium erupting in the tunnel below. Depending on which version of events you listen to it involved a good old fashioned dust up with skin and hair flying as the teams made their way towards the safety of their respective dressing rooms, kicking and punching, grabbing and pushing, shouting, yelling and cursing, Mullins going after Talty, players squaring up to each other, locked dressing room doors as officialdom scrambled around trying to restore order. When the dust eventually settled no more was said. It was over and done with, locked in the vaults of GAA legend. By the time the pubs had closed it had passed into folklore.

At the start of the second-half things seemed to have settled down as the sun came out. Dublin took full advantage of the temporary calm with another Rock free. Then disaster struck as the nasty undercurrent bubbled to the surface with Dully the next to go for kicking out at Pat O'Neill. It didn't matter whether he had connected or not, the damage was done. With 30 minutes to go only 12 Dublin players stood in the way of 14 Galway men and the Sam Maguire. The good news was the seven point lead they had in the bank. The bad news was a lot worse. With two men less and facing into the teeth of howling gale, the odds seemed stacked against them.

If Dublin were feeling sorry for themselves it certainly didn't show when Tommy Drumm's clever clearance found Joe McNally through on goal. As Coyne rushed out to meet him Joe fired the ball towards the empty net, only to see it clear the bar by inches: Dublin 1-7 Galway 0-2. It took Galway 10 minutes to record their first score of the second-half, but once they had broken their duck they quickly recorded a second. It looked as if the tide was turning, ever so slightly. Instead it was Dublin who registered the next point, another free from Barney. And then catastrophe: a goal for Galway, with The Hill tumbling dangerously downwards as the ball hit the back of the net. It was immediately followed by another point. Dublin's lead had been cut to three in the blink of an eye: 1-8 to 1-5. With 18 minutes left, it looked as if the Dublin goose was well and truly cooked.

But the players had other ideas, by some means they picked themselves up off the floor for the umpteenth time to hit back with another couple of frees from the ever reliable Rock. Crucially Galway failed to score for 12 minutes before they cut the deficit to 4 with 6 minutes left. With three minutes on the clock the lead was down to three, then two as Galway threw the kitchen sink at the Dublin defence in those excruciating dying minutes. Johnny Hughes shot wide from in front of the Dublin goal, P.J. Buckley blocked a Johnny Tobin pile driver and Barney Rock punched a ball out from under the crossbar as Galway turned the screw.

It was hard to see what was going on from the other end, so many bodies were massed in front of the Hill 16 goal. From a Dublin point of view, time stood still, in Galway it rushed by. In scenes reminiscent of 1974, the Dublin scallywags massed on the end line as the final minutes ticked by.

At the final whistle Dublin players sunk to their knees in exhaustion and thanksgiving at what had been achieved as Michael O'Hehir preached the gospel. "And so 12 men have won the All Ireland." Seconds later they were submerged in sea of riotous blue celebration. Galway's humiliation was finally over. Dublin had slipped under the radar to record their twenty-first All-Ireland success.

In that amazing last half-hour the twelve apostles held their ground, in the face of a repeated Galway assault, with one of the gutsiest displays ever seen on final day. Others like to call them the dirty dozen. From somewhere deep within the Dublin players found the will to keep going when all seemed lost. Every one of the players who came ashore at the end was a returning hero, different than the man who had taken to the field a couple of hours earlier. Boys had grown into men, great players had become legends. It was as if they were defending the Hill itself in that fateful second-half. All through the siege the Hill stood squarely behind their men defiantly roaring them home. Even though Galway out scored Dublin with the wind, it was Dublin's five points against the elements to the Tribesmen's two that proved to be the difference. In the last half hour Dublin played every minute as if it was the last. They looked no further than the next challenge – it wasn't about winning Sam – it was about winning the next ball. With the odds stacked against them, they defied the greatest battering the city had taken since Easter 1916, only this time the few came out on top, even managing to stay alive in the process. On this occasion the bloodletting was left to the national press in the days that followed.

The win was all the more special because the Dublin full-back line included my favourite ever Dublin player: Mick Holden. Mick was the joker in the pack but more importantly a bloody good defender. Like many of his team-mates, this was his finest hour.

As Tommy Drumm lifted Sam above his head, the inquest was only just beginning, not that we cared. The press boys could say what they liked; all that mattered to us was that Sam was home. The ghosts of '74 looked on with pride, as the rest of the country looked on in horror: the Jacks were back. The comedians on the Hill argued that they had never gone away. I was as happy as I'd ever been. I had made a mess of my Leaving Certificate, but it didn't seem to matter anymore. Nothing mattered. Dublin had won the All-Ireland and I had been there to see it. Life couldn't get much better. I had timed my arrival perfectly, two matches and one All-Ireland title, not a bad start to my Dublin career.

Chapter Eleven

The Centenary Final

Sunday 22 September 1984

All-Ireland Senior Football Championship Final
Dublin versus Kerry

Dublin were back to defend their title in the Centenary All-Ireland final in 1984. Somewhat shockingly, they had surrendered to Westmeath in the Centenary Cup, a special competition celebrating one hundred years of the GAA. This gave my Dad, a Westmeath man, a right laugh. He may have pinned his colours to the Kerry mast, but that didn't stop him rubbing my nose in it.

Having broken my attendance duck a year earlier I couldn't get enough of the Dubs. I had spent the winter months wending my way to Croker to watch the league games, most of which Dublin seemed to lose. It was always entertaining, if a little frustrating. But the league is the league and it was the championship that really set the pulses racing. On those cold winter days, it was the thoughts of summer days ahead that kept the cockles of the heart warm. It was on one such day that I spied one of Dublin's real heroes chatting away to a friend outside the ground: Phil Lynott who cut an imposing figure in his knee-length leather coat. It made my day. It was typical of Phil to be there to watch the Dubs on one of the days that mattered least.

With the confidence that comes with an All-Ireland triumph, Dublin eased past Wexford and Offaly to qualify for another Leinster final, but were in serious need of a more substantial challenge. It was no surprise that they got it from a Meath team coming off the back of success in the Centenary Cup. On a boiling hot July day, I was among the 56,000 who turned up to see if Dublin would retain their Leinster title. This was my first time at the provincial decider, my initial experience of Dublin and Meath. Little by little, Dad was setting me free. I was still watching from the Canal End, biding my time before I made the step up to the Hill.

The atmosphere was electric. There was no time to draw breath as three goals arrived early, two to Dublin, one to Meath. Meath also missed a penalty and Dublin were reduced to fourteen men when John Caffrey was sent-off before half-time. But once again, the side with the extra man ended up losing out, with goals from Ciaran Duff and Barney Rock enough to see Dublin home, 2-10 to 1-9. For Dublin at the time, it was a case of keeping Meath in their place, as they knew that there could be lasting consequences if the Royals usurped their place at Leinster's top table. Meath could sense our fear at 50 paces. For this reason games between the two began to take on an air of desperation reflected by a definite edginess between the two sets of supporters. A fight broke out to my right between a big Meath farmer and a short-tempered Dub, punches were thrown and panic rippled through the crowd. I felt sorry for the Meath man; blood was pumping from his nose as they were pulled apart. Apologies were made, hands were shaken, but the bitterness that had sparked the fight hung in the air. An uneasy peace settled for the rest of the game.

In the days leading up to the All-Ireland semi-final against Tyrone I had a big decision to make. I had served my apprenticeship and I knew that I was ready for the Hill. Playing against a northern side helped me make up my mind and I figured I would be safer in with the delinquents on the Hill. The North was out of control, I didn't expect their supporters to be any different.

Short on friends who were into Gaelic football, I was attending most of the games on my own. And, as I made my way onto the Hill for the first time, I looked nervously around me; the people seemed normal enough, chatting away as they awaited the arrival of the teams. Then, just as I was beginning to feel at home all hell broke loose: Tyrone were first out of the tunnel. But why were they running towards us? In their infinite wisdom they had decided to take over the Hill 16 goal for their warm up, part of the northern way, confrontation the order of the day. I wondered if I had made the right decision as people who had been a picture of calmness only seconds earlier began to spit venom at the Tyrone players. Their faces took on the contorted look of evil monsters as they vented their feelings and there seemed to be little else to do but join in. I loved it. The Hill was bristling with its usual righteous indignation that it gets when it feels that it has been sinned against. This was a declaration of war from Tyrone and there was no way that we were going to take it lying down. Things only got worse when Dublin entered the arena and immediately headed for the same end; for the next few minutes the kick around took on a farcical nature with both teams warming up in front of a seething Hill, a baptism of fire that I had never expected.

In the end that was as close as Tyrone got. When the actual game started, they proved to be no match even for a Dublin team playing within itself. It's one thing laying down the gauntlet but it's of little use unless you are able to back it up, as goals by Barney Rock and Joe McNally ensured an easy passage to yet another All-Ireland final. The 2-11 to 0-8 score line reflected Dublin's obvious superiority. During the second-half, the ruffians down in the bottom corner of the Hill decided that they had better things to be doing on a Sunday afternoon than watching Dublin coast home, bored by the course the game was taking they turned their attentions to the Garda Síochana. Missiles reigned down, doc martens meeting fence, batons crunching into flesh as both sides fought for the upper hand. The terrified faces of the pensioners in the Nally Stand reflected the ferocity of the skirmish. It was over as quickly as it had started. The police wisely withdrew and allowed the situation to calm down, the sight of a guard lobbing a shoe back into the Hill showed the more caring side of the other boys in blue. I was shocked by the outbreak of violence but more than impressed by the condemnation of the majority on the Hill who told the young hooligans where to go in no uncertain fashion: "Go Home, You Bums" was sung with gusto as we turned on our own for once.

The final against Kerry had an extra-special feel about it, a chance to relive the epic rivalry of the seventies, Kevin Heffernan renewing acquaintances with Mick O'Dwyer. Heffo must have been desperate to get one over on his Kerry counterpart. With O'Dwyer three to two ahead in championship victories over the Dubs since 1975, it was time to get even. It seemed apt that two of the biggest hitters in Gaelic football should lock horns in the Centenary final. Dad was looking forward to another Kerry victory. Getting a ticket was my main concern in the weeks and days leading up to the game and not surprisingly, they were like gold dust. In the end my Godmother in Cork came up with a precious ticket and popped it in the post on the Monday prior to the game. I was in the hands of the Irish postal service, a scary thought. Sure enough Tuesday and Wednesday passed with no sign. I was beginning to panic, my parents begging the post man to make enquiries. I could see it arriving the following Monday, the day after the game. By

Thursday I was frantic, until an envelope with a Cork post mark plopped through the door. I was going to my second All-Ireland final in three years. I was more than content with a seat in the Hogan Stand, even if I wasn't going to be on the Hill.

The press were finding it hard to pick a winner. Dublin's run to the final had been relatively trouble-free but they hadn't been particularly impressive, doing just enough to get the job done. If they were going to beat Kerry, they needed to reach the kind of heights they had scaled in the previous year's semi-final replay in Cork. Having finally shaken off the shock of the defeats to Offaly and Cork over the previous two years Kerry were beginning to look like their old selves again.

I was sitting amongst the members of the Cork County Board, who were looking somewhat bemused to find a uniformed Dub in their midst. They treated me as they would an exotic bird, monitoring my reaction to what was happening on the pitch. I am sure I was more entertaining as sadly, the game proved to be a massive disappointment. Dublin just never got going, as a clinical Kerry side suffocated the life out of them. The entire seventy minutes had that terrible feeling of inevitability about it from very early on as Dublin struggled in vain to break the Kerry stranglehold.

It felt as if I was stuck to my seat throughout. We were struggling to breathe as Kerry bossed the opening 35 minutes. A lead of seven points to three at half-time became nine to three early in the second-half and there seemed no way back. But hope springs eternal, and in the forty-third minute, Ciaran Duff fed the ball to Tommy Conroy who found Barney Rock free in front of goal. Barney gave Charlie Nelligan no chance with a well-placed shot into the corner of the Kerry net. My heart rose as the Hill danced with delight. But sadly, that was as good as it got: Tommy Conroy lost possession at the crucial moment when it seemed as if a second Dublin goal was on and following that it was a stroll in the park as late points from Ogie Moran and John Kennedy typified what had been a very comfortable afternoon for the Kerry men.

For once, Kevin Heffernan may have got it wrong. Kerry played on his mind more than any other side and he planned accordingly. Whereas the third midfielder had worked a treat in the past, his decision to use John Kearns to mark Kerry's danger man Jack O'Shea backfired as Dublin surrendered the initiative and became entangled in a tactical web of their own making. Instead of playing with their usual heart and flamboyance, they seemed strangely out of sorts. As with many of their displays that season, it seemed that Dublin were playing with the hand brake on.

Chapter Twelve

Heffo Says Goodbye To The Hill

Sunday 22 September 1985

All-Ireland Senior Football Championship Final
Dublin versus Kerry – Again

The 1985 All-Ireland final turned out to be a very different affair. It had everything that the Centenary final lacked, a titanic struggle which swung one way and then the other. I spent the first-half wondering what the hell was going on as Kerry unleashed shock and awe on a terrified Dublin defence and the second on the edge of my armchair as Dublin threatened to pull off one of the greatest comebacks of all time. It was only when Dublin were left with no choice but to throw caution to the wind that they broke loose, all their pent up frustration at Kerry's dominance pouring out in a frenetic last 25 minutes. Up to then the outcome had looked as predictable as it had 12 months earlier.

Dublin's run to the '85 final mirrored that of '84 with opening wins over Wexford and a rapidly fading Offaly, both of them on the road. I wasn't at either encounter; moving to the Hill was one thing but travelling outside the capital was still off-limits for me. Stories of ransacked trains and trails of empty cider bottles leading to the gates of tired provincial venues were the order of the day. They might not have been entirely true but they made for good press. I hadn't learnt to drive yet and without any immediate allies I was on the road to nowhere. My limited knowledge of Ireland's road network didn't help. I had done my best to learn as little in school as possible, there really wasn't much that interested me. It hadn't taken me long to find out that the Irish education system was not to my liking. Even though I enjoyed the odd aspect of school life, I spent most of my time itching to escape a system that was killing any spirit and creativity that was living inside me. It should have been preparing me for life, not just for the Leaving Cert. Knowing how to get to places like Wexford and Tullamore would have been a start. I desperately needed to hook up with some fellow travellers if I was to realise my dream of going to every Dublin game, but for the time being I had to be content with regular trips to Croke Park. And on some days even that was proving hard enough to find.

I was back there for the 1985 Leinster final against Laois with my brother John. We managed to get lost on the way to the ground. I felt like a bit of an eejit when I had to ask a Laois man for directions with my Dublin hat and scarf on. The rain was pelting down as we approached the turnstiles and there was no way John was going to spend the afternoon getting soaked on Hill 16. I had no choice but to go along with his decision. Secretly, I was quite happy to be sitting in the relative comfort of the Hogan Stand, as the downpour showed little sign of abating. It was never going to be a classic, Dublin running out winners by ten points to four, with Laois left to rue a number of wasted opportunities. Just like the year before Dublin were doing just enough, no more, no less.

I was back on the Hill for the semi-final with Mayo, with Dublin raging-hot favourites to reach their third consecutive All-Ireland final. With Kerry fancied to beat Monaghan in the other semi, yet another final meeting with Dublin looked odds on. The mid-eighties were beginning to feel like the seventies all over again. In total contrast to the Laois game, the semi-final was played on one of the hottest days of the year. Mayo hit the ground running: Noel Durkin's third minute goal shocked the Hill but after that it was Dublin who gained the upper hand to go six points ahead at half-time.

Early in the second-half the lead had stretched to seven and there seemed no way back for the green and red, but the introduction of Padraig Brogan and Tom Byrne changed the mood with Mayo hitting five unanswered points. And still they kept coming, rampaging towards the Hill, Dublin desperately trying to cling on. Another point cut the gap to the minimum before T.J. Kilgallon's point in the dying seconds brought the sides level. Leaving the ground, I was in a state of shock, Dublin failing to register a score for the final 26 minutes. As I wandered back into town, I met a bunch of Mayo supporters who asked me what I thought. They listened intently, a Dub preaching the gospel according to Heffo. I told them that their chance had gone, to enjoy today because this was as good as it gets. Dublin couldn't play as poorly again. Heffo wouldn't let them, one look at Mayo would be enough, he'd have them sussed by the time the following Sunday rolled around. They listened intently, nodded, said goodbye and headed on their way. I bet they didn't believe a word I had said. Amazingly, the other semi-final had also ended all square a week earlier. Perhaps a Dublin-Kerry final wasn't set in stone after all.

In the meantime controversy raged as to how Mayo's wing-back, John Finn had sustained a broken jaw during the game. Fingers were pointed at a few Dublin players but there was no evidence to back the accusations up. The days of multiple camera angles were still a long way off. It only added to the spice in the days leading up to the replay.

Finn wasn't the only one to miss the second game. I had a date with Amy Purdy, an American girl. At the time I worked in a tourist hostel in Gardiner Street; the reason I was bumping into girls from the other side of the pond. Amy and I were destined for the Phoenix Park as the blue-shirted hordes headed in the opposite direction. The things we do for love. I didn't think an afternoon in the company of the Hill's finest would impress Amy; she was far too nice for that. I would never ever make the same mistake again. I tried to block the game out of my mind, trying to pretend it wasn't happening; that I wasn't missing something special. Which I knew I was; that much was obvious when I finally heard the score on the way home: Dublin 2-12 Mayo 1-7. Another cracker apparently and a lot closer than the score suggested, with Mayo leading by two points nine minutes into the second-half. It had taken two predatory goals from Dully in front of a frantic Hill to turn the game on its head, one of his finest hours in a Dublin shirt. The afternoon also saw one of the greatest goals ever scored in Croke Park, a pile driver by Mayo's Padraig Brogan. Nevertheless, Dublin were back where they wanted to be. That was the good news. The bad news was that Kerry had also made it.

I knew that I shouldn't have missed the replay; bad karma. It was of little surprise when I subsequently failed to get my hands on a ticket for the final as I had messed with the natural order. So it was back to the sitting room, reliving the '74 experience with my Dad looking forward to yet another Kerry victory. Sadly, Michael O'Hehir had suffered a stroke and was replaced by Ger Canning as commentator. Ger was full of facts but lacking in the subtlety that O'Hehir would have brought to the table. It just wasn't the same without Michael's timeless commentary; he would have enjoyed the ebb and flow of what turned out to be an astonishing game.

By half-time, I was feeling glad that I wasn't there. With Jack O'Shea lording it at midfield, Kerry had been even more dominant than they had been twelve months earlier; if anything the scoreline of 1-8 to 0-2 flattered Dublin.

A second Kerry goal early in the second-half set the stage for a massacre of 1978 proportions, more humiliation staring Dublin in the face, when suddenly the afternoon turned on its head. Kevin Heffernan finally made the call he had been avoiding all afternoon when he pulled a struggling Brian Mullins ashore and introduced P.J. Buckley. Along with the switching of John Kearns to midfield at the beginning of the second-half, it changed the whole complexion of the game and tipped the balance in Dublin's favour.

Having cut the deficit to six points, Dublin had to regroup following Kerry's second goal; a kick in the teeth which should have quelled any chance of a fight back. But Kearns and company were having none of it and now they set about doing it all over again. Kearns was having his best game in a Dublin shirt, roaming the field like a man possessed. In the 17th minute of the second-half he floated a high ball into Joe McNally and Joe did the rest with a stinging shot. Goal for Dublin. Points from Barney Rock and Kearns cut the gap still further. Hope was replacing despair on the Hill.

In our sitting room the whole mood had changed. Dad was quiet now, worried about what was to come. He had spent the first-half pretending that he wasn't all that bothered, doing his best not to rub it in, talking absentmindedly about making a cup of tea at half-time. Well he wasn't thinking about a cup of tea now. He had the look of a man who had found out that the immersion had been left on, something that was guaranteed to scare the shit out of men of my Dad's generation. In contrast, I was moving towards the edge of my seat with every passing minute, screaming at the television screen.

With six minutes to go, Joe McNally punched a high ball from Kearns to the Kerry net for Dublin's second goal. We were in business, the good ship Kerry was listing, their lead cut to a single point: Kerry 2-8 Dublin 2-7. I still feel to this day that if Dublin had scored the next point they would have gone on to win, but it wasn't to be, as Kerry did what great teams do and held their nerve, the legacy of their past kicking in when they needed it most. Or maybe this was just meant to be their day. With two minutes to go, they stretched their lead to two and by the final whistle, they were four ahead. Having come within a whisker of one of the greatest comebacks of all time, Dublin had nothing left in the tank.

The referee's decision not to penalise Jack O'Shea for picking the ball off the ground in the Kerry square early in the second period didn't seem important at the time but in hindsight it could have made a big difference. Dad was smiling, more out of relief than any sense of immediate satisfaction. Or maybe he was just thinking about a fresh pot of tea. In the days following the final the usual post-mortem took place in the capital, the sporting pathologists meeting to pick over the bones of the Dublin carcass, visiting the local hostelries to listen to the victors and the vanquished. Just like the previous year, the finger of blame was pointed at Kevin Heffernan. In Dublin even our heroes aren't immune to criticism. Many felt that his loyalty to Brian Mullins had cost Dublin the game, it was only when the energetic P.J. Buckley was introduced that the tide began to turn in earnest. If it had been done earlier maybe Dublin would not have had as high a mountain to climb. It was easy to see Heffernan's dilemma, his loyalty to his captain who had done so much for him during his time in charge. It was a sad way for Brian's career to end; nobody could have given more for the cause.

The aftermath was littered with the wreckage of Dublin's dreams. One of Dublin's greatest ever players had played his last game in a Dublin jersey, with Kerry's recent domination of Dublin confirmed with another two successive wins over their greatest rivals. We were beginning to wonder if we would ever beat them again. It would be seven long years before Dublin would be back in an All-Ireland final. It was also the end for Kevin Heffernan, Dublin's two leaders on and off the pitch gone in one afternoon. They would prove impossible to replace. Four All-Ireland defeats on the bounce to Mick O'Dwyer's gifted Kerry side had sapped whatever remained of Heffo's strength. It was time for someone else to take up the reins.

Chapter Thirteen

Tipping Point

Saturday 10 July 2010

**All-Ireland Senior Football Championship Third Round Qualifier
Dublin versus Tipperary**

I did my best to avoid the inevitable fall out that followed Dublin's defeat to Meath. I suppose that's the good thing about supporting a county team, as long as you stay clear of the *Evening Herald* you can sidestep the hysteria, especially if you live in Carlow. For the previous fourteen days a sense of unease had settled over the urban skyline. People were fed up, sickened by another Dublin collapse. It didn't sound like they'd be coming back anytime soon. The good news was that Dublin had been written off as potential All-Ireland champions, leaving Pat Gilroy and the players to exist in a bubble without hype, the first time they had experienced such freedom in years. Left to just get on with it, they were finally in control of their own destiny. Nothing else mattered anymore; it was up to them were the story would end.

The Icelandic ash cloud had been replaced by the fallout that comes with every Dublin football disaster. The dogs are howling in the street, Dublin shirts are available on Ebay, the *Evening Herald* are laying off staff, Vodafone are counting the cost of their new sponsorship deal and the marketing gurus at Arnotts are giving themselves a well deserved pat on the back as they recognise the genius of their exit strategy. Dublin fans are planning their holidays for August for the first time in years. All are agreed, it seems only a matter of time before Dublin make an ignominious exit from this year's championship.

I find it better to retreat inside myself at times like this, introspection has become my only ally, that and Duff. Duff doesn't do crazy talk; he just smokes his cigarette and moves on, the calm in the eye of the storm. We've seen it all, it's nothing new. It's not like we haven't lost to Meath before. And we're still here. No matter how bad things look there is always hope, always the promise of a better tomorrow. And when it doesn't come we know that we have our DVD of the seventies to fall back on, the good old days that haunt us still, especially at times like this. Why can't it be like that all the time?

It's a typically grim Saturday evening as we step out of Duff's house and head for Croker, my loyal lieutenant by my side. I first met Duff towards the end of 1991. I was walking along O'Connell Street with one of my teacher friends Trevor when he pointed towards an approaching stranger and said "There's my good friend Duff." I couldn't help but notice that he had a striking resemblance to a young Shane McGowan as Trevor shouted out a big "Hello Duff, good to see you." Duff took one look at him, stuck his nose in the air and walked on by. I was amused and baffled as Trevor shook his head; "That must be to do with the fifty quid I owe him." Later when I got to meet Duff properly, and the debt had been repaid, I discovered that he was a Dublin supporter, one of the good guys. Suddenly I had an ally. I had walked a lonely road for over nine years, going to games on my own for the most part. I just needed someone to talk to. I had often found myself waking up at night wondering where Dublin's next All-Ireland was going to come from. But now there was Duff and it just got better, as he had other Dublin supporting friends and family; people who would understand my pain. Everything was going to be just fine. I had finally found my band of brothers.

As we wander down along the canal I look towards the grey sky. Pauline was right again, had warned us to bring our ponchos. The mood is sombre, the canal is deserted, the cider drinkers conspicuous by their absence. Again. Even the merchandise sellers seem subdued, slow business tonight. The touts haven't even bothered to turn up; two years ago they would have been out in force. It might as well be Corduff all over again. We don't even talk about the game, it'll have to look after itself, the time for talking long gone.

Maurice texted to say that he was running a little late, promises to meet us on the Hill later. Maurice is hanging by a thread, he has been losing the faith of late and I am surprised to hear that he is coming tonight. He hasn't been on the Hill for years. Duff tells him where we'll be standing, mentions something about a Centra sign. Duff knows the Hill like the back of his hand. Our line up changes from match to match depending on any number of influences: holidays, illness, family or work can all play their part in who turns up. P.O. and Niall are otherwise engaged tonight, both with acceptable excuses – a family dinner and a girlfriend's birthday – we let it pass. But lately apathy and disinterest have begun to rear their ugly heads, it seems like many have had enough. Many now see the hurlers as a better bet, underdogs on the way up, a far more enticing prospect than a washed out football team. But I rarely miss a game these days; I like to think I'll always be here. Over the years, I have become a lot more adept at planning my holidays so that they fall in between games, but the uncertainty of the qualifiers presents a whole different set of problems. You only have a week to prepare, to make your excuses and a few sandwiches before heading out the door. Win, and it means you get to do it all over again the following week. Come what may, I am determined to see this summer through. Holidays are off the agenda for the next few weeks. For all I know, such problems could be behind me in seventy minutes. Dublin stand on the brink of humiliation tonight, a loss to a hurling county could stymie our progress for seasons to come. The way things are going the likes of Kerry may well be calling us a hurling county soon.

It's hard to know what to make of the qualifiers. We haven't been here for awhile; five provincial titles in a row have allowed us the luxury of watching the qualifying dogfight from a safe distance. But now we're back with all the uncertainty that it brings. Drawing Tipperary certainly seems a stroke of fortune for us, but will we be able to capitalise on it?

A half-empty Hill tells its own story, even the upper tier of the stands are shut tonight. About 22,000 turn up in the end, giving the night the feeling of a meaningless league game, but it's anything but. It's hard not to feel lonely, but also somewhat cosy in a strange way. We are the diehards, the chosen few. The good time boys and the corporate whores have moved on to pastures new, but they'll be back when Dublin reawaken, waffling on about how they were there on that cold, dark night when Dublin squeezed past Tipperary.

Marty Morrissey was made for nights like this. He lives for the humdrum of GAA life and worships the gods of the game. I know that there is a good chance Marty will be here tonight, his tan and his never-ending enthusiasm brightening up an otherwise dull evening. You can always count on his colourful jackets to raise a few eyebrows, not least his own. I sometimes wonder whether Marty was the result of some strange biological experiment carried out deep in the bowels of Gaeldom in an attempt to produce the perfect reporter, who would convey the magic of our wonderful game as if it was a matter of life and death. Marty has a way of making a squabble in Limerick hurling seem as if it holds the key to our very existence. Sometimes I get the feeling that he may well be right.

The Dublin players look straight ahead as they run out onto the pitch, they're almost afraid to look at us; apprehensive about what they might see. With empty concrete terracing reminding them of their recent sins, they must have known that it would be like this. They look guilty, even though they owe us nothing. They do the training and make the sacrifices. We do the drinking and the giving out. They must feel deserted right now, but they can't afford to feel sorry for themselves. They have us to think about, the ones who bothered their arses to turn up. Like it or not, they are stuck with us, if we're here on a night like this we'll be back the next day and the one after that until it ends. Losing to Tipp is not an option. The Dublin football team need to let us know that they are still around, that their heart is still beating, however faintly.

Really, we're on a hiding to nothing tonight, we should beat Tipp but this game is all about staying in the championship. We will get no credit for a win and if we lose... lose and bonfires will burn all over the country and the *Herald* will fold. It's time to circle the wagons, get the win – go home – see what the next round brings. If that doesn't happen, it'll be time to turn off the lights.

The Hill is restless. I get the feeling that more than a few are here to watch a car crash, to have a good moan when it all starts to go wrong. The odd 'Gilroy Out' placard here and there. Like me, others are here because they have to be, because they can't stay away, because even in the bad times this is where they find peace. We live for nights like this one just as much as those sun-drenched days when the place is packed to the rafters with Dublin on a roll. You can't have one without the other. How else would we know the difference?

Rain sweeps down as the referee prepares to throw the ball in. Time to get the poncho out, I had to buy another one tonight, having left my previous purchase at home. The plastic ponchos sold by the street vendors around Croke Park seem to be the new bags for life, important but not important enough to remember when you leave home. This one is blue: cheap and cheerful, they sell out in minutes on nights like this, turn up late and you'll have to make do with a white one. I no longer care about how I look; the last couple of Irish summers have been all about survival. Getting into one of these ponchos isn't easy, I generally confuse one of the arms with the hood part and wonder how the hell I am supposed to get my head through such a small hole. It doesn't help that l always leave it too late, hoping against hope that the dark clouds will pass us by. I almost fall over as I frantically squeeze into the dryness of the blue plastic. I look to see if there are any telltale rips in the fabric. These things are paper-thin and the ferocity of putting them on usually leads to a couple of tears. That's the other problem; you sweat like a pig, especially on a wet muggy night. The life expectancy of a poncho is very short. If they don't disintegrate at the match then you are bound to lose them in the pub. Either way, it ends up necessitating another purchase.

Maurice texted again to say that he is on his way; he shouldn't have much trouble finding us on a night like this. Pat Gilroy cuts a solitary figure as he watches his team warm up, our leader has the look of a Buddhist monk on a three month retreat, he never seems surprised by the places his team bring him to. He always looks calm, self-contained, knows what needs to be done if Dublin are to get back to where they belong. But even Pat must know that tonight is do or die. Lose and I can't see him surviving. Losing to Meath is one thing, losing to Tipperary entirely another.

Dublin led by six points to one after just ten minutes, but the game was far from over. Dublin's early flurry of points included a 45 from goalkeeper Stephen Cluxton. As he strode up field to take the kick we looked at each other and wondered if Gilroy had lost it: a goalkeeper taking a 45? Seconds later, we were cheering as the ball sailed over the bar. What a great tactic! We were soon celebrating a goal as Eoghan O'Gara gathered the ball on the right, rounded his marker, sprinted towards the square before delivering the perfect pass to Michael Dara MacAuley, who punched the ball past Paul Fitzgerald in the Tipperary goal. Alan Brogan added another point to stretch the lead to seven. There's still no sign of Maurice. Surely he should have been here by now.

The goal should have settled Dublin. Instead it led to another mini-implosion as Tipperary fought their way back into contention. We had a perfect view of the horror unfolding below as Barry Grogan stole in behind a static Rory O'Carroll – who slipped on the wet pitch as he tried to change direction – to fire past a stunned Stephen Cluxton. Yet again, Dublin's rearguard had been sliced apart by one simple long ball and our lead was down to four. I am becoming increasingly worried about O'Carroll, he has the makings of a good player but there is a real risk that his confidence will be damaged irreparably if he has to endure much more of this. By half-time the lead was a mere two points – 1-9 to 1-7 – and my eight point winning prediction was looking extravagantly optimistic. But I have other things on my mind: I am beginning to fear for Maurice's well being. How could he have got lost in such a small crowd? Maybe he's forgotten his way to the Hill; it's been years since he's been here, his migration to the stands at the turn of the century down to the onset of middle age and fatherhood.

We began to ready ourselves for the worst when Tipperary reduced the gap to a single point after the restart. The only good news being the arrival of Maurice; not for the first time he had wandered too far to the right and found himself in amongst the cider drinkers behind the goal – the Bermuda Triangle of the Hill – not a place for the faint-hearted. He blamed it on the wrong Centra sign. We blamed it on old age. It was good to have him back; I was worried his referee burning past had caught up with him at last and he had been captured and brought to some GAA version of Guantanamo Bay off the west coast. Having survived his trip to the dark side Maurice was quickly into his stride, taking note of the referee's name and county after a questionable decision early in the second-half. He hadn't gone away.

Bernard Brogan gave the Dubs some breathing space with another point, but Tipperary hit back to cut the deficit to a single point once again. We began to think the unthinkable before the Dubs' superior fitness gradually kicked in, resulting in a late flurry of points: 1-21 to 1-13 in the end. My prediction had been spot on. Relief all around; we had survived the opening round of Russian roulette.

As we make the long walk back to the pub, we feel a little better. Not much but at least we know that there will be another day. Still there's no getting away from another disappointing Dublin performance, the ease with which Tipperary worked their way back into the game all too familiar. Tonight was a step in the right direction but still the doubts remain: Gilroy needs to decide on a system and stick to it. Confidence will only come with winning. But there were encouraging signs too, MacAuley and O'Gara impressed again and it was good to see Bernard Brogan approaching his best form. The power and no-nonsense that MacAuley and O'Gara bring to proceedings is something that Dublin are badly in need of. Players who are prepared to do the dirty work that allows the more gifted to shine. Once again MacAuley was relentless but it remains to be seen whether O'Gara will be able to up his scoring ratio to the level that will be required. But he is a raw talent. He needs time but judging by some of the comments on the Hill he will be lucky to get it. Understanding and compassion are in short supply. The Hill doesn't do age; you're either good enough or you aren't. Young players are often seen as a luxury we can't afford, unless they're winners. When you've been waiting for an All-Ireland for 15 years it's hardly surprising . It's never easy coming into the Dublin team, but right now it must be hell.

The following day I go through the television coverage of the game. Another consequence of Dublin's descent into the qualifiers is that they now find themselves at the mercy of TV3. Only a belated appearance in the All-Ireland quarter-final will see them returning to the tender loving arms of RTÉ. Even Matt Cooper and the TV3 boys seem to be struggling lift their enthusiasm for this one, with Peter Canavan particularly sombre in his appraisal of how far this Dublin team has fallen. And you can't really blame them, Saturday night wasn't exactly a barrel of laughs. But it's Peter who seems to be suffering the most, he looks all Dubbed out. Been beaten by the Dubs in 1995 must have hurt, but I get the feeling it's not that. It's more likely to be the disproportionate amount of coverage that Dublin have received over the years, especially at a time when his beloved Tyrone were at the top of their game. In the end it's left to former Dub Senan Connell to tell us what it's like to be a Dublin player with all the hype and pressure that brings. Not much fun right now by the sounds of it.

I turn next to *The Sunday Game*. Des Cahill, Cuala man and Dublin fan, has taken over the presenter's chair from footballing fundamentalist Pat Spillane. I always got the feeling that the former Kerry legend seemed to think that every man, woman and child should be able to kick a ball over a set of posts from 60 yards in front of 60,000 screaming nutcases, and still be able to take a few digs at the same time. If you had these attributes then in Pat's eyes, you had what it takes to make a useful county footballer. A rare breed of fellow it must be said but if you don't meet these exacting criteria, you don't exist in Pat's perfect world. I can handle Pat in short bursts, but a whole programme devoted to his worship of the finer points of the game, especially the kick pass, was a bridge too far. Naturally Dublin were a perfect target for Pat's high standards – effete athletes rather than footballers – they failed the acid test time and again. And how he loved them for their weaknesses, salivating at their wondrous ability to snatch defeat from the jaws of victory. And all of this at a time when Kerry were at their fluent best. In typical Kerry style, he even talked us up before the horror of 2009. Kerry men have a habit of doing that, they talk up their opponents and talk themselves down, sowing the seeds of complacency. I know better now. 2009 has left me scarred. I'd rather get lost than ask for directions down around Killarney. I will never believe a Kerry man again.

So it's been Des Cahill since the start of the season. I'm fond of Des. He has a relaxed style, enjoys the game, Marty Morrissey without the rough edges and the Kim Jong-il hairdo. Des understands that the players are amateurs giving it everything that they have. He has a way of guiding the audience through the most painful of experiences with a light touch. An hour of Des and you're guaranteed to feel better about yourself and your team.

It's hard not to like a man who stood up and was counted during some of the darkest days that our troubled state has known. In the aftermath of Italia '90 everybody was an expert, with a new breed of armchair and barstool pundits stalking the land in search of anyone who would listen, driving those of us who had revelled in our sporting anonymity further underground. Suddenly sport belonged to the masses. On the radio, in the shops, in the pub, in the bloody pub toilet, there was always someone ready to tell you something that you knew already. There was no escaping them, they would rabbit on for hours as if their opinion was the only one that mattered. And when the great World Cup juggernaut rolled on, they couldn't bear to wait another four years for another shot at self-importance, so they duly hopped on the next bandwagon that appeared: Manchester Fecking United.

The Red Devils, up to then a nasty blister became a rancid boil that gripped much of the nation for the next 20 years and it's not over yet. Thankfully it doesn't seem to matter as much anymore. Seeing a kid in a Man United top now is much the same as seeing Kerry winning the All-Ireland. It happens all the time. Time dulls the brain. But none of us who lived through those dark days will ever forget the part played by Des Cahill. Des was the self appointed and undisputed king of the ABUs – a term that came to define the resistance movement – Anybody But United. With Cantona in full bloom Des displayed a willpower that kept many of us going as the evil empire from the north west of England threatened to destroy everything that we believed in. They even opened a shop in Dublin, the only time that I considered committing a criminal offence by employing a tactic whereby I would place Arsenal memorabilia in the shop, the opposite to shop lifting. Our innocence, our very existence was at stake.

Nineteen ninety-nine was our *annus horribilis*, the year that United won the treble. I watched on in horror as the League and FA Cup slipped out of Arsenal's grasp. And worse was yet to come when two late goals gave our arch-nemesis Alex Ferguson the European Cup, the trophy he most wanted to get his grubby hands on. I held my head in my hands at the final whistle and wondered how I would make it through the night, never mind the next day. But somehow I survived. And I learnt that anything in life can be overcome. Yesterday's sports news is always the next day's fish and chip paper. Life goes on, something that we Dublin fans have found to our benefit over the years.

It was Des that kept our spirits up, he was relentless as he waited patiently for a bad United result to come along. Often that meant waiting for months, sometimes years. But it was all water off a duck's back to Des and when it happened he pounced like their was no tomorrow, ignoring the retribution that would follow a week later. He had the ability to view a bad United result in splendid isolation. So when I find myself staring at Des on a Sunday evening in 2010 I do so through misty eyes. Without him, many of us might not be here now.

Maybe it's because I'm a little older but it doesn't seem to matter as much these days. United win so often that it barely registers on my radar anymore. It helps if I avoid seeing the latest trophy being presented. It's still possible to retain some control over what enters your mind and even more importantly your soul. That's why the Hill empties so fast on the worst of days.

Chapter Fourteen

Why Does It Always Rain On Me?

Sunday 27 July 1986

Leinster Senior Football Championship Final
Dublin versus Meath

Following three All-Ireland final appearances in a row from 1983 to 1985, the dark days of the early eighties returned to haunt Dublin in the latter half of the decade. To make matters worse Meath were in the ascendancy. All we could do was wait impatiently for the balance of power to shift back in our favour, whenever that might be.

Dublin football might have been struggling but those years gave us cause to widen our horizons; it was around this time that Ireland lost its sporting innocence with Stephen Roche's Tour de France victory. It didn't matter that we knew nothing about cycling. The economy may have been in tatters, with Charlie Haughey exhorting us to tighten our belts while he was loosening his own, but there was nothing like a sporting day in the sun to help us forget our woes. Even Charlie managed to make it to Paris to bask in the sweet smell of Stephen's success. He probably picked up a few of those expensive shirts while he was at it.

It was then that Jack Charlton appeared. At first it looked as if he would be just another name on the long list of managers who had failed to take Ireland to the finals of a major soccer tournament. Even a 2-0 home win over Bulgaria in our final qualifying game for Euro '88 seemed to be too little, too late. All Bulgaria had to do was draw with Scotland in Sofia and they were through and we were out. As the game kicked off in Sofia, Dublin was going about its business, waiting for the bad news to arrive. Very few teams won in Sofia. At least RTÉ were up for it even if the Scots weren't. Their decision to show the match was expected to heap yet more misery on an already demoralised public; first Haughey and now this. It was a typically dark Wednesday afternoon in Dublin, a city that had the feel of post-war Eastern Europe during the winter months, dilapidated buildings waiting for an economic upturn. This particular evening had nothing to distinguish it from any other evening in Ireland's capital as the city's introspective commuters made their way home through the smog.

The news wasn't good. The game was still scoreless with very little time left. The vast majority of the population were blissfully ignorant, but not me, I was sitting at home watching the match deep in prayer. Come on. Just give us a break. It's not like we don't deserve it after all we've been through. A little bit of happiness never hurt anyone. There were four minutes left on the clock when Gary McKay of Hearts scored the most important goal in Irish football history. One nil to Scotland. The final few minutes seemed to go on forever, there was something quaint about not knowing the amount of injury-time the referee would play, but it had heart attack written all over it.

After what seemed like an age, the referee brought our agony to an end. People cried and buses burst into song as the news of the extraordinary events in far-off Eastern Europe travelled by word of mouth. Things would never be the same again. We were off to Germany. First U2 and now this; we suddenly felt invincible.

Over the next eight years, Jack changed our world. We started to believe that we were someone, that we mattered. Barriers were broken down, and it was Big Jack's hand that was shaking the barley. I watched Ireland beating England in Stuttgart with my father and mother. There wasn't a dry eye in the house when the final whistle blew. We cried again a week later when the Dutch ended our dreams. But this was just the beginning. The bar had been raised; we were no longer content with just making up the numbers. From now on we wanted to win.

But the winds of change came too late for me. Increasingly frustrated with the Ireland I was growing up in I wanted out. I decided to head for London. I knew that I would miss two things the most of all: my parents and Hill 16, but it was a decision I had to take. There was no getting away from it, it was time to say goodbye to the Hill. But not before I had to endure the agony of watching Meath winning three Leinster titles in a row.

These were tough times for Dublin football. Kevin Heffernan had said his goodbyes to the Dublin job prior to the championship in 1986. His successors, the caretaker triumvirate of Brian Mullins, Seán Doherty and

Robbie Kelleher, lasted only six months, one Leinster final defeat to Meath and they were gone. Three former players doing their best to replace a legend. I remember the rain that day, rain that got heavier and heavier as the afternoon made its way towards its terrible end. Bad weather suited Meath and Dublin; the greasy surface making a vicious tackle look mistimed rather than nasty.

I decided that it would be a good idea to bring Jessie, my American girlfriend, along. I wasn't about to repeat my Mayo mistake. I thought that an afternoon on Hill 16 would show her a side of Dublin only a cherished few got to see. As the day got darker and darker and we got wetter and wetter, it dawned on me that I had made a mistake. This was no place for a pretty American girl. I'm sure she didn't know what to make of it. The idea that standing on an uncovered terrace getting soaked could be construed as enjoyment must have crossed her mind. The fact that she was standing amongst the unhappiest bunch of people on the planet didn't help. To make matters worse Dublin lost by nine points to seven in a game to forget, the winning points coming in front of a pissed-off Hill, wet, cold and beaten. At the end, we turned as one and left. Squelching home, I knew Meath were here to stay. Unfortunately, Jessie wasn't; she headed off home at the end of the summer.

Gerry McCaul was the next man to try his luck in the hottest seat in Gaelic football, a low key appointment that left a lot of the Dublin public underwhelmed, with the Dublin County Board going down a different route for once, choosing a coach as opposed to a former player in an attempt to challenge Meath's dominance. Even though Gerry had been very successful with Ballymun Kickhams, we knew very little about who he was or where he had come from. We preferred the big names. Still, despite our misgivings he made a promising start with Dublin beating Kerry in a cracking National League final thanks to a superb Ciaran Duff goal. It might not have been the championship but beating Kerry in a final, any final, should be enjoyed. For a few short hours it felt like we had gotten the monkey off our back. By the start of the championship it had jumped right back on with Meath cementing their place as the dominant force in Leinster.

Winning the league was about as good as it got for McCaul. His job as a headmaster must have prepared him for the disappointment that characterised his time in charge; so much potential, so little return. Not surprisingly his approach was rumoured to be authoritarian, leading to an element of friction between players and manager, never a recipe for success. It seemed that Gerry found it hard to leave the classroom behind when he turned up for training. As well, winning the league increased the pressure on him to deliver Dublin's first All-Ireland since 1983. Timing is everything in management and although Kerry's dominance was coming to an end, their place was taken by a Meath team at the height of its powers, along with an equally impressive Cork side. With Dublin in the process of rebuilding it was a frustrating time all round.

Chapter Fifteen

Thousands Are Sailing

Sunday 20 August 1989

All-Ireland Senior Football Championship Semi-Final
Dublin versus Cork

At the start of the 1988 campaign new names were beginning to appear on the team sheet, players who would become household names over the next few years. Charlie Redmond had been around since the 1985 campaign but he was becoming an integral part of the team as the decade moved on. Mick Galvin was another useful forward who had made an impact over the last couple of years. Then there was Eamon Heery – fit, hungry and ready to die for the cause – everything that would come to symbolise a Dublin footballer in the 1990s. These fresh faces were mixed with the players who had made up the nucleus of the 1983 side. The likes of Barney Rock, Gerry Hargan, Ciaran Duff, Jim Ronayne and Joe McNally had clocked up a fair few miles at this stage. But none of this seemed to matter as Dublin eased into another Leinster final with a comprehensive win over a poor Longford side in Mullingar. So, inevitably, the stage was set for yet another showdown with Meath.

The final turned out to be another massive disappointment. I watched from the Hill in absolute horror as two early Meath goals set the foundations for another sickening victory; Dublin left chasing a game that they never looked like winning from then on. It was an awful day; everything that could go wrong did. The final score of 2-5 to 0-9 revealed the importance of Meath's early dominance. The sending-off of Dave Synnott didn't help, but despite this crippling setback, Dublin actually managed to draw level, only for Meath to pull clear again with three unanswered points. In the closing minutes we had a golden chance to rescue a draw, but sadly Charlie Redmond fired the penalty over the bar. This was the beginning of a long sequence of penalty misses that would haunt Dublin, and in particular Redmond, over the next few years. It also told us something about McCaul; when he needed a slice of luck it was never forthcoming. The small margins always went against Gerry, each Meath triumph raising the stakes even further. Somewhat predictably the summer ended with a whimper when Meath captured their second successive All-Ireland title with another win over Cork in September. Thankfully, I was already in London.

I said my goodbyes in August. I was glad to be leaving, I needed my independence, my parents had done everything they could have done for me but it was now time for me to show that I could stand on my own two feet. I also needed to get away from Meath. Thousands were sailing, but I took the plane. Three hours later, I was sitting in a London pub with my cousin David wondering what the hell had I done? Here I was in a massive city without a job and without a home. My cousins kindly agreed to take me in for the first few weeks and I ended up staying eight months. So much for being independent.

I drifted from job to job, trying desperately to find something that I enjoyed doing. Part-time postman was my favourite, the post room was full of colourful characters and I didn't mind getting up early in the morning as it meant I was finished by lunchtime. But I needed something a bit more permanent, and when the opportunity to work in The British Library came along, I grabbed it with both hands.

Perhaps the main reason I chose to go to London was tied to another sporting love that I had developed from a young age. I have been an Arsenal fan since the age of eight and the chance to watch them on a weekly basis was too good to miss. So I became a regular at Highbury throughout the 1988-89 season. It turned out to be quite a season with George Graham leading Arsenal to their first title in eighteen years, culminating in the famous 2-0 win against title rivals Liverpool at Anfield. It mirrored my experience as a Dublin supporter in that I found myself going to the matches on my own for the first half of the season. Once again, I was ploughing a lonely furrow, but I was in my element. For some strange reason I felt as if I was coming home; I may well have left one band of brothers behind, but it hadn't taken me long to find another tribe and I immediately felt at one with these people. The feeling on the North Bank at Highbury was exactly the same one I had experienced the first day I set foot on the Hill; this was my place. I have always loved London and its inhabitants; I like their attitude to life and their sense of humour. Londoners come in all colours, creeds, shapes, and sizes and after the mono-cultural nature of life in Ireland in the eighties, London was an amazing shock to the system. I found everything I missed about the Hill on the North Bank.

Going to away-games was even better. I travelled down to see Arsenal win at White Hart Lane and Upton Park and the atmosphere was electric. The terrace culture in English football was wild and exciting and I couldn't get enough of it, there was an edge to it I had never felt on the Hill. Whereas the Dublin fans created their own momentum, here both sets of fans drove each other on. The win at Tottenham was clinched with three goals in nine electric first-half minutes right in front of a rapturous Arsenal support. I hugged strangers and sang and danced my way through an afternoon I will never forget and, despite being deep inside enemy territory, I arrived home safely, much to the relief of my cousins.

As winter turned to spring, Arsenal were in pole position to win the League, but results tailed off as Liverpool began to reel them in. My season on the North Bank was set for a grandstand finish.

Going to an English football ground in the eighties was the polar opposite of what it was like wandering down to Croke Park to watch the Dubs. In Croker the tension was to be found on the pitch, but on the terraces and in the stands, we kept ourselves in check. We might have been burning up inside and our language was never less than colourful, but that was as far as it went. Outside the ground, the mood was generally one of polite respect; we didn't bother the other supporters and they didn't bother us. Going to an English away game was a far edgier experience, the mutual antagonism between the fans carries a much greater threat of violence. Not least between Arsenal's followers and the other London tribes like those of Tottenham, Chelsea and West Ham. I knew full well that I was heading into uncharted waters when I made my first trip to see Arsenal play the Hammers at Upton Park.

I left anything that might identify me as an Arsenal fan at home, even travelling down early to avoid any mass confrontation that might occur outside the ground closer to kick-off. My heart was the only red and white part of me that remained as I stepped off the tube and into the lion's den, trying hard to look as if I knew where I was going. I was surrounded by Hammers, hoping that they couldn't hear my heart thumping. I was headed for the relative safety of the away end, which I knew would be heavily policed. In my head, I was a West Ham fan and if anybody asked me that's what I would say. I wanted it to roll off my tongue as if I had been saying it all my life.

I looked around for any fellow Arsenal fans but if they existed, they were keeping themselves to themselves. I found it interesting that I didn't feel afraid; I was getting an adrenalin rush from the danger, the feeling of being in enemy territory. I kept my head down and kept moving. Inside the ground, standing amongst the Arsenal travelling support, I relaxed. We roared out our defiance as the West Ham fans left us in very little doubt about exactly what they would do if they managed to get their hands on us. Fingers were raised to throats in a cutting motion. But we laughed at everything that they threw at us. Safety in numbers. Not to mention the lines of police separating us from claret and blue. The wire mesh fencing that penned us in gave us an air of reckless invincibility.

On the pitch Arsenal ran out easy winners by 4-1; one of the good days. As usual after an away match, getting home would be the difficult part. We were kept in the ground afterwards as the West Ham fans were given time to disperse, but when we were finally let out, it seemed as if every last one of them had waited to say goodbye. The police radios crackling in anticipation of a potential ambush after some West Ham fans disappeared down a side-street. We were penned in outside the ground as a police helicopter tried to locate them. It was an anxious few minutes hemmed in by mounted police on edgy looking horses. I was getting pretty nervous too, but eventually we were led back to the tube station through a mile-long line of police, some of them in riot gear. The Saturday afternoon shoppers watched us go by with a look of horror on their faces. We were an unwanted element. It was only when I was back on the train that I could finally relax; it was time to go home.

But everything was about to change. The football world was turned upside down on Saturday April 15, 1989. Arsenal were playing Newcastle in a must-win game, the perfect opportunity to pile the pressure back on Liverpool, I set out for Highbury at about noon. Liverpool were involved in an equally important game that day, an FA Cup semi-final against Nottingham Forest at Hillsborough.

At Highbury, the North Bank was abuzz with nervous excitement and the early minutes were typically tense with little to separate the two sides. But then the mood changed as rumours began to percolate through the crowd that there were problems up in Sheffield. Transistor radios were held against ears as the fans around me tried to make sense of what was going on hundreds of miles away. It appeared that the game had been stopped and that a number of fans had been injured. With the images of Heysel still fresh in our minds perhaps it wasn't surprising that some sections of the North Bank began to blame the Liverpool fans for what was happening. But it soon became clear that this was a very different scenario. News of the first fatalities was met with a hushed silence. On the pitch, the Arsenal and Newcastle players played on, unaware that a catastrophe was happening elsewhere. Surely the reporters had got it wrong. People don't die at a football match. But then we thought of Heysel again. And Ibrox. And Bradford. The game below us lost all relevance as the death toll mounted; even Arsenal's late winner was met with pained indifference. I got the tube home in a daze. How could something like this happen?

Football was at its lowest ebb, the fans caged like animals in segregated sections. When I finally made it home, I sat down and watched the news, feeling numb as the horrific scenes of fans trying to escape the crush were replayed. I didn't sleep that night; it was clear that football had to change. Lord Taylor was given the job of fixing a terminally ill game. His conclusions would have far reaching consequences: standing areas would no longer be permitted with fenced enclosures a thing of the past. The age of all seater stadiums was upon us. Ironically, Highbury had been overlooked as an FA Cup venue that season because of the lack of fencing at the ground. Everton fans had poured onto the pitch following a semi-final winner against Southampton a couple of years earlier. Better a few fans dancing around than 96 people dead. Very few people probably even remember that incident. How many will ever forget Hillsborough?

As usual, the game dusted itself down and got back to business as if nothing had happened, there was still money to be made. I headed home to watch Ireland take on Spain in a crucial World Cup qualifier at Lansdowne Road with the old ground looking more ancient by the day. The atmosphere was charged with emotion and security tight as the officials nervously worked to ensure that there would be no repeat of the tragic events in Sheffield. On a day to recharge the soul 56,000 Irish voices roared Ireland to a famous 1-0 victory. We were on the verge of history as our first World Cup finals appearance was a real possibility now. I had decided in the days after Hillsborough that I would never take sport as seriously again. But here I was, biting my nails down to the bone as Ireland held on in the dying minutes. Old habits sure die hard.

The season ended with Arsenal winning the League at Anfield. By that time, I had even managed to find some mates to accompany me to matches. I met Tony in work, he had drifted away from football having supported Tottenham in his teens but I soon had him making regular trips to watch Arsenal at Highbury. His friend Alf was a QPR supporter and even he was persuaded to watch the Gunners on the odd occasion, although he invariably ignored what was going on and tuned his Walkman into QPR's match. His indifference said it all, Arsenal meant nothing to him; he was only there for the drinking that would come later. They might as well have been Meath for all he cared.

The news from across the Irish Sea was equally good. With Arsenal crowned champions for the first time in eighteen years, I turned my attention to what Dublin were up to, and early June brought good news. Apparently Kildare had been defeated in Newbridge; their steely resolve finally broken by a second-half goal from Dully. Wicklow were next up, Dublin running out fairly comfortable winners with another second-half goal from Joe McNally wrapping things up. I might as well have been a million miles away. By this time, I had made the decision to return home to Ireland to pursue a teaching qualification. I knew that it would break my heart to leave London and Arsenal behind, but at least I would be close to my parents again. They were growing old and I needed to be there for them. There was also the small matter of the Dubs. But I wasn't going to be home until late August which meant that they would have to do without me for most of the summer.

For the fourth year in a row Dublin and Meath contested the Leinster final with 56,000 there to see another cracking encounter. I cried with joy when Dad shouted the result down the phone: Dublin 2-12 Meath 1-10. After three years of disappointment Dublin had finally redressed the balance. Another Dully special settled the Dublin nerves and they were ahead by four points at half-time, before Meath clawed their way back with Mattie McCabe putting them ahead with time running out. But Dublin rallied and a new hero was born when Vinny Murphy scored a crucial second goal. Dad never missed an opportunity to keep me in touch with my roots and a few days later a newspaper cutting of the match report from *The Irish Times* arrived over. I stuck it up over my desk in work. He knew only too well what this victory meant to me. I also knew that he was glad that I was coming home.

Next up was Cork, a good omen if recent clashes were anything to go by. Our last two semi-final meetings with Cork had been the prelude to Sam returning home to the capital. The thought of a trip to a Kilburn pub to watch the match never crossed my mind, so I found myself desperately trying to tune my cousin's radio into RTÉ. It wasn't looking good when all of a sudden I heard the names of various Dublin players struggling to make themselves heard through the frenetic buzz with the reception dipping in and out at regular intervals. The frequency seemed to match the flow of the action on the pitch, with the culmination of an exciting move disappearing in a haze of white noise. But, to my amazement, I was able to make out the score. Surely it couldn't be right: Dublin 1-4 Cork 0-0 after only fourteen minutes, Vinny Murphy's goal the highpoint of a whirlwind start. It seemed that Dublin had one foot in the final.

Not so fast. By half-time, Dublin were trailing: 2-2 to 1-4. Two Cork penalties, both converted by John Cleary, and the sending off of Dublin's rookie centre-half-back Keith Barr had turned the game in Cork's favour. Barr was left lying on the ground in front of the Hogan Stand with what later turned out to be a broken jaw. The referee booked the culprit Dinny Allen. But before Dublin's centre-half back could be replaced, he had wreaked his revenge and, unlike Allen, he was sent off. Allen was no darling of the Hill; one of the names in our little black book after raising his fist in triumph after each of his goals in the 1983 semi-final clash. Dubs have a long memory when it comes to crimes against the Hill. The boys tried their best to claw their way back but the damage was done: Cork 2-10 Dublin 1-9. Bad luck following Gerry McCaul around like a stray dog. I dejectedly switched off the radio and returned to what was left of the last few days of my London life.

Before I packed my meagre belongings, I made my final visit to Highbury. A boring, scoreless draw against Wimbledon meant I was leaving with a whimper. Sport doesn't do fairytales. As I turned towards the tube, I took one look back at the famous old ground, I would miss my days following Arsenal, but at least I knew I would soon be back on Hill 16.

Two days later I was back in Dublin. My father was there to collect me at the airport. I laughed when he told me the news that Arsenal were following me home; they were lined up to play a friendly against Dublin side Bohemians on the following Wednesday. But it was the Dubs that my heart was longing for. Next year's championship couldn't come quick enough.

Chapter Sixteen

Reasons To Be Cheerful

Saturday 17 July 2010

All-Ireland Senior Football Championship Fourth Round Qualifier
Dublin versus Armagh

We have serious history with Armagh. It doesn't matter that the manager and many of the players that inflicted so much pain on us have now moved on, the mere sight of an orange jersey is enough to shake a Dub to the very core of his being. In fact, there are a number of northern shirts that bring back bad memories. With a few notable exceptions, it seems our northern cousins have had us in the palms of their red hands since 1992. The sight of Stephen McDonnell lining out at full-forward for Armagh is another scary reminder of days gone by. McDonnell was one of the pillars of an Armagh team that achieved so much. Ruthless in their efficiency, they bullied their opponents into submission before they unleashed playmakers such as Oisín McConville to do the real damage. They were the pioneers of a physical, simple but effective style that later became known as 'puke football'. The rest of us bit our tongues and marvelled at the physique and fitness of these men from across the border. Why couldn't Dublin be like that? With Dublin busy thinking up another way to lose a match, Armagh finally broke the mould to land their first All-Ireland in 2002. It goes without saying that they beat us along the way and just for good measure they repeated the dose a year later to leave us shattered and broken. Unlike us, their defeats were rarely self-inflicted. Either luck went against them or they ran up against a better side on the day. No shame in that.

Thus far, they have managed only one All-Ireland title, but looking back, it feels like they have won more, they certainly deserved more. Of course, they had Kerry and Tyrone to contend with. Once they were usurped by Tyrone, they hung around like a bad smell, their mojo long gone. And, unlike Austin Powers, they never got it back. They're like us now, left to reminisce about the good times, searching desperately for a return to former glories.

But Stephen McDonnell is still going strong and he wanders menacingly towards the Hill as we ready ourselves for what's to come. McDonnell is not one for gesturing towards the opposition supporters. He has no bone to pick with us: he keeps his celebrations for his own. He strikes me as a straightforward sort of guy – he has always played his football that way – putting the ball in the back of the net with the minimum of fuss; the Jimmy Greaves of the Gaelic world. Inevitably, time has taken its toll as it does with all great players, but McDonnell's guile and experience, as well as his brute strength, are sure to be a severe test for Dublin's rookie full-back Rory O'Carroll. Rory has had a tough start to his Dublin career and the last thing his fragile confidence needs is an afternoon up against one of the greats of the modern game. One thing is certain, that Armagh will test O'Carroll early on. That's what Armagh do, they prey on your weaknesses, knocking at the door until it collapses inwards. They will have spent endless hours watching the Dubs in action, picking up on their frailties, noting their vulnerabilities, and relishing the opportunity to put their plan into action.

Absent due to work commitments, Duff hasn't made the game today. Duff is another exiled Dub and the qualifiers are sure to play havoc with his bi-weekly sorties from Ennis. Without Duff there is no one to punch me on the back just prior to throw in. But all that will be forgotten if we win today. Maybe then, we will even begin to doubt the powers of Duff; maybe he is the jinx who hinders Dublin's ambition year after year. Maybe he has been the problem all along. Our suspicions grow with our superstitions. P.O. is also absent. So today it's just Niall and I on the Hill, along with about 8,000 others, of course. I met Niall in college. I was queuing for a cup of coffee one morning when a mutual friend introduced me to a Morrissey look-alike. Niall stared at my Arsenal scarf in disbelief, surprised that I was wearing it on this day of all days; we had just been thumped 6-1 by Everton at the weekend. Niall was a Gunner, a fellow traveller; another boy with a thorn in his side. Within minutes, we were lost in conversation as we pondered all things Arsenal. It was only years later that I discovered that Niall was a Dublin enthusiast as well. Now we had even more to moan about. We have been going to games together ever since. Still, life on the Hill just isn't the same without my trusty companion, he's probably settling down to watch the match in some Ennis pub. Poor old Maurice has had enough; he's at home minding the kids.

This is payback for those two defeats at the beginning of the century. The first, although it rocked us to the core, wasn't as bad as we were on an upward curve, having lifted our first provincial title in seven years. But when we met again a year later, we were heading in the opposite direction and another galling defeat seemed to confirm our worst fears. We know what to expect today. Armagh may not be as good anymore, these days they are back in the pack with the rest of us mortals chasing Tyrone and Kerry, but they will be no different. This will be a dogfight that will be decided by a point or two. And it certainly won't be pretty.

Today is a big game for both sides. This result means everything. A win will push the victors within sight of a place in an All-Ireland quarter-final, as for the losers, the usual recriminations and calls for the manager's head will surely follow.

Not least Pat Gilroy. He's already a dead man walking in the eyes of some supporters, if he doesn't win this one he will be toast. Not that he seems to care; he's kept his dignity and got on with the job without any fuss. He's not one for excuses, he knows what he needs to do, dignity and stoicism will only get him so far. Winning games like this one is what it's all about. Win this and people will start to sit up and take notice again.

In McDonnell and Jamie Clarke, Armagh certainly have the players capable of derailing us, and Rory O'Carroll and the rest of the full-back line will really need to be on their game today. Up front, we will need the Brogans and Eoghan O'Gara at their creative best to overcome the blanket defence the northerners will surely deploy. Paddy O'Rourke's Armagh side has as many questions to answer as their Dublin counterparts and this is what makes today's encounter such a mouth-watering prospect; both teams seem to lack the leadership required, but one of them is destined to advance. Like ourselves, Armagh's summer has been riddled with inconsistency. Let's hope that today is one of their off days. We need all the luck we can get right now.

Sure enough, Armagh win possession from the throw-in and launch a high ball in towards McDonnell. We hold our breath as we look to the blue skies in a vain attempt to catch a glimpse of the dangerous object hurtling towards us. I am terrified but it could be worse, I could be Rory O'Carroll.

At least I don't have to do anything about the impending danger, apart from move a little to my left so that I have a full view of the disaster that is about to happen. My head says goal to Armagh and my heart agrees. The next ten seconds of my life don't look good. More importantly the next seventy minutes don't look good for Dublin. It's as if the outcome of the game depends on what happens next and in many ways it does. This must be what it is like sitting in your house in downtown Baghdad as you listen to the sound of an incoming missile... only a game... not a matter of life and death... I know, I know! But right now Rory knows that if he loses this particular battle, he is more than likely going to lose the war as well. The ball seems to be in the air for an eternity as if making up its mind what to do, as if it has a choice. It could stay up there forever for all I care. Come down you bastard. Let's get this over with. Rory rises majestically and steals the ball right from under McDonnell's nose, directly in front of an ecstatic Hill. He doesn't look back as he goes on to have his finest hour in a Dublin shirt yet. Where only seconds ago there was doubt, now there is hope and we roar our appreciation as our latest hero releases the ball to a team mate who sets up Dublin's first attack of the day.

Despite O'Carroll's promising opening the signs are worrying as Armagh make the early running. Soon they are three points to one ahead and the denizens of the Hill are already starting to grumble. The orange shirts continue to dominate, but their propensity for overplaying in the build-up keeps the game tight until they spark into action knocking over three quick fire points to make it six points to two. At this stage of proceedings the future looks decidedly orange, but Dublin refuse to wither. It's the Bernard Brogan show for the next few minutes as he bangs over three unanswered points to drag Dublin back into the game. In contrast, Eoghan O'Gara is having a quiet game, the experts on the Hill grumbling if the ball happens to go anywhere near him. The sides go in level at the break when Stephen Cluxton knocks over a 45 to become only Dublin's second scorer of the day.

Dublin start the second-half as they finished the first, with the younger Brogan continuing his personal crusade as he trades early points with Stephen O'Donnell, who has to be content with scoring from frees. The full-back line look a lot more assured now and Rory O'Carroll is turning in a man-of-the-match performance as he continues to frustrate O'Donnell in open play. In fact, the whole team looks more compact. Dublin are playing a different game today: hunting in packs, chasing down their opposite numbers and dispossessing the opponent in the tackle, leaving the defence much less exposed than before. It's a return to the type of game plan they used to such good effect in the league. Forward Niall Corkery is one of the new breed, always prepared to work hard without the ball. As we win back possession for the umpteenth time, it suddenly occurs to us that we are actually out Armagh-ing Armagh. We are finally giving them some of their own medicine.

Gilroy's game plan is clearly working as Dublin surge into a three point lead with scores from Bernard Brogan (who else?), substitute Kevin McManamon and Philly McMahon. McMahon's point is a corker. It involves our corner back sprinting down the left and combining with McManamon before firing over a truly inspirational point. McManamon has made a big difference since he replaced an out of sorts O'Gara at half-time, he has been tormenting the Armagh defence, his strength and low centre of gravity making him difficult to dispossess. It shows the unsentimental side of Gilroy and reveals a little more about an intensely private man. He might have a soft spot for O'Gara but ultimately the team comes first. The atmosphere on the Hill is slowly changing, our optimism growing; this could be shaping up to be one of Dublin's gutsiest displays in years.

We won't lose the run of ourselves just yet of course; momentum can disappear in an instant, especially in Gaelic football. There is no let up, with Dublin it's usually all or nothing; 10 minutes of brilliance followed by a shuddering collapse. It's been like this for so long now that we're used to it. It doesn't make it any easier to accept, it's just that we know it's coming now. Dublin thrive on the pace of the game one minute and revile it the next. What is needed is a more measured approach, a more resourceful use of time over the full 70 minutes. The really good teams, Kerry and Tyrone, have learnt to ride out the storm, to nick a crucial point when the waves are crashing against their coastline. Strategy goes out the window in such a high pressure environment and players play from memory alone, doing what has to be done, it's impossible to take stock, the game is moving so rapidly around them with bodies coming at them from every angle. Up on the Hill it's different. We have all the time in the world up there.

So – we knew what was coming next – having put so much effort into getting ahead, it was now time for Dublin to surrender the initiative. The energy levels dropped, tired bodies retreating into themselves, as Armagh said thank you very much and hit three unanswered points to draw level, each one ratcheting up the tension on the Hill as the mood swung with the rhythm of the match. We curse ourselves for being there; surely there are better ways to spend a Saturday afternoon. I must ask Maurice the next time I see him. For all the dark days in our past, it still feels as if this is the first time they had done this to us. It always feels like the first time because it hurts so much. Some day we will win an important game without having to go through this. Just for once, it would be nice to walk out of Croke Park with our sanity intact.

Despite the ebb and flow of the scoreboard, the game itself is patchy; a stop-start affair with too many frees disrupting the flow. It boils down to the survival of the fittest, which side will blink first? We punch the air with relief as Bernard puts us back in front. We scream when Jamie Clarke's pass puts an unmarked Brian Mallon through on the Dublin goal and his shot beats Stephen Cluxton, a certain goal. But Philly McMahon arrives at the last moment to clear the ball away from the goal-line; the moment that rescues Dublin's season. Dublin breathe a huge sigh of relief and pour forward with a fresh impetus; Paul Flynn hits a point and another Bernard Brogan free leaves Dublin three points to the good with time running out. The Hill is getting cocky when a Joe Feeney point for Armagh makes us think again. It is left to Eamonn Fennell to apply the coup de grâce with an injury-time point. The final score: Dublin 0-14 Armagh 0-11.

The Dublin players turn to the Hill and applaud us. This is the first day that they have felt able to acknowledge us this season, the type of day when team and supporters become one. The Hill is a mixture of emotions: tiredness, relief, quiet satisfaction at a job well done, perhaps a smidgen of disbelief that we won after all. For a little while we stand together, taking it all in. Gaelic football has a relentless feel to it that leaves you gasping for air at the end. That's why the Hill stays together for a few precious moments before heading off to the pub. It's a collective catching of the breath before we re-enter the mainstream.

As we make the long walk back towards Hedigans, there's a bounce in our step. Niall spends most of the trip advancing his latest theory; that today's unexpected triumph is down to the absence of Duff. In the end we decide to give him the benefit of the doubt. One day is never enough to copper fasten assumptions based on superstition. It looks as if Duff could well be absent for our next outing, so only time will tell.

True to Gilroy's style, today's was a very pragmatic, realistic approach; it was clear that Dublin set out to concede less than Armagh. Something contrary to the way Dublin normally play the game but right now it is a necessary evil, we can't expect to blow teams away any more. At the moment winning is more important than anything else; victories breed the confidence that allows a team to express itself. There was one moment just before half-time that summed up Dublin's new approach: Armagh were forced back from the Dublin goal through sheer weight of numbers and when Kevin Nolan turned over possession, Dublin raced to the other end of the field to register a point. It might not be pretty but it sure is effective. The winning comes first. It might not satisfy those Dubs, brought up on the feast that was the seventies, who feel that winning with style is as important as winning itself. But needs must right now.

Today was a huge step in the right direction. Redemption is never easily won, but there was an honesty and resilience about this Dublin display that bodes well for the future. When this Dublin team goes up to lift Sam it will be days like this that will be remembered.

Pat Gilroy is the same as ever, no sign of a smile at the end, just a respectful handshake and a nod of his head as he towers over his opposite number. Pat makes everyone look small. It's job done. The work in progress set to continue for another week at least. He has had the look of a condemned man all season, but as he walks towards the tunnel I spot a glimpse of the 'I told you so, but you wouldn't listen' about his leisurely amble. He knew this was coming, he just didn't know when. His substitutions worked well; gave the team the impetus it needed to get across the line. McManamon brought a freshness to the forward line, his bustling style bringing back fond memories of another darling of the Hill: Dessie Farrell. Darren McGee and Eamonn Fennell breathed new life into a tiring midfield. Michael Dara MacAuley had another superb game; his distribution and link-up play has given Dublin a dimension they have been lacking for years. He is the type of player who would have brought the best out of Ciarán Whelan. Too often, Whelan was left to do the donkey work when he should have been driving into the heart of the opposing defence. It was equally good to see Dublin's more experienced players such as Bryan Cullen and Barry Cahill doing their bit. And then there was Bernard Brogan: simply magnificent. He proved to be the difference between the sides. Despite his nine point salvo the worry remains that too much of the scoring burden is been placed on him. Bernard can't be expected to pull a rabbit out of the hat every day.

This was payback time. The players stood up and were counted; giving their beleaguered manager some valuable breathing space. The tactics helped, this was as pumped up a Dublin as we have seen in a long while, the return to the tactics that had served the team so well in the league a huge success. But tactics are only as good as the players that put them into action. Today there was a togetherness and a will to win that was most impressive. The full-back line was superb; repaying their manager's faith when many were calling for their heads. In many ways the performance reflected everything that Gilroy stands for: honesty of effort, no bullshit and definitely no startled earwigs.

Given the good weather, the attendance was a bit disappointing – just under 26,000 – slightly up on the Tipperary game, thanks mainly to the greater number of Armagh fans who made the long journey down in the hope of witnessing another famous victory over the Dubs. The Hill is developing a cosy feel – 'we band of brothers, we happy few' – as an Englishman said once. We'd better enjoy it while it lasts. More wins like this one and they'll be back: the fair-weather fans. Oh ye of little faith.

For the third time in a row, the draw is kind: Louth are stuck in a moment they can't get out of as they try to come to terms with the nature of their Leinster final defeat to Meath. The news that the game will be played in headquarters only adds to my conviction that the gods are on the side of the Dubs this year.

No doubt, there is still scope for disaster, Louth might find the prospect of a day out with the Dubs a reinvigorating prospect. But, on the whole, even for a determined pessimist like me, things are looking up. We might even see some that famous Dublin swagger next Saturday. You could almost see the weight being lifted from the players' shoulders in those final few fateful minutes today. Surely that will count for something when they take to the field in seven days time. The news that Duff has been def-in-ITELY ruled out for the second week running lifts our spirits even further. I know that I will miss him but if it means that Dublin are guaranteed another win then it is a price I am willing to pay.

Chapter Seventeen

Paddy Cullen's Penalty Blues

Sunday 20 September 1992

All-Ireland Senior Football Championship Final
Dublin versus Donegal

You could call the early 1990s the bridesmaid years for the Dublin football team. Each year, they looked set fair to end the famine, only to come up against a different set of opponents who destroyed their dream: Meath in '91, Donegal the following year, Derry in '93 and Down in '94. With the exception of an exhausted Meath team, the others went on to win Sam. Dublin were unquestionably the most consistent team throughout this period, but it was that very consistency that seemed to become as much of an enemy as a friend. They were the stepping-stones to other people's dreams -shadow artists.

As with all sporting dramas, luck – in our case rotten luck – played a huge part during these heart-breaking summers as time and again, the roll of the dice went against us at decisive moments. Time and again, the Dublin players were left scratching their heads as they left the field wondering just what they had done to deserve this. The answers didn't come easily in the months that followed. In many cases there were no answers; it was simply a case of circling the wagons and trying again next year, and the year after that. Failure came in many different guises: a missed penalty one year, a crucial interception the next and after that, an inspirational point from an unlikely source. Strange things seemed to happen when Dublin took to the field. When a small bit of good fortune was needed most it was always the other side that got the bounce of the ball. They say you make your own luck but not in the case of this Dublin team. No group of players could have done more. In the end it was their sheer bloody-mindedness that drove them on despite all their misfortunes, they simply would not give up. Bringing the Sam Maguire back to Dublin had become an obsession.

The pain began with the seismic defeat against Meath in 1991, what happened in that epic series would have killed off most teams, but, to their credit, the players picked themselves up off the floor, dusted themselves down and got ready to go again the following summer. As for the fans, we tried to make some sense of where it had all gone wrong but it didn't do us any good. If this is what it felt like just watching, then what must the players have been going through? For weeks afterwards, I would find myself lying awake at night in a cold sweat as the ghost of David Beggy bore down on the Dublin goal. I swear I even saw him standing at the end of the bed one night laughing. We passed the winter months putting our shattered lives back together – September to Christmas was usually spent finding the pieces – but as winter turned to spring new hope would return. The time had finally come to set things right. And once more, with the sunny optimism of a horde of lemmings, we would approach the championship cliff edge once again.

This year we'll go all the way, we'd tell ourselves. And then we'd think of Meath and the other sharks lying in wait and reconsider. Better to take it one game at a time then: wake me up when September comes, that fateful month would have to look after itself for the time being. The past never really left us and we never expected it to. It would only say goodbye when the next Dublin captain lifted Sam above his head and slammed the door shut on another chapter in Dublin football history. Only then would we be free.

I often wondered if the journey would ever end. I found that it was best to keep quiet about my football obsession in non-sporting company; people couldn't understand how my personal happiness could be so tied to the fortunes of a team of perfect strangers. They thought I was a bit mad to be honest, and I could see their point. Most of what they said made perfect sense but I was way beyond rational at this stage. So, this code of silence left me to endure my sporting pain alone. Many of us are at our happiest there, wallowing in our misery. We pour it out in disguise, dressed up as the shitty weather or the state of the economy. The average Irish male may be a talkative creature, but he says remarkably little of consequence and his true feelings are almost never expressed. Sport and talking about sport in particular, is a vital safety valve for the Irish male to express his anger and frustration – and his love and sentimentality – in a socially acceptable forum. Take that away from us and we have lost our only way of expressing our innermost troubles in a constructive manner. Take that away and we are fucked.

That is unless you are Maurice. In addition to being the bane of referees everywhere he is a Liverpool supporter. He is also the only one of us ever to have had an out of body experience; this miraculous event took place on the night Liverpool beat AC Milan in Istanbul to win their fifth European Cup. Maurice had decided to share this night of all nights with his new work colleagues, not a very good idea really, because witnessing Maurice watch his team in action is to see the man, warts and all, with all his psychological tics and idiosyncrasies exposed. In short, in a state only his closest friends or his analyst should witness. I asked his wife Margaret how he had coped with what was an extraordinary evening by any sporting standards and something about the relish with which she recounted the story told me that she, at least, had enjoyed it immensely.

Hope had turned to fear for Maurice when Liverpool went one down, and fear had turned to despair by the time they trailed by three goals after 45 minutes. At this stage a stony-faced Maurice was revealing parts of himself that he probably wished would remain hidden forever. Sport does that; it tears away the mask. Here he was stripped of the coping strategies he had carried with him all of his life: never look beaten, always keep the chin up. Except now his chin was dragging along the floor as he reached for his pint. Maurice the charming and urbane new workmate was gone. His newfound friends tried their best to talk him round but there was no getting through to him. Humiliation was staring him in the face. He knew now that he should have stayed at home where he could have endured his own private hell. As he re-emerged for the second-half he tried to put his best foot forward. At 3-1 he dared not to hope, at 3-2 he tried not to say 'I told you so' because he had said nothing of the sort, at 3-3 he did his best not to knock over an entire table of drinks and when the ensuing penalty shoot-out ended in victory he did what only a man can do when he has seen the light. He burst into tears.

Now and again I wonder what it would be like to sit down and enjoy a match and not worry about the eventual outcome, to see its beauty and logic unfold with a detached eye. Instead I always find myself seeing a game through the eyes of the team I am rooting for. My life as a sports anorak is never ending, just as the English Premiership resolves itself with another trophy-less season for Arsenal, Dublin's championship campaign kicks into action. And by the time Dublin bid farewell to another summer, Arsenal are back up and running. Throw in all the other sporting distractions that crowd the calendar and it's no wonder that there is very little respite. A three-week break where no sport is played anywhere in the world is the obvious answer. Maybe that would allow me to recharge my batteries and do some of the things normal people get to do on a daily basis. But it's all wishful thinking. I know I'm trapped in a world of my own making.

The defeat to Meath in '91 was followed by another devastating day against Donegal in the 1992 All-Ireland final. Former seventies goalkeeping hero Paddy Cullen had taken over the reins of leadership from Gerry McCaul after the 1990 campaign came to an end. Paddy's approach was admirably straightforward; his teams were instructed to blow the dastardly culchies away. As plans go, it didn't seem like a bad idea and we loved him for it. Paddy was a man who knew how to win and he wasn't lacking in confidence when it came to sending his team into battle. Whereas McCaul had been quiet and workmanlike, Paddy believed that Dublin needed to get back to playing with the customary swagger that had been so successful when he had been a player. It was as if we could reach out and touch our glorious past. But Paddy had reckoned without Meath and by 1992 he found himself having to pick the players off the canvas in readiness for another crack at winning what was becoming a frustratingly elusive All-Ireland. The first hurdle was the Leinster title, and in early June we were delighted to hear that Meath were early fallers, beaten by Laois. Suddenly and most unexpectedly, our road to September was clear. From the Hill, Cullen's leadership seemed somewhat laissez-faire. The tactics, if you could call them tactics, were pretty simple: quick ball was launched in the direction of Vinny Murphy as Dublin charged at every team they came up against. For most of the season this worked a treat, but there were voices of concern on the Hill; what was our fallback if this swashbuckling style failed? But as the campaign gathered pace, such thoughts were brushed under the carpet as the Dubs marched happily on.

We sliced through Leinster with gay abandon to set up a meeting with Mick O'Dwyer's Kildare side in the Leinster final. This was a special game for Paddy and his backroom staff, a chance for some payback against their seventies nemesis, losing this one was unthinkable. Instead of playing their football, the Lilywhites decided that an aggressive approach was called for and when the fists began to fly after only twelve minutes Dublin responded in kind. The ensuing dust-up seemed to go on for ages and the sight of one of the Kildare players running away from Keith Barr gave us all a good laugh.

Kildare may have started the fight but there was little doubt that Dublin ended it, and the dust settled to reveal Kildare on the retreat and Dublin in cruise-control. We went on a scoring blitz with Barr, high on the adrenalin of it all, driving a further stake through the Lilywhite heart when he scored one of the great Dublin goals at the Hill 16 end. His rasping shot from twenty yards left the half-time score line reading: Dublin 1-10 Kildare 0-4. After that, there was nowhere to go but home for the Kildare men. Dublin coasted through the second-half to run out comfortable winners by 1-13 to 0-10. And O'Dwyer had finally been put to the sword. For only the second time since 1985, Dublin were high kings of Leinster. Down south, the news was even better. Incredibly, Clare had beaten Kerry in the Munster final. This meant that Dublin would be meeting the Banner men for a place in the All-Ireland final. Everything was going to plan. With Donegal beating Mayo in the other semi-final, Sam seemed closer than ever.

And so the day of the Clare semi arrived. The Hill was a blue canvas as usual but as for the rest of Croker, it seemed the prospect of taking on the mighty Dubs had brought the whole of Clare to the capital. It felt like we were the away side as a sea of saffron and blue washed over the stands as Clare took to the field. But they weren't cheering for long. It was vintage Dublin: quick direct ball into Vinny Murphy who unleashed an unstoppable shot into the top corner at the Railway End. The Hill went crazy with delight. But the contest was far from over; every time Dublin seemed ready to take the ascendancy, Clare hit back. More than once, we found ourselves biting our nails as Clare threatened to upset the script. In the end, Dublin ran out winners by 3-14 to 2-12, but it had not been the comfortable passage that many had expected. Vinny's brace of goals had been decisive. In the pub later, we talked in usual clichés about the benefits of a good test. It was just good to be back in the final, tomorrow could wait for now.

Confidence was sky-high in the weeks leading up to the final. In the papers and on TV, the pundits were writing Donegal off as if they were a nothing team. It seemed that redemption was finally close at hand. But something was gnawing away at my insides. Time and again, we were told that Donegal had never won an All-Ireland. Well, there always has to be a first time, I thought. Dublin had beaten Donegal in the league only a few months earlier but everyone seemed to have forgotten the two late Dublin goals that had turned a game dominated by Donegal on its head. I prayed that the Dublin team weren't buying in to all the hype and hoopla building up around them in the run-in. But, judging by the rumours that began to circulate, it seemed that the heads of some players might have been turned. Needless to say, I was a bag of nerves in the days leading up to the game, with my usual cheery optimism, I could see it all going pear-shaped. It didn't help that Kevin, a Kerry teaching colleague of mine, outlined on a daily basis exactly how Donegal would beat Dublin. Having a Kerry man explain to you how Dublin can be beaten is something akin to a top doctor telling you that it's time to start arranging your own funeral. If Kevin knew what needed to be done then I was sure that the wily Donegal manager Brian McEniff would also have a few tricks up his sleeve.

Dublin started well enough and were leading by four points to one when we were awarded a penalty. A bloody penalty. Instead of rejoicing, we peered through our fingers as Charlie Redmond stepped up to take the kick at the Canal End. Charlie went for power but his shot lacked direction as it flew high and wide. The whole of Donegal rejoiced and that was pretty much that. They never looked back as they embarked on a points scoring spree. Dublin had no answer, their one dimensional approach floundering on the rocks of an impressive Donegal defence. They knew that if they negated Vinny Murphy's threat, then they would be a long way down the road to a famous victory and it soon became clear that pumping high ball after high ball into Vinny wasn't having the desired effect. The deliveries were too slow and even when he managed to win possession he was smothered by two to three Donegal defenders. At the other end Donegal were scoring points for fun. The second-half was excruciating; we were reduced to praying for a goal that never came. And in the end, we were well beaten: 18 points to 14.

I was understandably grumpy afterwards and had words with Maurice when he mentioned that he was thinking of going to Donegal for his holidays. In the heat of the moment, I vowed never to set foot in the north-west ever again. But in the days and weeks that followed, I came to accept that it wasn't Donegal's fault. Someone has to win and someone has to lose. There were no hard feelings. Maurice didn't even have the strength to burn the referee when we got back to Hedigans, there was only one thing to do on a day like this; get totally pissed. As supporters it is our sacred duty to pick over the bones of defeat, consecrating the ceremony with a good feed of pints. But one thing is certain, we drink even more after a good win. Nothing gets in our way. It didn't matter that Donegal had played out of their skins. There was nothing lucky about their triumph. They were simply the better team on the day. But this wasn't about them, this was about us. We had left the game behind. By the time I bumped into Kevin later that night, all I can remember him saying is "I told you so".

I awoke the next morning with the mother of all hangovers. At some point in the darkness, I knew that the light would begin to creep back in, but I just didn't know when. And until then, drink was the only option that I thought I had. No amount of talking about it could erase the sense of desolation that followed this defeat. Something told me that it would take a lot of getting over. That's what we do in Ireland when we have something that we need to forget. We try to drink it out of our systems, hoping against hope that when the hangover subsides, the pain will go with it, but it only seems to make it worse. Dublin football has taught me to face up to my demons over the years, to look them in the eye and tell them that I'll be back for more of the same next year.

Somehow I managed to make it through the teaching day before I collapsed into bed, drew the curtains and pulled the duvet over my head. When I woke up the next day, Paddy Cullen was gone. It was becoming clear that all had not been well in the Dublin camp leading up to the final; heads had indeed been turned by the hype. To make matters worse, Paddy's comments the day after the game in which he laid much of the blame for defeat at the door of the Dublin players didn't go down well. After that, the writing was on the wall. As supporters, we live in a parallel universe to what is going on behind the scenes. We like to think we know exactly what's happening but we only see the public side of the show. We had enjoyed Paddy but losing changes everything. Losing to Meath was understandable, but losing to Donegal was downright careless. On Sunday morning Paddy Cullen was the Messiah in waiting but by Sunday evening he was a dead man walking. The strengths that people had talked about over a couple of pre-match pints turned to major weaknesses as we drowned our sorrows.

I was kind of sad that it had to end this way for Dublin's former goalkeeping king. It was ironic that a missed penalty should seal his fate after his own heroics against Galway and Armagh. It would have been great to see Cullen delivering an All-Ireland before he rode off into the sunset. It would have suited his style: a big cigar, a glass of whiskey in one hand and Sam in the other. But sadly it was not to be.

Chapter Eighteen

Down And Out In Croke Park

Sunday 18 September 1994

All-Ireland Senior Football Championship Final
Dublin versus Down

So, yet again, Dublin were looking for a new manager. The County Board was back in the groove, turning to yet another hero from the seventies to turn our fortunes around. If they kept this up there wouldn't be many left to pick from in the future. It was as if they were honour bound to relive our glorious past. Pat O'Neill was appointed soon afterwards, with Fran Ryder as trainer. The connection to the seventies was strengthened further with the news that Bobby Doyle would be a selector under the new regime. Pat was a totally different kind of manager to Paddy: a medical doctor, his approach to securing an All-Ireland would prove to be as intense as it was forensic. He wasn't a man for sound bites and there were no false promises as he settled into his new job. With Pat, everything was done for a reason.

And O'Neill's retooled Dublin side looked promising, like his two predecessors, he won the league at his first attempt. The nucleus of the side had been together for a few years now with established stars such as John O'Leary, Eamon Heery, Paul Curran, Keith Barr, Mick Galvin, Gerry Hargan Charlie Redmond and Mick Kennedy providing the backbone. The likes of Paul Clarke, Jack Sheedy and Davy Foran were the link between the more experienced warriors and the young guns such as Dessie Farrell, Paul Bealin, Vinny Murphy and Pat Gilroy. The fact that we beat Donegal by 10 points to 6 in the 1993 replayed National League final showed that we had been caught with our pants down nine months earlier. The Hill was on fire that day and the team responded by scoring eight unanswered points before Donegal finally registered their first point just before half-time.

Despite the improvements, Leinster proved a tougher nut to crack in the 1993 championship campaign. We started with a hard fought four point win in a low scoring game against Wexford in Wexford Park. This day is probably best remembered as the one when a Dublin fan went through the roof.

Having climbed onto the roof of the dressing rooms at half-time, he crashed through the ceiling, landed in the middle of the Wexford team before making his apologies as he exited through the dressing room door. I was more than a little worried that Dublin's opponents in the semi-final would be Meath. It didn't help that I was on holiday again, but this time the news from the other end of the phone was good. In the end, I needn't have fretted as Jack Sheedy's late point gave us some measure of revenge for 1991. Jack was notable for his tireless running as well as his wayward shooting, but this was a beauty. I was back in time for the final and for the second year running Mick O'Dywer's Kildare side were Dublin's challengers. Kildare liked to think that they could put it up to Dublin. However the Dublin players didn't seem to be too bothered by their antics and it was obvious that they felt that they held the upper hand. Yet again, Kildare seemed to think that their best chance lay in throwing their weight around and the signs looked promising for the Lilywhites as Dublin turned around only a point ahead with a stiff wind blowing into their faces. But despite this, Dublin found much more space in the second period to run out winners by 11 points to 7 in a hard fought encounter. Six unanswered points at the beginning of the second-half proved to be the key to another satisfying victory for the backroom staff. O'Dwyer had been put to the sword again.

Derry were up next in the All-Ireland semi. With Sam having headed across the border on the previous two occasions, the Derry men were aiming to make it three in a row for Ulster. The excitement surrounding the match meant that we couldn't get our hands on any Hill tickets so we had to be content with the Canal End. We thought we'd be clever and get there early to secure a good spot. The minor game was just starting as we wandered up the steps towards the terrace. All was quiet; we would be in position long before the Derry hordes arrived. But as we stepped out into the light, an amazing sight panned out before us – the place was already packed – red and white flags were raised in a spectacular explosion of colour and noise. These guys were going to enjoy their day in the sun no matter what. I let out a bewildered "Fuck This" much to the amusement of a pretty Ban Garda. She laughed and said that she would come and rescue us if we got into any trouble. We needn't have worried; the Derry supporters turned out to be some of the nicest people that I have ever had the privilege to stand amongst. In the end they would break our hearts, but the memories of that day and what it meant to them will remain with me to my dying days.

Derry broke from the parade early as it approached Hill 16, a statement of intent supposedly orchestrated by captain Henry Downey. Despite losing full-back Dermot Deasy early on to a pulled hamstring, we held our nerve to lead by nine points to four at half-time. Vinny Murphy was dominating Danny Quinn with Charlie Redmond taking advantage of any frees that came Dublin's way. Even Pat Gilroy, not renowned for raising the white flag, had chipped in with a couple of points. But Derry never gave up. Tony Scullion had managed to quieten Murphy and the Derry half-backs were bringing Joe Brolly into the game. Slowly but surely, Derry cut the Dublin lead and with only seven minutes left on the clock, the sides were level. The winning score came right at the end – I still blame Duff to this day – with Johnny McGurk tight to the right touchline on the Hogan Stand side, the Dublin defence seemed to have everything under control. "Keep him out there. Keep him out there" roared Duff. The Dublin players must have been listening because they did exactly as Duff said. But it still wasn't enough as Johnny picked this precise moment to hit one the most incredible match winning points I have ever had the privilege to witness. The ball travelled directly towards us as it split the posts ending Dublin's All-Ireland dream for another year. We hugged the Derry supporters, said our goodbyes and headed for the pub. The Ban Garda smiled as we passed by. She seemed to be glad that we had survived. Unfortunately, there had been no need for her to rescue us after all.

Hedigans again, beaten again, picking over the bones again. Would our torture never end? It was clear that the atmosphere generated by the Dubs was bringing out the best in Dublin's opponents. For what seemed like the umpteenth time, Dublin had lost a game that was there for the taking. A seesaw battle if ever there was one, a minute more and Dublin might well have drawn level. Even though Derry were coming on strong in the second-half, it was still impossible to pick a winner in those last hectic 10 minutes.

I was sitting in a pub in Enniskillen a few months later when I overheard two old age pensioners discussing Derry's All-Ireland triumph. One of them turned to the other and said: "I'll tell you when that All-Ireland was won." The moment I had been thinking about came drifting back into my head but I was sure that he would point to some incident in Derry's win over Cork in the final. "When was that?" said the other. "When Jack Sheedy was through on goal only to be dispossessed in the semi-final against Dublin." I couldn't believe it. Here I was, sitting in a pub miles from Dublin and two old men were confirming the thoughts that had been running through my head over the last few months. I couldn't seem to get away from it; I had rerun the moment over and over again in my mind. We were getting ready to jump for joy as Jack had the goal at his mercy after rampaging through a seemingly impregnable Derry defence; a goal then for Dublin would have been enough. But it wasn't to be. The history of sport is littered with the ghosts of defining moments. They don't make it into the record books, but it is often forgotten that they are the very reason those books tell it the way they do.

For the umpteenth time Dublin put their latest disappointment behind them and moved on. 1994 was one of those World Cup summers when the Gaelic boys had to compete for the attention of a sports-mad nation. Dublin had drawn Kildare in the opening round of the Leinster championship and, somewhat appropriately, Ireland were due to play Italy in their opening group game later on. All our thoughts were focused on the boys in green but the Dublin-Kildare match would be a tasty starter before we all sat down to our main course later that night. The boys in blue were big enough and old enough to look after themselves now, we thought, after all, beating Kildare was a given.

Kildare were within seconds of finally getting one over on the Dubs when Charlie Redmond kicked a last gasp equaliser to save the day. None of us would have denied Kildare their victory. Dublin, who had been awful, looked like a tired team that had taken one too many punches. The idea that they had the energy to go after Sam with the same relentless purpose that had characterised much of the previous three seasons looked to be beyond them as we headed for the exits. A few hours later Ray Houghton's goal secured a famous win. The summer was up and running.

For the Dubs, it was as if they had needed that massive fright to kick start their season and two weeks later, the real Dublin reappeared. Maybe seeing Ireland beating the mighty Italians had shown them that anything was possible, even beating Kildare. Whatever had happened in those two intervening weeks, their hunger was back. By half-time Dublin were 11 points to 2 ahead. The sending-off of Paul Bealin allowed Kildare back into the game and at one point they had cut Dublin's lead to three before a very strange event took place: Dublin scored a penalty. Charlie Redmond must be one of the bravest men in Dublin, not only is he a fireman but time and again, he had put his neck on the line. After that Kildare were history; opening the way for yet another Leinster final clash with Meath.

In a welcome break with recent tradition, I made it along to this one. The news that Alex Ferguson and his Manchester United players were at the match left us wondering what they must have made of it all. I'm sure Ferguson would have loved the bruising intensity but in truth it was a poor game.

Meath recalled their veteran goalkeeper Michael McQuillan only for him to fumble a Charlie Redmond free into his own net. The ball seemed to stay in the air forever as a hypnotised Hill 16 followed its trajectory before it slipped through McQuillan's hands to nestle in the corner of the Meath net. All goals against Meath are special, and the Hill erupted in an outpouring of joy that would have made you think that one of the greatest goals ever had just been scored. Sure enough, it turned out to be the precious difference between the two sides. A young Meath man by the name of Graham Geraghty stood out and his goal towards the end had us biting our fingers down to the quick. I liked to think that we had played our part. Trevor Giles had struggled to convert some crucial frees into a baying Hill during a typically tense first-half and poor Mickey McQuillan must have felt the power of thousands willing him to drop Charlie's free. The final score read Dublin 1-9 Meath 1-8.

For the second time in three years, Dublin found themselves facing unexpected opposition in the All-Ireland semi-final. In 1992 it was Clare and now Leitrim were readying themselves for their tilt at the Dubs. The hype was even bigger with the whole country backing Leitrim. This was nothing new, we were well used to being the big bad wolf. I expected Dublin to run out easy enough winners if they could weather the expected Leitrim storm in the early minutes as we had better, more experienced players in every position. Yellow and gold replaced the saffron and blue of Clare when Declan Darcy led his team onto the hallowed turf of Croke Park for the first time. For the second time in three years the Hill stood defiant and alone.

Although they gave it a good lash, the final score of 3-15 to 1-9 in Dublin's favour was just about right. Once Charlie Redmond scored Dublin's first goal, the writing was on the wall. Just before half-time, Mick Galvin scored the goal of the season after a sublime passing movement that started with

Dermot Deasy deep in Dublin territory. Dublin were back where they wanted to be: seventy minutes away from realising their dream. It was just a pity that Down seemed to be blocking the view.

There was no room for complacency in the build up to the 1994 All-Ireland final. Down were a serious outfit, they had built on the legacy of the great team of the sixties by winning their third All-Ireland in 1991 and but for the vagaries of getting out of the Ulster championship, it was widely felt that Pete McGrath's team should have added another by now. Winning Ulster was becoming almost as hard as winning an All-Ireland but having made it out, they were now many people's favourites to make it two titles in four years. We knew we were up against it, if we were going to win that elusive All-Ireland we were going to have to do it the hard way.

In Mickey Linden, Down had one of the greatest players ever to play the game. If Dublin were to emerge victorious, Linden would have to be stopped. But when Ciaran Walsh, the man detailed to mark Linden, was injured in a club match just weeks before the final, Pat O'Neill faced a difficult decision. Get this one wrong and any hopes Dublin had would be blown away in a flurry of early Linden points. In the end, he chose Paul Curran, a player who normally played at half-back, but with his pace and skill it was thought that he was the best option. Only a few months earlier, Curran had done a good job on Linden when he was switched onto him in a league game. O'Neill's decision was based on what had gone before -the doctor was at work. But Paul was only back from injury himself and many felt that putting him in the full-back line would damage Dublin's attacking intent. In a desperate attempt to calm my nerves the night before the game, I met Duff in a city centre pub and we spent most the evening wondering if Curran would be up to the pace of the game, especially in those crucial early minutes. As we headed for home we were nervous wrecks.

I had a ticket for the Cusack Stand, but even the darkening skies over O'Connell Street couldn't dampen my ardour as I searched desperately for someone with a spare Hill ticket. Just as I was about to give up hope, I got lucky. I quickly offloaded my Cusack ticket and headed down to meet Duff. He was delighted to hear that I would be accompanying him to the Hill. It seemed like a good omen. After the defeat to Donegal, this final had a double or quits feel about it; lose it and this Dublin team would be history. A lot of the players had a serious number of miles on the clock and any further mental anguish was sure to take its toll. Defeat was unthinkable. Maurice had just married the lovely Margaret and was on his honeymoon in Crete, so this time it was his turn to wait for the hours to pass in a foreign land before picking up the phone to find out the result. I didn't envy him as we made our way up the steps towards Hill 16.

The skies finally opened on a jam-packed Hill about an hour before throw in. Because of the crush, only our shoulders and heads would get wet, the least of our worries as we prayed for salvation. We sang our hearts out as the teams paraded in front of us, happy that Dublin would be defending the Hill in the first-half. That's the way we liked it and it was always good to have our team attacking into the Railway End in the second-half, something to hold onto if the going got tough.

Down struck first. The first point of the game gave Ulster's finest the vital psychological edge they had been looking for. Linden got the better of Paul Curran, who slipped as he attempted to get out in front of his man, to set up Gregory McCartan. The Hill was quiet, a younger or lesser player would have received a collective bollocking but Paul Curran was a hero and we could feel his pain. Paul knew the score. Unless he got to grips with Linden, the game would be over before it had even started.

Within minutes our very worst fears had been realised with Curran looking lost at corner-back, Linden took full advantage to put Down in the driving seat. Although Dublin had initially managed to stay in touch, everything changed when the second defining moment of the game arrived midway through the first-half. Curran and Paul Clarke were left on the Croke Park turf as Down ripped the Dublin defence apart with a swift incisive move. Linden and McCartan advanced on John O'Leary in the Dublin goal. At the last moment, Linden flicked the ball to McCartan and he did the rest to leave the score: Down 1-5 Dublin 0-3. Pat O'Neill reacted by moving Paul Clarke onto Linden and releasing Curran back into his natural habitat of the half-back line. Perhaps O'Neill would have acted earlier if he hadn't been dealing with a player of the calibre of Curran, but winning an All-Ireland requires a ruthless streak and the delay had left Dublin with a mountain to climb. Memories of 1985 came flooding back, Kevin Heffernan refusing to countenance the removal of his captain Brian Mullins. By half-time, Down were ahead by 1-8 to 0-7 and the Hill was mumbling darkly as it always does when things don't go to plan.

The first few minutes of the second-half would be vital, Dublin had to up their game, more of the same and it was curtains. Paul Bealin came in for Pat Gilroy at midfield, but little changed and soon Down were six points ahead. Dublin couldn't seem to get any sort of a foothold in the game. Hanging on to Down's coat tails, we readied ourselves for what was to come. With the minutes ticking by we began to accept our fate.

But that would have been too straightforward. Little did we know it at the time, but Down had registered their final score of the day. Paul Clarke was keeping Linden quiet and the Down hurricane had blown itself out. Now it was Dublin's turn to brew up a storm. With 20 minutes left, they had the ball all to themselves and began to sweep forward in wave after wave of relentless attack. For the second time that day our minds turned to the 1985 comeback against Kerry as we prayed for the goal we so badly needed. If we were going to force a replay or even win a game that had looked lost only minutes ago it had to come soon.

It was torture to watch. Down were flooding the area in front of their goal in a desperate attempt to hang on. Even though Dublin cut the lead to three with the game entering its final ten minutes, they were making hard work of it. But Dublin's forwards seemed determined to smash a way through the wall of defenders when creeping quietly around the side might have been a better idea. Time and again, the blue shirt in possession failed to spot a teammate in a better position. It was as if the whole Dublin team was trying to squeeze through a tiny door at the same time. When cool heads were required, Dublin were found wanting. Their approach was too frenetic. I was as nervous as I have ever been in those last few agonising minutes.

And then the break we had been praying for arrived, with only eight minutes left, Dessie Farrell was bundled to the ground by a posse of overanxious Down defenders and referee Tommy Sugrue had no hesitation in holding his arms outstretched. Penalty to Dublin. We danced for joy and hugged each other. And then we stopped. We looked anxiously to see who would take the kick. By the law of averages we were due to score one by now. It looked like Charlie Redmond was placing the ball down. Poor auld Charlie, the darling of the Hill, had suffered more than any other player in Ireland when it came to penalty heartache but this was no time for sentimentality. This one simply had to go in, our time had come.

Thousands of desperate voices rained their advice down on Charlie as he put the ball on the spot. "Hit it hard Charlie." "Break the fucking net." "Send him the wrong way Charlie." "Don't miss it for fuck's sake." I clasped my hands together and looked to the heavens again. "Please God let it go in." Charlie steps up. Hits it. It flies high to the goalkeeper's left. Niall Collins dives. The ball comes back of his body. Back towards Charlie and the on-rushing Johnny Barr. We don't have time to be disappointed. There's a rebound to be gobbled up. Both Dublin players slide towards the ball. Down captain D.J. Kane puts his body on the line by throwing himself in front of them. Three bodies collide. The ball slides towards the Down goal and slips wide. A grateful James McCartan jumps into his goalkeeper's welcoming arms. We curse our luck. More misery. We knew that was it. FUCKING PENALTIES. No good to anyone. Especially us. No one was blaming Charlie. He was brave enough to step up to the plate.

To their credit, Dublin refused to bow to the inevitable to cut the lead to two. But it was too little, too late. The final whistle sealed our doom. One of the Down players felt the need to taunt the Hill. We didn't need that on a day like this. We got out as quickly as we could. Apparently, Charlie did the same, collected his gear and got the hell out of there. It was that sort of day.

Within minutes, Duff and I had scuttled up Clonliffe Road and were rounding a corner towards the canal when a lone Down supporter couldn't resist having a pot-shot. He wasn't even in the ground to see his team receive the cup. "Cheer Up Lads," he chirped. I wanted to tell him where to go in no uncertain terms but Duff dragged me off by the scruff of the neck. We had a couple of pints and said our goodbyes. We were too disappointed to drink. Over in Crete Maurice was struggling with an antiquated phone as he attempted to contact home. He hit the wine when he heard the bad news.

I didn't even watch the recording of the match when I got home. A couple of days later, a teaching colleague asked me if I had a tape of the game as he had a Down pal in the States who would like to watch it. I handed it over the next day, glad to be rid of it, glad to make someone else happy.

Over the next few days, I tried to make some sense of the last four years. I was irritable and argumentative, ill at ease with the world. Whereas before, I had managed to retain some small sense of hope of better things to come, now there seemed to be nothing to hold onto. It felt like the end. Dublin had given it everything and yet they had come up short, beaten by the better team on the day. Again. They had lost big games over the last few years from every possible position. Ahead, behind, level pegging. It didn't seem to matter. I wondered how they were coping with this latest setback. Another nine months down the drain. They had tried desperately to batter the door down but Down's dominance in the opening 50 minutes had left Dublin with too much to do. In the immediate aftermath, the players were angry and out of sorts. Johnny Barr ran into trouble outside a nightclub and there were rumours that Niall Guiden had attended a wedding in the days leading up to the final. He was subsequently banished from the squad. Apparently it wasn't Maurice and Margaret's.

Chapter Nineteen

If At First You Don't Succeed

Sunday 17 September 1995

All-Ireland Senior Football Championship Final
Dublin versus Tyrone

We needed Pat O'Neill more than ever now. His ability to approach the wreckage of another heartbreaking season with a clinical eye was invaluable. Doctor Pat was the perfect man for the job and nothing was left to chance, no team would be fitter or better prepared. But what was needed now was the final piece in the jigsaw, an instinctive player who would swing games in our favour, someone with a magic touch. And, as we readied ourselves for the opening encounter with Louth in Navan, the name of Jason Sherlock began to be touted as Dublin's next bright young thing. It was a hell of a lot of expectation to heap on such a young pair of shoulders; it showed how desperate the media were to find a new angle to the Dublin story. The Dubs sold newspapers. If anything, the recent torment had brought the players and fans closer together. But in the days leading up to the Louth game, we started to get the feeling that maybe this could be our year after all. It had taken eight long months but finally we began to believe again. We had our mojo back.

Louth in Navan; slip up here and the dream is over before it has even started. But now we have Jason. He may have impressed on the minor stage but that has never been a guarantee of success at senior level. However, Jason had added to an already impressive pedigree with a league goal against Kerry in Tralee, a rite of passage for any Dublin player and no matter how hard Pat O'Neill and his back room team tried to play down the Sherlock factor, the buzz just wouldn't go away. But to me, it still looked a little too early to be tossing a 19 year old into the hurly-burly of senior championship football. I worried that some vicious county back would break him clean in two. It didn't take a wild imagination to wince at what the likes of Colm Coyle might do to Jason if he ever got his hands on him. But Meath were a long way off. First of all Dublin needed to beat Louth.

Duff's brother Vivian and his mate Tom were driving to the game so we cadged a lift with them. These guys were veterans of the seventies and I listened intently to their memories as we moved into enemy territory. I had packed a survival kit to cater for all eventualities: a return bus ticket in case I got separated, enough food and water to get me back across the border and my passport. Vivian's other friend Brian had declined the trip on the grounds that he rarely set foot outside the capital. As we approached the outskirts of Navan, we waited to see if there were any late changes to the team that had been announced earlier in the week. Dublin managers have always enjoyed messing with the media, an uneasy relationship that has existed for years. O'Neill was no different. You could sense the disappointment amongst the travelling support when it became clear that Jason was starting on the bench. Another youngster, Keith Galvin was selected in the full-back line while Dessie Farrell was switched to centre forward. In Farrell's case, it seemed like a sensible move as Dessie's game has always been built around close-control allied to the ability to link up with better placed team mates, but too often, his good work was wasted out on the touchline. The game was being played on a Saturday evening to suit television, so the sizable Dublin contingent were in good spirits on the back of a sunny, boozy afternoon. Navan was overflowing, any opportunity to invade the capital of Meath grabbed with open arms.

In the end, we ran out fairly comfortable winners by 0-19 to 2-5, but things had been a little hairy either side of half-time when the Dublin defence had shipped two goals. For an anxious few minutes it had looked as if Louth might be capable of causing an upset. Dublin's penalty hoodoo had also struck again; this time it was Paul Clarke's turn to try his luck but it turned out to be no better than those who had gone before him. Charlie Redmond had obviously had enough and who could blame him, however his nine points proved crucial as Dublin pulled away for an impressive opening day win. But the biggest cheer of the day came after 20 minutes when Jayo came on and his introduction paid a dividend when he won a penalty within a minute of his arrival on the pitch. He went on to register a point and looked more than comfortable. Inevitably, he shipped one heavy blow as the elbow of Louth's Gareth O'Neill let him know that he would be a target for the bully boys. But to his credit, Jason just got up and got on with it; his enthusiasm was boundless and the Dublin supporters howled with outrage if anyone went near him. It was as if we had taken on the role of protective parents.

Towards the end of the game, I was too busy worrying about myself to worry about Jason. We had ended up beside a bunch of Louth supporters around the halfway line and whilst at first the banter was friendly, slowly their mood worsened as the effect of their afternoon drinking wore off and Dublin pulled clear. It wasn't long before they began to get more and more abusive towards anything Dublin, including us. Thankfully, they decided to leave with a few minutes to go and I looked at Duff with a certain degree of relief. We had become a little cut off from Tom and Vivian who were standing to our right. But just when it seemed that the danger had passed, Vivian decided to pipe up from his relatively safe vantage point: "Cheerio boys. We might see you next year." It stopped them in their tracks. Time stood still as we awaited our fate but luckily they just scowled and moved on.

The GAA seemed to be determined that we should spend the summer in Meath and we were back in Navan three weeks later for the game against an improving Laois side. There was an even bigger crowd this time as Jason-mania had begun to take hold of the capital. It was a beautiful sunny day as we rolled into town in the back of Tom's car. I loved the whole idea of away days, the chance to get out of the city and the bond that builds between the travelling supporters. An army on the march, with lines of cars and buses stretching out into the countryside. Tom regaled us with endless stories of Keaveney and the good old days.

Laois should have been a goal up through Damien Delaney after just fifteen seconds but he blasted the ball past John O'Leary's right-hand post with the goal at his mercy. After that, it was nip and tuck with the scores level at five points each at half-time. But Dublin seized the initiative at the start of the second-half with three quick points. Thirteen minutes from the end, the moment we had all been waiting for arrived. Jason, who had hit the post earlier, collected a ball from Jim Gavin and evaded Ger Doyle before hammering home the decisive score of the day. The fact that Sherlock had scored his first championship goal without his boot only added to the legend that was growing around his every move. A star was born that day in Navan. Hopes of another tilt as Sam were growing as the Dublin bandwagon gained momentum. As usual, one giant obstacle stood in our way – Meath – next up in the Leinster final.

Once again, I was missing in action, on holidays in the south of France, and

I spent the day trying to keep myself busy as I waited to pick up the phone. Lose and this Dublin team would be history. We had been saying this for a few years now but this time it really felt like the end of the road. And it was no different for Meath; too many aging bodies with too many miles on the clock. So the game had a last chance saloon feel to it. In the end Sunday 30 July 1995 turned out to be the perfect day, a blue-lettered one when this Dublin team reached for the sky and finally cast off the shackles of frustration and ill-fortune that had dominated them since 1989. This was payback for '91. I couldn't believe it when my father announced the final score over the phone. Maybe he was struggling to believe it himself. Meath 1-8. Followed by a massive pause – he liked to build up the tension – Dublin 1-18. I dropped the phone and jumped around the room like a lunatic. Ten fucking points.

When I returned home, I watched every minute of the game. I could almost feel the heat and the tension coming off the screen in those early minutes. At first, the script seemed to be following a familiar pattern as Dublin's early dominance was rewarded with a lead of eight points to four at half-time. The inevitable backlash followed as Meath hit back to take the lead courtesy of an Evan Kelly goal and a point from Graham Geraghty. But today was different, Meath had hit the front early giving Dublin sufficient time to recover.

Meath had no answer to the onslaught that followed with Charlie Redmond and Paul Clarke leading the charge and the game was effectively sealed when Jason Sherlock's speculative shot came down from the heavens only for Clarke to punch the ball to the net for a stunning goal. Sherlock survived the attentions of Colm Coyle to kick a wonderful point towards the end. Coyle must have been boiling up inside as his young tormentor raised his arms in defiance to a frenzied Hill, even taking some time out to kiss the referee. Jason certainly looked like he was here to stay. It was also a great day for Paul Curran who gave a man-of-the-match display, which must have gone a long way to restoring his confidence following the disappointment against Down a year earlier. The final whistle unleashed an outpouring of blue joy not seen in Croke Park since the 1983 All-Ireland final.

Of all the days I missed, not knowing what it was like to be on the Hill for this sweetest of victories haunts me most. But, of course, the job was still only half done, and one of Dublin's greatest displays since the seventies would count for nothing if we didn't bring Sam home. Everyone in Dublin knew as much as they raised their glasses to one of the great Dublin displays of recent times.

Perhaps it was just as well that Dublin's next opponents would be Cork in the All-Ireland semi-final. Matches between the two sides have always had a special intensity to them. This is urban warfare at its very best. Dublin had ambushed the Rebels as the same stage in '74 and '83, but their fresh-faced innocence had allowed the Leesiders to gain some measure of revenge in '89. This Cork team had been around the block having lost to Derry in the 1993 All-Ireland final. They had a little bit of Dublin in them, the same hunger born out of disappointment making this the clash of the bridesmaids. Such was the interest in the game that tickets proved hard to come by and our usual gang was scattered to the four corners of the ground on match day. I ended up in the brand spanking new Cusack Stand with Declan, a curly haired Dublin nut and a friend of Duff's. I cast an occasional envious glance at those on the Hill throughout another nerve-racking day.

For the fourth time that summer, the life of this incarnation of the Dublin team was on the line: each day they had taken to the field the stakes had been raised and each day felt like it could be the end. Another failure now was unthinkable. The outlook wasn't looking too good as Cork started well, before another dramatic intervention from Jason Sherlock changed the course of the afternoon. Cork were leading by five points to two when Keith Barr's quick free kick put Jason in possession about thirty yards from goal on the Hogan Stand side. He had to get past Cork's full-back Mark O'Connor first but as Dublin's new pin-up spun on a sixpence, O'Connor slipped. In an instant, Sherlock was free and through on goal, his rasping finish gave Kevin O'Dwyer no chance in the Cork goal. Dublin were back in business. Cork's early dominance faded as Dublin picked up the pace to lead by 1-5 to 0-6 at half-time.

In the second-half, Dublin controlled the midfield with Brian Stynes giving another towering performance alongside future Dublin manager Pat Gilroy, who had replaced the injured Paul Bealin just before the break. Each day, a different player stepped up to the plate, it was Mick Galvin's turn to kick four vital second-half points. With Charlie Redmond keeping the scoreboard ticking over, Dublin ran out comfortable enough winners by 1-12 to 0-12. Nevertheless, I was still a nervous wreck in those dying minutes as I waited for a Cork goal that never came. As the final whistle blew I hugged Declan. We were back in another All-Ireland final. Just for tonight, I was going to enjoy myself.

The lead up to Dublin's third All-Ireland final in four years was a typically nervous one. The Jason factor was thwarting us at every turn in our frantic search for tickets. It was every man for himself this time: Duff was already sorted, relegated to the Canal End, at least he was in. I couldn't get a ticket for love nor money. It was bad enough worrying about the game without the added pressure of wondering whether I would be there. Maurice was in the same boat, ticketless having lost out in a draw of family and friends, six tickets and seven names, he had been the unlucky one. His wife Margaret ended up on the Hill; now if that's not love then I don't know what is. Poor Maurice ended up watching the match in the pub, ruling out his opportunity to witness Dublin lifting Sam in the flesh for the first time. Still there was always next year and the year after that... With the game only twenty-four hours away, P.O. rang with the news I had been waiting all week to hear.

I was in, or so I thought until I saw the tickets he'd got. He showed them to me when he arrived to pick me up the next day. They looked a wee bit dodgy to say the least. The price had been scratched out and a scribbled £30 had been written in. It didn't look good. I was caught in two minds. Should I try to get another ticket off a tout or should I trust P.O.'s instincts that everything would be fine? I even showed the tickets to a Garda manning the barrier at the top of Clonliffe Road to see what he thought. He looked at them and said in a thick country accent: "Ah sure, why not give it a go." I had to laugh. As we approached the entrance to the new Cusack Stand, I began to notice a high proportion of suits. I was dressed in my usual pair of jeans and Dublin shirt and if I looked a little bit out of place, P.O.'s sandwiches wrapped in tin foil really took the biscuit. The fact that he was carrying them in a tired old looking plastic bag, the man bag of the nineties, only added to a growing sense that we were out of our usual milieu. Aghast, I realised we were in the corporate whore section, but any qualms I had about where we were sitting would have to wait until afterwards. First we had to get through the turnstiles. Would those iffy tickets pass inspection? My heart was thumping as we presented the tickets, the sweat beading on my brow. He waved us through. WE WERE IN! I let out a huge sigh of relief. I felt exhausted already and the game hadn't even started.

Once in, we were confronted with the slightly surreal sight of a bunch of Aer Lingus hostesses. I was ready for take-off but this wasn't what I had in mind. Still I did my best to keep my mind on the game. Today is the day, I thought to myself, I can feel it in my bones. There was little doubt that this Tyrone team was the weakest of the four to come out of Ulster since 1991; surely Dublin would be too strong for them. But then the doubts began to creep in. Relief only came when I was jolted back to the present as one of the Aer Lingus ladies welcomed us before directing us towards an escalator. At this point I was completely confused. Was I in a plane or a department store? It seemed a very long way from Hill 16, but as we took our seats, I realised that we were sitting just above the hallowed concrete, I was as near to my tribe as I could be, a tiny crumb of comfort. As we wandered back up towards the bar, P.O. pulled out his sandwiches and opened the tin foil, the sound competing with the hum of people enjoying themselves. All around us, the suits were filling themselves with beer, high on the octane of their own self-importance. I bit into a ham and cheese sandwich and wondered why sandwiches always taste better when someone else makes them. It was good to get some food on board. Better to be prepared.

We headed for the toilets and I chuckled to myself as P.O. conducted a detailed discussion about the minor final with a supporter of the winning team even though he had only seen the final two minutes. Back in our seats, I got the feeling that a lot of these people didn't really care if Dublin won or not. They thought they did, but deep down it wouldn't affect their lives all that much if Sam headed back across the border for a fifth year in succession. They couldn't give a fuck. They were just here to have a good time. I looked down longingly at a packed Hill 16.

Looking back on the week leading up to the final, I was glad that the search for a ticket kept me busy and stopped me from worrying myself silly. As it stood on the day, my nerves were shredded with fear.

Reason to be fearful number one: Peter Canavan. Canavan was one of the most gifted footballers in Ireland and he was guaranteed to cause the Dublin defence all manner of problems. With full-back Dermot Deasy ruled out with a hamstring injury, Ciaran Walsh, who missed last year's final was handed the job of keeping Tyrone's main threat quiet.

Reason to be fearful number two: Stage fright. Would Dublin be gripped by fear? Would they be able to shake off years of disappointment? Would the fear of losing be greater than the will to win?

Reason to be fearful number three: Charlie Redmond. Rumours had been circulating that Charlie had injured his leg in training and that even if he played, his movement, particularly his free-taking, would be badly affected. Without his free taking, Dublin would be shorn of one of their most potent weapons. As Charlie went through his warm up routine, the signs weren't looking good.

Reason to fearful number four: Goals. Dublin have lost the knack of scoring goals in big games, goals win games and we knew that they would need at least one today.

Reason to be fearful number five: The loss of Deasy. For the second year running, the Dublin full-back line had been pulled asunder by injury, but a defence containing Paddy Moran, Ciaran Walsh and Keith Galvin looked better equipped this time around and if they could limit the effect of Canavan then Dublin would be well on their way to a famous victory.

I was desperate for the game to start, to finally be able to stop thinking.

Tyrone raced into a three-point lead leaving a shell-shocked Dublin rocking. Dublin were playing with a strong breeze at their backs. I bent over in my seat in an effort to try and relieve the sickening pain that had gripped my stomach. The Dublin's players looked out of sorts and the Hill was ominously quiet. Fear was everywhere, on the Hill, in the stands and on the pitch. Someone needed to do something fast and then Keith Barr stepped forward, the man for a crisis, to belt over an incredible seventy yard free.

At last we were up and running. Within no time the sides were level. But Charlie Redmond was clearly struggling. The shaky start was forgotten when Dessie Farrell put us ahead in the twenty-fourth minute and two minutes after that, we were in heaven when the goal we had been waiting for arrived at last. Jason Sherlock (who else?) chased a long ball into the square and bravely slid the ball past the massive Finbarr McConnell in the Tyrone goal, but the ball didn't have the legs to make it across the line, as it trickled towards goal a scramble of bodies converged with Charlie Redmond winning the race. The Dublin fans on the Canal End went berserk as the ball nestled in the net. GOAL FOR DUBLIN. In an instant, Charlie had blown away the bitter memories of his penalty heartaches. By half-time, Dublin were five points to the good: 1-8 to 0-6.

But still there were more questions than answers, as we tried to pass the time during 15 minutes that seemed to last forever. I thought of Maurice, drinking his pints, going backwards and forwards to the loo, wishing he was one of us. It was Tyrone's turn to take advantage of the wind. The signs were looking ominous as Canavan started to exert his considerable influence, drawing fouls from an increasingly frazzled looking Dublin defence. In a repeat of the first-half, Tyrone opened with three unanswered points, all from Canavan. Same old Dublin, doing things the hard way, as that all too familiar feeling that it was all slipping away settled back into my stomach.

Directly below us Charlie Redmond moved his head in a threatening manner towards Fergal Logan's forehead, the referee Paddy Russell took Charlie's name and pointed to the line. But Charlie stayed on, and it was another couple of minutes before Russell realised he was still on the pitch and sent him to the sidelines again. Thank God he didn't score in the meantime, that could have been a real headache for the GAA and more importantly us. We were a man down with 25 minutes to play. Unwelcome memories of the 1983 final came flooding back as Dublin turned their attention to holding onto what they had. Dessie Farrell, who was having a marvellous game, hit his fourth point to calm our nerves, the first score for 24 minutes. We were hanging on. With 13 minutes left, Paul Clarke kicked only Dublin's second point of the half, a superb effort into Hill 16. The Dublin lead now stretched to 1-10 to 0-10. One more score would seal it, instead, Canavan cut the deficit to a single point with time running out. With only minutes to go, John O'Leary prevented a goal as Dublin hung on for dear life. At one point, one of the hostesses came down to ask me if I was okay. Apart from the nervous breakdown I was fine. Alongside us, a father and his young son couldn't bear to watch.

Still the gods weren't finished with us. Peter Canavan slipped as the ball broke to him and all he could do was flick it towards Sean McLoughlin. Time stood still. I could hear nothing; the world blocked out by what was happening in my head. A replay and we would be without Charlie with a team that looked out on its feet. If we were to win it we had to win it now. McLoughlin collected the ball, swung his boot, his kick high and straight: the equaliser. The Canal End erupted in a sea of red and white as I buried my head in my hands, the white noise cutting me off from my feelings. I looked to the Hill for comfort, but found none; trauma written across the toughest of faces. Until I heard P.O.'s Antrim accent: "Free Out! Free Out!" Slowly I lifted my head and rubbed my eyes. He was right; Paddy Russell was pointing up field. The scoreboard still read: Dublin 1-10 Tyrone 0-12. Seconds later, Russell blew his whistle for the final time. I hugged P.O. who was yapping on about how shite Dublin had been. I didn't care. None of that mattered now. Winning was all that counted. I hugged the father and son who had come back to life. The Aer Lingus girls were all smiles. Sam was coming home.

I was sad that I wasn't with Duff and Maurice at the final whistle; the celebrations had to wait until we got to the pub. I watched John O'Leary and Paul Curran lift the famous old trophy through misty eyes. I said goodbye to P.O., who was still muttering about the poor standard of the match as he headed for his car, and I wandered off to join the lads. It was nice to be on my own for a few minutes; to take stock of what had just happened.

There was lots of hugging, backslapping and shaking of hands in Hedigans. As I looked around at all the smiling faces, my mind drifted across the last few years. The bitter memories were fading now, our journey at an end. Maurice was telling us how he was thinking of framing a picture of Paddy Russell and sticking it up in his front room. Hopes of peace talks with the refereeing associations were being mooted in the national press. The pub was rocking and ballads were sung as day became night. One poor culchie couldn't take it anymore. As he got up to leave, he shouted at one of his tormentors about how long it had been since Dublin's previous All-Ireland. "Twelve years" he scoffed. The reply came fast. "Sure it's only a few hours since we won the last one." It seemed that nothing could stop us now.

Nothing but a Tyrone appeal that is. It wasn't long before rumours started to circulate that Tyrone were unhappy at the circumstances surrounding Charlie Redmond's sending-off and it took a couple of days before the furore died down. The team paraded the trophy through the capital. There had been so few supporters outside the Mansion House a year earlier that Maurice had been offered a sandwich by one of the players who came out to greet the loyal few who had turned up to pass on their condolences. I had a feeling that the sandwiches would be thin on the ground this time around, still it was nothing that P.O. and his tinfoil couldn't sort out.

When the dust settled and the fear of an appeal receded, we were finally able to enjoy our victory. I was back on the Hill a few nights later for the annual Goal challenge when the newly crowned All-Ireland champions took on an All-Star selection. It was all good clean fun, but still some of the veterans of the Hill couldn't resist a dig at a bad pass. Perhaps the perpetual criticism comes with the territory; it's a Dublin thing. You're only as good as your last game, even if it was an All-Ireland final win. Sunday may as well have never happened. In the end, the game had to be abandoned as thousands of teenybopper Jacks chased Jason Sherlock around the pitch, but nobody really cared. After all the pain that had gone before it was a perfect ending.

Chapter Twenty

Louth And Clear

Saturday 24 July 2010

All-Ireland Senior Football Championship Fourth Round Qualifier
Dublin versus Louth

This game was effectively decided on Sunday 11 July, the day of the Leinster final, with the Louth men chasing their first provincial title since 1960. But first they had to beat Meath.

I couldn't have cared less, what Meath did in their spare time meant nothing to me. I was out for a walk with Jane and Samuel; minding my own business. But life isn't that simple anymore, the first text from Duff said "Typical Meath". I didn't bat an eyelid. I was beyond Meath, they could have Leinster, winning it hadn't exactly done us much good over the last five years. My only worry now was the ramifications for the qualifiers. A Meath win would mean that we would avoid them for another round; one bout of madness is enough for any summer. I was focussed on the bigger picture. It shows how much I have moved on over the years, I suppose.

If Meath had run out easy winners, that would have been that. But that would have been too straightforward. Duff's use of the word 'typical' had drawn me in, it's not a word I would normally associate with Meath; different maybe but not in any way typical. It was as if they were clamouring for my attention: forcing me to listen, forcing me to watch. And it was beginning to work as another text arrived: "Robbing Bastards". I was starting to realise that something strange was happening in Croker, so I texted Ger to find out more. Ger knows his stuff and his reply was typically succinct and to the point. Unusually for a Waterford man, he has a real sense of right and wrong. "Meath won with goal in last minute. Ball thrown into the net. Referee attacked by angry Louth supporters". Quite an afternoon at headquarters then.

With the game deep into injury time Louth were clinging to a precarious lead, having spurned numerous chances to kill off the game. Always dangerous against Meath who have a habit of making you pay: no team senses fear like Meath. The inevitable followed when an avoidable goalmouth scramble ended with Joe Sheridan throwing the ball into the Louth net for the winning goal. Referee Martin Sludden conferred with his umpires and despite the shrill Louth protests, the goal was allowed to stand. Seconds later, the final whistle unleashed the kind of anger that is usually left to the club circuit as several irate Louth men (and women it has to be said) chased Sludden across the pitch with a pitiful number of Gardaí trying to keep up.

If it was a bad day for the GAA, it was an even worse day for Louth: not only had they missed out on a first Leinster in 51 years, they now had the added burden of carrying with them a sense of injustice that no team should be expected to bear. The whole county knew that they had been wronged. Even Meath seemed ashamed, but not ashamed enough to offer a replay. They don't do ashamed in Meath, leaving the ball firmly in the GAA's court, who hand-passed it back to Meath. As the drama unfolded late into the Navan night, the intrepid Marty Morrissey appeared on the news to inform us that it would be a few hours before any decision would be reached. Marty looked as if all his Sundays had come at once. He spoke of feelings running high as the delegates assembled; feelings always seem to run high in the land of the Gael. In the end, Meath stood firm, they were keeping the cup. Louth tried to put a brave face on it in the days that followed, but their hearts were broken. This wasn't anger; anger can be used to generate a backlash. They had lost what was rightfully theirs and there would be no coming back from what had happened to them on that fateful day in early July.

I chuckled to myself. Meath had bypassed us as the villains of the GAA world and for a few short weeks, we basked in the glory of our new found popularity. Second most hated team in Ireland was a huge leap up the ratings for us. This was perfect. Louth were in the qualifiers and Meath had lost whatever credibility they had left, weeks later they were gone, bad karma and Kildare ending their ambitions for another year.

It was universally agreed that playing Dublin in Croke Park would be the perfect pick-me-up for Peter Fitzpatrick's men. A big crowd on Hill 16 and the prospect of a quarter-final place would surely reignite the fire in the Louth bellies. But the pendulum had swung significantly in Dublin's direction. From our point of view, this was the perfect draw, the Wee County haven't beaten us since 1973. That's twelve defeats in a row and there is very little to suggest it would be any different this time.

We might feel sorry for Louth but we can't afford to show any mercy, we are on our own journey, with our own recovery to prioritise. The referee will be important; he might feel that he owes Louth something. In the run in, the papers are full of the Louth challenge. I lost count of the number of times in the last week that I have read about Louth's midfield partnership of Brian White and Paddy Keenan being the best in the country. In fact I've read it so often that I'm actually beginning to believe it. The Louth forwards are also earning lots of plaudits but the evidence of the Leinster final suggested otherwise. I'm hoping that the press are just winding us up, but you just never know. As for Dublin, it looks as if Pat Gilroy is going to stick with the same team that started against Armagh. Eoghan O'Gara's ability to run directly into the heart of the opposition should be better suited to a lighter Louth side. Dublin certainly need the likes of Alan Brogan and the other forwards to start chipping in score wise, otherwise the pressure will grow on Bernard Brogan to produce another five star performance.

As I drive up from Carlow, I know Louth are there for the taking. The continued absence of Duff is another cause for optimism. No P.O. either. On and off the pitch it's the same line up for the second week running. We may well have to apply for a banning order before the quarter-finals if this keeps up.

As we walk up the steps leading to the Hill, I sense a different atmosphere – for the first time this summer a sense of expectation fills the air – we expect to win today. It can't have been easy for the players getting up at the crack of dawn and heading into training in the days and weeks following the Meath defeat. But the good ship Dublin is pointing downstream again. No need to fight against the current any longer. Whatever happens after today will be a bonus. But a win today is a must. Lose to Louth and the whole edifice will come tumbling down on top of Pat Gilroy's head.

It's obvious that the players sense the new mood. No longer the reluctant gladiators, their entry onto the field is forceful and aggressive as they move towards the Hill. The warm-up is fast, concentrated, to the point. I get the feeling they can't wait to get going. The fear is gone, the hunger is back and the haunted looks a thing of the past.

Louth burst onto the field full of righteous indignation, ready to right the wrongs that had been done to them. Heads down, they charge across the pitch as if they have been released from purgatory and the wrath of the Wee County is released in a guttural welcome from their loyal support. But when they look up, they see only blue shirts – Meath are at home with their feet up, polishing the trophy – this has nothing to do with Dublin, we're not the enemy. It's as if Louth realise that all the anger that has built up over the last two weeks has nowhere to go, all that energy wasted, they have nothing left for the task at hand. They look around as if wondering what is going to happen next. At the other end, Dublin are ready.

Some of the players even steal a glance at the Hill. Each day, a few more prodigal supporters seem to have returned to the fold, citing the usual excuses: holidays, the wife wouldn't let me or a trip to the barbers. Bullshit – the whole lot of it – no mention of a lack of faith. They like to think that nothing has changed since they took their sabbatical and they'll carry on exactly where they left off: moaning when the first pass goes astray, spreading disharmony. But it won't matter, they know and we know that they weren't there against Tipperary. They were in the cinema or pontificating over a pint with their other absent friends when the rest of us where standing in the rain as we faced into our darkest hour. Back then, they couldn't give a shit but now they're back showing their caring side. Part of me would like to see them fuck off back to where they came from. But I know that it's better to live and let live. I let it go.

For all those reasons, today is kind of special for those of us who have been here for the last three weeks. This is our day and maybe the last one before the trickle of the fickle turns into a flood.

I look towards the Canal End where the Louth players are going through their paces under the watchful eye of manager Peter Fitzpatrick. Peter is a character, just one of many that exist within the strange world of Gaeldom. You have to be slightly mad to take up the reins of a county team and Peter cuts a heroic figure right now. He speaks in a strange language that many of us struggle to understand; long reels of what sounds like undifferentiated psychobabble that makes less sense when he has finished each sentence. Over the last couple of weeks, he has done well to keep his head given the injustice that was done to his team. For a while, it even looked like he was enjoying his time in the limelight. Winning would have meant fame and kudos in Louth but losing had put him on the national stage. And now he has the Dubs in his sights.

Down in front of Hill 16, Pat Gilroy has the strut of a man who can finally see some light at the end of the tunnel. He has been getting right up the noses of TV3 over the last few weeks with his refusal to do a pre-match interview. Pat has better things to be doing in the minutes before a match, like making sure that his team is ready. Seems sensible to me, if you want to talk to Pat, eight o'clock on a Friday morning is where it's at, Dublin's early morning training sessions starting to make waves as our recovery gathers pace. Pat is a realist, sees himself as the Dublin football manager, nothing more, nothing less.

Any post-match interviews he does deign to give are always worth a listen, no spin-doctor, Pat tells it as it is. From his first day as leader, he has sought to build a cocoon around the team – he knows how damaging media hype has been – and his protection has worked. Where there was once blind optimism, there is now a quiet confidence. Great expectations tempered by a gutsy realism. He has come a long way in a few months. And for that he deserves a whole lot of credit.

Dublin are quickly into their stride, their midfield totally dominating, as they go about sowing the seeds of doubt in the already troubled Louth minds. Dublin players are everywhere. In contrast, Louth are struggling to keep to the pace of the game, chasing blue shadows and showing no stomach for the fight. Michael Dara MacAuley and Ross McConnell are lording it at midfield. So much for the newspaper hype. At least John O'Brien is keeping Bernard Brogan quiet. Unfortunately for Louth, Eoghan O'Gara chooses today to have his best game so far in a Dublin shirt with two well-taken goals. His first on 11 minutes sees him run directly at the Louth defence before unleashing a deflected shot that flies past Niall Gallagher. Perhaps the Louth keeper should have done better, but there is little he can do about O'Gara's second goal two minutes before the break. Having received the ball from Alan Brogan, Dublin's newest enigma cuts inside his marker before placing a lovely side-footed finish past a helpless Gallagher. It takes Louth eighteen excruciating minutes to register their first score. At half-time Dublin lead by 2-6 to 0-3.

There is more good news when the attendance is flashed up on the big screen, just under 48,000, slowly but surely the Jacks are coming back. After only a few minutes the Hill was alive to the sound of music. "C'mon You Boys In Blue" rings out in unison as we celebrate our rebirth. But amazingly, some of our flock are still far from happy. As Dublin take their foot off the gas during a routine second-half, not surprising considering it's their third game in three weeks, the moaners on the Hill find their voice. They're not happy so we all have to be unhappy too as Louth try to make a fight of it, but it's too little, too late and Dublin run out comfortable winners by 2-14 to 0-13.

I even feel a little sorry for Louth as they do a lap of honour to thank their loyal ranks of supporters who have turned up in great numbers today. There's nothing like a sense of injustice to get a Gaelic crowd going. We embrace it as if it is a long lost friend. Even the Dublin supporters stay behind to give them a roar of approval; we were never going to miss the chance to put the knife into Meath. "C-H-A-M-P-I-O-N-E-E-S! C-H-A-M-P-I-O-N-E-E-S!" drifts down from the Hill as the red shirts wave back. After that near death experience in Navan back in 1995, I never thought I'd live to see the day when I would be cheering on a Louth team. But Meath have a strange way of changing your approach to life.

Louth aren't the only ones hurting today, it has been another bad day for Duff and P.O., they must be beginning to ask themselves some real questions about this jinx business. Niall smiles knowingly as we join the happy throng heading for home. "C'mon You Boys In Blue" is belting off the concrete walls under Hill 16 as we head down the steps towards an All-Ireland quarter-final.

The draw will be crucial; we have had our fair share of shit draws over the last few years. Surely this time we are due a bit of luck, Roscommon would be good. No baggage. No mental scars. Or we could get Meath again, one of the drawbacks of the back door system, as if it isn't enough to beat your greatest rivals once. It is one of the reasons the current Cork team have failed to lift Sam: they go and beat Kerry in the Munster final only to lose out to the same opposition a couple of months' later in the wide-open spaces of Croke Park. Beating the likes of Kerry once is hard enough, doing it twice is almost an impossibility; the one part of the present system that doesn't make sense. It is also the reason why Kerry and Tyrone have been able to carve up the All-Ireland feast amongst themselves over the last few years. The element of surprise exited the championship with the introduction of the back door system. Winning an All-Ireland is harder than ever. Prior to the change, one result could open up a summer, like Laois beating Meath in 1992. The qualifiers have helped the strong as much as the weak. As I pull up outside our house I am jolted into the present as a little bundle of joy pushes his way out the front door and rushes towards my open arms. I bend down to meet Samuel's smile with one of my own. As I pick him up, I shove all thoughts of Tyrone and Kerry to the back of my mind.

The GAA make us wait a week to know our fate. And then the axe falls: for the third time in seven years we draw Tyrone. That's it then. The end is in sight.

Chapter Twenty-one

Back To The Future

Sunday 28 July 1996

Leinster Senior Football Championship Final
Dublin versus Meath

Having delivered Sam, Pat O'Neill and his backroom staff stepped down. You couldn't blame them – they had achieved what they had set out to do – they had given the job everything they had and more but the well was probably empty and there seemed little point in going back the following summer to find out.

Mickey Whelan had little or no managerial experience when he became Dublin boss in 1996, his reputation built on his past deeds as an All-Ireland winner, another ex-player given the task of bringing success to the capital. It was an intriguing appointment, one that caught everybody by surprise. Mickey was part of the Heffernan era, he might have looked old but his ideas were cutting edge, with players being encouraged to spend more time with the ball. Mickey didn't see the point of running up mountains. The game was played with a ball, so why not use it in training. It might have worked with a group of impressionable young players, but it quickly became clear that the older players were worried about where the new regime was taking them. Having finally tasted success under O'Neill they wanted more of the same and fitness was the altar at which they worshipped.

It was clear that Whelan wanted to make his mark, to have some players he could call his own, with the result that Eamonn Heery, Niall Guiden and 1983 hero Joe McNally were all recalled to the squad. Nobody questioned Heery's recall; he had always shown fierce commitment to the cause and had only left the squad following a falling out with Pat O'Neill. But the situation regarding Guiden and McNally was a different matter altogether. Guiden's attendance at a wedding in the days prior to the 1994 defeat to Down still rankled with the more senior members of the panel and it was felt that his return sent out all the wrong signals. And while Joe McNally was still one of the best forwards in the Dublin club game, many doubted he would be able to get up to the required fitness levels required for inter-county football, the days of the bustling full-forward a thing of the past, lean and mean was everything now. Those who had spilt blood to win an All-Ireland were left scratching their heads when all three names appeared on the team sheet at the beginning of the 1996 championship season.

Whelan may well have felt that the hunger that had driven the team on during the last few years was on the wane, and he could have been right, but his heavy-handed tactics alienated the senior players and it was no surprise when the cracks began to appear. Jason Sherlock had been dropped, yesterday's man only months on from being Dublin's saviour. The All-Ireland winning full-back line was torn asunder. Vinny Murphy headed off to Kerry in a huff, even Mick Galvin threw in the towel for a few weeks before returning as the euphoria of the previous summer dissipated.

If the opening day championship win over a poor Westmeath side papered over the cracks, then Louth in Navan brought all the problems bubbling to the surface. Louth could and should have won, before losing their nerve in the final few minutes as a lucky McNally goal saved Dublin at the death. The signs did not look good with a Leinster final only weeks away. But, having beaten Meath by 10 points 12 months earlier, we had every right to be confident. I felt so positive that I headed off to Galway to see Radiohead.

With Sean Boylan building a new team with the likes of Darren Fay, Graham Geraghty and Trevor Giles included in the squad, this was no time to be letting Meath rise again. Ten years ago Dublin had found to their cost what can happen when you let the Meath Genie out of the Leinster bottle. It was probably just as well I was in Galway. Back in those days, being at a rock concert was akin to being cut off from the outside world, there was still no texting and the size of a mobile phone meant that it was better to leave it at home. Radiohead had just finished a storming set when I wandered over to a bored looking Garda. I asked him did he know the result from Croke Park. I couldn't see Dublin losing, surely this game was too early for this rookie Meath team. But the news that greeted me stopped me in my tracks; Meath had won by 10 points to 8. I asked him a second time, hoping that I had misheard him, but he nodded his head with a satisfied smile, it was just as well that he was trained to deliver bad news. I walked away in a daze. I felt guilty; I should have been there.

We wandered back into Galway and settled into a pub. I saw some of the highlights of the game on the telly as a Dublin trad band belted out some rousing tunes. It looked like a typical Dublin-Meath encounter with tackles flying in and no room to breathe. The sight of the Meath players celebrating at the end stuck in my throat. How did we let this happen? I felt a little better when the band played my request, I have always found The Ferryman an uplifting song and I needed its consolation now more than ever.

To make matters worse, Meath's young upstarts went on to win the All-Ireland, achieving in one year all the success it had taken Dublin seven to construct. It was sickening to watch. Dublin's hunger was gone. Just like 1986 Meath's victory 10 years on set the agenda for years to come.

Duff gave me the lowdown when I returned to a capital in mourning. Anger was in the air. Apparently the hero of last year's All-Ireland win, Paul Clarke, had spent the afternoon watching the match from the Hill, along with Ciaran Walsh, another man with an All-Ireland medal in his pocket, leaving Whelan to toss untried players such as Shay Keogh and Dermot Harrington into the Meath cauldron. It was crazy stuff.

How much of the disaster was down to Whelan and how much was down to a loss of hunger, we will never know, but Pat O'Neill would have spotted the danger signs and acted accordingly. Despite the poor season Whelan remained at the helm. The pressure increased with another uninspiring league campaign. Unable to work with him any longer, John O'Leary stepped down as captain, before retiring from the panel following defeat to Meath in 1997, a sad way for such a distinguished career to end.

New captain Keith Barr tried his best to pick up the pieces, but he could do nothing about the luck of the draw, with Dublin facing Meath in the first round. Whelan did his bit to mend the broken fence with Clarke, Galvin and Walsh back in the team. But it made no difference as Meath ran out winners in front of over 62,000 spectators. 1997 had gone the way of '96.

Yet again, a penalty miss sealed Dublin's fate and this time it was Paul Bealin's turn to crash a shot off the crossbar with the last kick of the game. It would have rescued a draw, but it wasn't to be. Despite another disappointing campaign the Dublin County Board continued to stand by their man.

Eventually Mickey Whelan walked the plank following a league defeat to Offaly in Parnell Park, the atmosphere poisonous as we left the ground that day, as big men with bulging muscles, shaven heads and contorted faces shouted dogs' abuse at Whelan who, head bowed, made his way to the sanctuary of the dressing room. I felt sorry for the man. Nobody deserved what he was going through. He had been a dead man walking for going on two years now. It was clearly time to say goodbye.

It turns out that Mickey Whelan was in the wrong place at the wrong time. He tried too hard to force a transition that had to come eventually, but the team of '95 deserved the right to have a go at retaining their title in '96. Whelan's time in charge lacked direction and discipline; too many rumours were making it into the public domain and the evening papers were full of stories of unrest. What is remarkable is that Mickey Whelan lived to fight another day. He was indeed ahead of his time; his managerial success came later, culminating in an All-Ireland club title with St Vincent's in 2008. Two weeks after that he stepped down as manager, to become part of Pat Gilroy's backroom staff as his former player became the new Dublin manager. Ten years after he had left his Dublin post Mickey Whelan was back in the big time. And he doesn't look a day older.

Chapter Twenty-two

What Have We Done To Deserve This?

Saturday 12 August 2000

Leinster Senior Football Championship Final Replay
Dublin versus Kildare

Enter Tommy Carr, another former player and one of my former school colleagues. He may have been a few years ahead of me but I knew Tommy well. His brother Declan, who went on to captain Tipperary to the Liam McCarthy Cup was in my year, so we got to know Tommy. He was one of my heroes even back then, the full-back on the school rugby team, a position I had big hopes of filling in the years to come.

But this was different. I wasn't sure that Tommy had what it took to be Dublin manager as he had only recently stopped playing. Surely he would be too close to the current players. I wondered would he be strong enough to do things his own way, to take on the older players who wanted a return to the days of Pat O'Neill. I knew that Tommy was a nice guy, but apart from Sean Boylan, nice guys seemed to be a liability in the dog eat dog world of GAA. I really hoped that he would prove me wrong. As a player, he had always been wholehearted and uncompromising, and if he could bring those qualities to his management style then he would do okay.

As it was Tommy had no time to stamp his authority on the team before the start of the 1998 championship season, and it showed, as Dublin lost to Kildare in a first round replay. For the second year in a row, Dublin's season had ended before it had even begun. It didn't help that we had been abject on both days, a shadow of the side that had brought Sam home. For some reason, I ended up in the Canal End for the replay. A bad day all round, it was the first time that a Dublin side had lost to Kildare in the championship in 26 years.

It was becoming clear that Dublin were entering a transitional period. Tommy had picked the worst time to take the reins, with Meath experiencing a second coming, from day one he must have known that time wasn't on his side. The jury was still out as the 1999 season began, with the winds of change blowing through the dressing room as John O'Leary and Keith Barr retired and the burden of captaincy passed to Dessie Farrell. It wasn't just Meath that were growing strong again, a revitalised Kerry were back in the big time, inspired by the mercurial Maurice Fitzgerald. Whatever solace we Dubs had taken from Kerry's fall from grace in the nineties was long gone. In Connacht, the emergence of another great Galway side further muddied the All-Ireland waters. But Tommy couldn't afford to look beyond Leinster, and with Meath and Kildare flexing their considerable muscles it was obvious that the road ahead would be a rocky one.

At first things seemed to be going pretty well. Tommy almost succeeded in doing what so many of his recent predecessors had done by winning the league at his first real attempt, but a disappointing performance against Cork in the final in Páirc Uí Chaoimh scuppered his chances. Having dodged a significant bullet in the Leinster semi-final replay against a dangerous Laois side, Dublin were back in the Leinster final for the first time in three years.

Despite the final score – Dublin 0-12 Meath 1-14 – this remains one of my favourite days on the Hill. The support given to the Dublin players was magnificent as we sang our hearts out. Meath were better than us, we knew what was coming. This was a day to show our pride. As the teams paraded, we gave it everything we had in a desperate attempt to lift the Dublin players. It was only when the superb Ollie Murphy scored Meath's goal that Dublin's resistance fell away. At the end, as the players sat exhausted on the Croke Park turf, we clapped and sang our way through the presentation. "C'mon You Boys in Blue, C'mon You Boys in Blue," rang out as a defiant thank you to a set of players who had given us everything they had.

The manner of the display didn't stop Tommy getting it in the neck. His failure to switch debutante Peadar Andrews off the rampant Murphy was seen as a major error, but maybe Tommy had no one else capable of doing the job. As it stood, Murphy had been almost unplayable and the panel wasn't exactly overflowing with options. Not for the first time Meath rubbed our noses in it as they went on to lift another All-Ireland. With Manchester United winning the treble, my sporting life couldn't really get any worse.

In 2000 it did. With a first Leinster title in five years within their grasp Dublin faced Kildare in an intriguing provincial decider. If I could change history, I would stop Collie Moran scoring the late point which ensured a replay in what had been a rip-roaring clash. Ironically I was sitting high up in the Cusack Stand with Ciaran Whelan, my Kildare-supporting friend, not his namesake who was down on the field doing his best to sink the Lilywhites. Tickets were hard to come by, Kildare were at the top of their game and the capital was finally beginning to believe that Tommy had the team pointing in the right direction.

Thankfully, I was back on the Hill for the second instalment the following Saturday. I was confident that this day would tell us a lot about Tommy, about the team. Were these Dublin boys ready to become men?

As the half-time whistle blew the answer was a resounding yes. Dublin had played as well as I had ever seen a Dublin team play, with Collie Moran's long range point one of the best I had ever seen in Croker. Six points to the good. The Hill was luxuriating in the summer sunshine as the sides remerged for the second-half. Duff was his usual self, well prepared, with a fresh bottle of water for the second-half. Maurice was basking in the sweet smell of success as he worked on his sun tan. Hill 16 was a good place to be. I couldn't see Kildare coming back. They had been blown away in that first-half. Even Micko would find it hard to lift their shattered spirit. There seemed to be very little to worry about.

In the space of 90 awful seconds Kildare were level with 2 goals in quick succession at the Hill end, so quick that some people watching on TV thought the second was a replay of the first. We had no such luxury, a knock-out punch that none of us had seen coming, thousands of people concussed by the force of the blow. The Hill died there and then. We knew that there was no way back. For the rest of the half we stood in stunned silence trying to make some sense of what had happened. In the meantime Kildare toyed with us, making the most of our slow death. Duff was as tense as I have ever seen him, a broken man, I tried to speak to him but the words wouldn't come. In the space of five minutes he had drank the bottle of water that was meant to last him for thirty-five minutes, the shock of what had happened driving it to his lips every couple of seconds. I wanted to go home. I always wanted to go home at times like this, but I couldn't. I knew I had to stay, leaving has never been an option for me. I was tied to this team come what may.

Today that's two paltry points in a terrible second-half performance, all of Dublin's good work forgotten as they pressed the self-destruct button. The brilliance of the opening half only made the second-half collapse all the harder to understand. Bodies lay slumped on Hill 16, tears rolling down our collective face, a place in mourning. How would we get over this one?

I was speechless for about an hour afterwards, staring dead-eyed into my pint. I've lost count of the number of Dublin related pints I've stared into over the years. But the storm clouds slowly lifted. Life has to go on. We have always found some way out of the darkness. What else was there to do but drink our way out of the gloom? Two hours later, we were having the time of our lives. The afternoon's events pushed aside in a drink induced haze. Maurice was in flying form. Big Brother was the latest craze and our refereeing consultant had printed out a Big Brother scenario off the Internet. He had entered our names in the slots provided. So after every round of drinks, Maurice's booming voice would inform us of the latest news from the house. "WEEK TWO: Dublin lose a six point lead in less time than it takes you to open your front door… In the diary room, Duff downs a bottle of water in record time… By the pool, Paul gets a new pair of troosers…" and on it went all night. Maurice was certainly no Jimmy Nail, his Geordie accent taking on a Northside slant, but his performance did much to lighten the mood.

The following morning, the pain was as bad as ever and no amount of drink could wipe away what had taken place. I got dressed and headed over to see my rock of sporting sense. Nothing surprised Dad anymore. He approached sporting disasters with a sense of calm that comes with ninety-one years of experience. For once he was speechless; he'd missed the whole thing. He thought it was on the following afternoon. In hindsight, he was one of the lucky ones.

I was going through the different phases that follow such a harrowing defeat. The sense of loss that comes with the final whistle was soon replaced by disbelief, followed in the case of last night, by a worrying amount of manic hilarity. The Irish often rely on humour to get them through the darkest of hours. We often have a better laugh at a funeral than at a wedding.

The next phase is anger – anger that yet another Leinster title has slipped through our fingers – anger that only time will heal. Ciaran Whelan, the happy Kildare version, rang me from some far-off island near Spain to pass on his condolences. I got the feeling that it would be a long time before we would be allowed to forget this one. The sadness comes later and lasts for months.

For Tommy it was the end of the road for another year. There was nothing to be said, no words that would make us feel any better. He did what he had to do; he kept his head low and got on with the job. He must have known that the nature of the defeat would damage the team irrevocably, a pivotal moment that there was no coming back from, a collapse that would define his time in charge. If Dublin had won that game they would have gone onto bigger and better things, but they lost their nerve – the pendulum had swung – for some reason they could no longer see a way past the Lilywhite jersey. For years we had lauded it over Kildare and now all of a sudden they were the new Meath.

Chapter Twenty-three

The Trip To Tipp

Sunday 4 August 2001

All-Ireland Senior Football Championship Quarter-Final
Dublin versus Kerry – for the first time since 1985

A year later we were ready to go again. Tommy had survived the inevitable fall out that followed the Kildare debacle, luckily for him the Dublin County Board much preferred their managers to endure a slow painful death. We had seen it with Mickey Whelan and now it seemed to be Tommy's turn. Wins over Longford and Offaly set up yet another provincial decider against Meath. Tommy wasn't the only one that cut a worried looking figure in the days before the game as I was faced with a dilemma that no man should have to go through.

Maurice has decided that the time had come for him to announce his official retirement from the Hill. To be fair it had been coming for a while: rumours of a bad back accompanying little jibes at the standard of beverages available at the Railway End all added up to an unhappy man. After years of active service he was heading for the stand. I couldn't get my head around it. He had been coping with the onset of middle age admirably up to now. No matter how hard I tried to talk him down he was adamant, he no longer wanted to stand. Naturally his wife Margaret was standing by him, or should that be sitting. The trouble was that Duff had gone along with it, leaving me with the prospect of a lonely vigil should I decide to stand my ground and head for the only place I wanted to be. To further muddy the waters, my girlfriend and future wife Jane had decided to come along to see what all this Dublin fuss was about. After the Jessie disaster I wasn't exactly looking forward to introducing her to the Hill. There are things in life that a man and woman shouldn't do together, for me standing together on the Hill is one of them. I could never be myself, love and the Dubs had never mixed. I had learnt the hard way.

In the end I had no choice, I watched from high up in the Canal End, spending the majority of the afternoon staring longingly at the Hill when I should have been looking at Jane. I yearned for that sense of togetherness that comes with being on the Hill, up here I felt like I might as well be watching the game on TV. If I was to get back there, I knew that I needed to convince Duff that he needed to be there too.

Dublin were left chasing the Royal tail after an early Graham Geraghty goal and to be honest, Meath were in control throughout and ran out more comfortable winners than the three point gap suggested. Meath were revelling in their turn in the sun, so much so that they didn't seem to be all that excited about beating us anymore, we'd become irrelevant, just a stepping stone to greater things. The recent history between two such evenly matched sides defied understanding, with one team dominating for years before the other regained the ascendancy. But then there has never been anything logical about Dublin and Meath.

But all was not lost. The GAA had introduced the back door system, allowing losers a second bite at the championship cherry. Losing to Meath was no longer the end. A week later we found ourselves back in Croke Park facing Sligo for a place in the All-Ireland quarter-finals. It didn't seem right but there you go, beggars can't be choosers. At least we were facing a side from outside Leinster for the first time in years. It also gave me the chance to beat a hasty retreat to the Hill. The atmosphere was strange, we knew that we shouldn't be there, any other year we would have been coming to terms with what had happened a week earlier. Now we just put it to the back of our minds and moved on, strange days indeed.

It was soon clear that we weren't the only ones struggling to come to terms with this whole backdoor malarkey. At first the Dublin players seemed as confused as we were, but thankfully they pulled themselves together to wallop Sligo by 3-17 to 0-12. Maybe this qualifier system wasn't so bad after all. The draw for the quarter-final set the trend for years to come – Dublin against a resurgent Kerry – but we didn't care, we were just happy to be there at all. We quite liked playing Kerry, the law of averages said that we had to beat them in the championship sometime soon. It was going on 24 years since our last victory; 1977 a distant dream. We still yearned for the seventies, even though we tried our best not to, but there was no getting away from those glory days with the present Kerry team led by a man who had played a considerable role in our downfall back then.

Páidí Ó Sé, the cutest whore of them all, was back in town. I liked Páidí, he would have made a great Dub. Like many of his fellow Kerry men he speaks with a lyrical intensity that tells us how important football is to our way of life. His never changing hairstyle has always amazed me, it has a Sheriff Street quality to it that must be difficult to replicate down in the wilds of Kerry.

So Kerry would do just fine – it's not that we expected to beat them, we didn't – at least it was another day out. The news that the tie would be played in Thurles was greeted with great enthusiasm, at last we had the chance to re-enact the 1983 pilgrimage to Páirc Uí Chaoimh. We're creatures of habit: any chance to retrace our steps is taken with both hands.

Having missed the Sligo game Jane was back on board, along with Trevor, a fellow teacher and veteran of Meath '91; he had the aura of someone who had been touched by the sense of loss that we all carried in our hearts from that day on. We travelled cross-country from Carlow, arriving with a couple of hours to spare. It turned out that we were the lucky ones: a whole generation of Dubs got swallowed up in the traffic jams that stretched out along the route from Dublin to the home of hurling. Many were never seen again, some settled in the country, others simply disappeared. Typical Dubs, we treat every journey as if we're popping down to the shops, underestimating time, traffic and distance. We like to think we're the only ones travelling. As a result we had to endure the usual shite the following Monday as our country cousins slagged us off, the usual jibes trotted out as the phone lines of every conceivable phone in show buzzed to the sound of hundreds of cackling culchies, with the odd heartbroken Dub thrown in to give the other side of the story, the poor roads, the nobody told us it would be like that sob stories. As usual we took it on the chin and plotted our revenge. Many had given up halfway, if they were lucky enough to get that far, abandoning their cars to watch the drama unfold in some quiet pub which had found itself jammed to the rafters with match tickets floating through the air as the realisation set in that their owners were going nowhere. Accounts of extraordinary fortitude and bravery from the bars of middle Ireland brought tears to the eyes. It was heady stuff; it is always is when the Dubs are involved.

For those who had made it, the big match atmosphere in Thurles was to be savoured. The Square was rocking with the mood at fever pitch as we ambled down towards Semple stadium, Dublin wit mixing with Kerry flamboyance. Many had questioned the sense in sending two of the land's footballing heavyweights to a hurling town but it had worked.

Despite the tales of woe emanating from the midlands, the good news was that Maurice, Margaret and Duff had made it safely. It didn't take long for my fashion sense to be the centre of attention. I had dressed up especially for the day, having gone to the trouble of buying the latest Dublin tracksuit in Arnotts on the previous Friday. Trevor was clearly enjoying himself, drinking in the good vibrations as we lined up outside the turnstiles. We hadn't seen Trevor at a Dublin match since 1991 but he seemed to be enjoying his comeback; he has always been a character and even the fiercest creatures on Hill 16 were left a little bemused when he announced that he was going for a snooze just before one of the games against Meath. The Hill was packed but still Trevor managed to crouch down and nod off for a few precious minutes.

When we found our seats in Semple Stadium, we discovered we were surrounded: to our right was the Wexford ladies camogie team, and on the left was a family in the process of digging into their beetroot sandwiches. P.O. would have been mad jealous, but not me, I'm more of a tomato sandwich man myself and I watched transfixed as purple dots of beetroot juice glistened in the sun as they dropped onto the tinfoil wrapper; needless to say these farming folk weren't from Dublin. Behind us was a Kerry supporting father and son, always a dangerous combination. The seating wasn't what we were used to, moss covered wooden planks nailed onto concrete, it was distinctly old school. I felt like I was stepping back in time, I might as well have been at the 1985 All-Ireland final. Same teams, same seats.

Kerry raced out of the blocks to leave Dublin chasing shadows all over the field. Páidí was urging his men on, leading the charge. They were doing what Kerry do best, winning battle after battle and allowing the war to take care of itself. I even found myself yearning for a beetroot sandwich as things went from bad to worse. We simply couldn't gain a foothold in the game, any opportunities that came our way were wasted as Dessie Farrell and Collie Moran both squandered a couple of golden chances to keep us in touch. For my part, I was getting more and more annoyed with the Kerry tactics. Time and again they cynically fouled Dublin players either side of the halfway line, stopping Dublin gaining any forward momentum and hampering the likes of Declan Darcy taking advantage. It was clever and orchestrated with a different Kerry player fouling each time, meaning that the referee failed to realise that a pattern was emerging. Much to the embarrassment of Jane and the others, even Maurice seemed shocked, I screamed my disgust at the officials. I was told to sit down and be quiet. It didn't help that the annoying Kerry teenager and his arrogant father standing against the wall behind us were twisting the knife at every opportunity. As if it wasn't bad enough having to deal with teenagers for a living, here I was being forced to listen to them during the holidays as well. I wasn't the only one getting hot under the collar. Tommy Carr marched onto the pitch and confronted referee Mick Curley; his passion seemed to inspire the team. Out of the corner of my eye, I could see Maurice licking his lips in anticipation and it wasn't at the thought of a beetroot sandwich; Mick would probably end the night burning in an ashtray. From then on it was all Dublin. Nineteen eighty-five all over again.

With Kerry eight points to the good I was preparing myself for the long drive home when I noticed Vinny Murphy getting ready to come on. Even this was beyond Vinny. There were eight minutes left when he scored Dublin's opening goal. Three Dublin points followed. Then, incredibly, Darren Homan fisted the ball beyond a helpless Declan O'Keefe in the Kerry goal and Dublin were ahead. Our world had been turned upside down. Páidí was marching up and down the sideline like a demented hare, his Kerry side doing a Dublin. It was nice to see the boot on the other foot for a change.

The ground was rocking to the sound of the Dubs in full voice. We were nearly there. I was standing on my excuse for a seat as the game entered injury time when I felt the urge to celebrate. I couldn't resist having a go at the mouthy father and son combination behind us, I swivelled and let fly: "You're Gone." I must have looked like a demented mad man if the frightened glances from the Wexford girls were anything to go by. To our left, the sandwich eaters were too busy crying beetroot tears to bat an eyelid. I like to put it down to the heat or to the years of teaching, either way, I should have known better, but we were on the crest of a famous victory and I couldn't help myself. I looked back at the pitch to see Dublin's goalkeeper Davy Byrne lining up a kick out – surely the whistle would go any second –

all he had do was put it as far up the field as possible and that was that. Instead he sent it flying into touch down below us. I closed my eyes and prayed, surely it was too far out, but when I opened them my worst fears were realised. Maurice Fitzgerald was walking over towards the ball. Please God, not Maurice Fitz. He had come on a few minutes earlier to be met by a barrage of charging Dublin shoulders but had just calmly walked way. Fitzgerald was here to play football, now he had his chance. All eyes were on him as he picked the ball up and ran it through his hands before he looked towards the posts. They must have seemed miles away. Tommy Carr gave him a few words of advice as he wandered along the line. We were right behind him as he kicked the ball out of his hands with the outside of the boot. It soared into the heavens before bending to the right as it locked its sights on the Dublin posts, slicing the sticks in two as it sailed over from 45 metres. The whole of Kerry erupted in thanksgiving. Only a Kerry man could have produced such a moment of brilliance.

But there was still time for more drama, another opportunity for Dublin, a 45 straight in front of the posts. Into the wind and too far out, it was no surprise when Wayne McCarthy's kick fell short: Dublin 2-11 Kerry 1-14. I even managed to shake hands with my teenage tormentor on the way out. What happens in the heat of the moment stays in the heat of the moment, for me at least. I looked back at Tommy Carr shaking his head at the sheer bad luck of it all. Páidí Ó Sé was his usual self, doing his customary impression of the cat that had got the cream as he made his way towards the tunnel in his beige slacks and runners, an outfit that defined fashion in Ireland at the time. Even my ninety-two year old father had taken to wearing runners with a jacket and tie, something I blame Páidí for. Factor in Páidí's haircut and Kerry's manager was well on the way to approaching iconic status as a culchie sex symbol. It's no wonder that the modern Kerry man has such a keen fashion sense. The likes of Paul Galvin didn't lick it off a stone.

As we made our way back out onto the streets of Thurles, we knew we had blown it, our one and only chance of beating Kerry gone. It was hard to see Dublin catching them with their pants down again. We may have missed our chance but at least we hadn't missed the match.

Streams of cars left Dublin at first light the following Sunday. Our worst fears were realised with the second encounter following the same script as that of the previous week. With Tommy Carr banished to the stand as a result of his altercation with Curley, Dublin were left chasing green and gold shadows for the second week in succession. Curley was looking well, if a little singed around the edges. Jane was with us again, determined to see this particular story through to the end. I could have saved her the trip. We ended up sitting next to Liam Lawlor who was up to his eyes in allegations of political corruption at the time. On the other side of the ground Maurice, Margaret and Duff had Jackie Healey-Rae, man of the people and TD for South Kerry, to keep them amused. Even after all these years, I still can't understand a word he is saying. Sitting beside Jackie was another Kerry native who spent the entirety of the game shouting the same thing: "C'mon Mike Frank" in homage to the great Kerry forward Mike Frank Russell. It was enough to do their heads in. Darren Homan's second-half goal threatened to ignite another Dublin comeback but this time it was not to be as Kerry held on to win by three points: 2-12 to 1-12.

A little over a month later, Tommy Carr was gone, sacked by the County Board. It was a sad way for it all to end. It didn't matter that the players liked playing for Tommy. It was all to no avail. Tommy had given it his best shot but it was never going to be enough, seven years without a Leinster title was too much to bear, even for the usually patient suits. Timing played a big part in his eventual downfall. Left to pick up the pieces and start again as the 1995 All-Ireland team reached the end of the road, he laid the foundations for the success that was to come. From one Tommy to another: Tommy Lyons was about to reap what Tommy had sown. If the trips to Tipp proved anything it was that winning wasn't everything. Whenever I think of Tommy Carr my mind always drifts back to those wonderful couple of days in Thurles.

Chapter Twenty-four

The Summer Of Love

Sunday 1 September 2002

All-Ireland Senior Football Championship Semi-Final
Dublin versus Armagh

Tommy Lyons announced his arrival on the county circuit by leading Offaly to a Leinster title in his first season in charge, and by slaying Meath en route, it meant he was already something of a hero to us before he became Dublin manager. He had been tipped by many to take the job in 1995 but nothing ever came of it. Unlike the taciturn Carr, Tommy Lyons was all razzmatazz, tailor-made for the showbiz side of the Dublin job. Stick a microphone in front of Tommy and he was likely to pour his heart out. It was hard not to get caught up in the sheer infectious enthusiasm of it all. If the players played as good a game as Tommy talked then we were in for some exciting times.

The team that had lost in Thurles was given a makeover with fresh young faces coming into contention: Alan Brogan, John McNally and Ray Cosgrove started up top while Darren McGee, brother of centre half-back Johnny, brought strength and athleticism to the midfield with Paul Casey and Barry Cahill settling into defence. Colman Goggins was appointed captain. It was soon clear that Lyons wanted a change of emphasis; quick ball rather than high ball delivered into the likes of Brogan and Cosgrove so that they could fully utilise their pace.

The capital was badly in need of a pick-me-up and not just because of the lack of GAA success; the whole country was still reeling from the fallout from Saipan. Our World Cup dream had soured as we watched Roy Keane walking his dog in Manchester when he should have been leading the line in the Far East. With Mick McCarthy looking older by the day we turned to Tommy Lyons to lift our spirits.

The excitement was building as Dublin prepared for a trip to Dr Cullen Park in Carlow to take on Wexford. I was already spending a lot of time in Carlow, and within two years I would be living there. I felt at home in my new surroundings as Jane dropped me off at the Dinn Ri pub in the centre of town so that I could meet up with Maurice, Margaret and Duff who had travelled down from Dublin for the day. However within minutes it became clear that we were not welcome, the suspicious scowls of the local townies followed us wherever we went. Two charming young local chaps drove by slowly in their car shouting "Go Home You Dublin Scum." Maybe they were just pissed off about Roy going home, it affected people in different ways. Thankfully, nobody reacted and we waved them on their way. It was already feeling like it had been a long day, most of the country had been up at the crack of dawn to witness a Roy-less Ireland rescue a point in their opening World Cup encounter with Cameroon.

I was feeling pretty tired as we approached the ground. But at least we had a convincing Dublin win to look forward to. This was the beginning of a new era after all, and Wexford weren't expected to put up too much resistance. Of course, our blithe confidence was sadly misplaced and Dublin hung on by the skin of their teeth to win by two points after a dreadful display. Many of the players looked as if they had never met each other. In the final few minutes, Dublin teetered on the brink of disaster as Wexford began to realise the opportunity that now stood before them. The main entertainment was the constant supply of streakers who kept the police and stewards busy as the travelling hordes made their mark. They'd be leading one exhibitionist away when the cheers would go up to greet another. Keeping our heads down, we had a few quiet pints in Carlow afterwards. There was little to shout about anyway, especially with Meath up next.

I arrived on the Hill with very little expectation to weigh me down. I often find it is best to travel light in situations like these. My lack of confidence worked a treat as Dublin ran out convincing winners by 2-11 to 0-10. A massive seven-point margin had finally ripped the Meath monkey from our backs, our first victory over them in the championship for seven years. It was a strange game, I kept expecting Meath to respond to the Dublin lead, but the comeback never came. Two goals from Ray Cosgrove had put Dublin in control and, unrecognisable from their Carlow incarnation, they never looked back. Ciarán Whelan bossed the midfield on what was a very satisfying day all round. Croke Park was looking wonderful as it finally neared completion and the Dublin forward line was looking a bit more like the finished product too as Cosgrove bagged 2-3 and Alan Brogan, son of

Bernard Senior, notched up three points of his own. It was great to see the offspring of the seventies team beginning to make waves. As a result, Dublin were within touching distance of their first silverware since Paul Curran and John O'Leary had lifted Sam in '95.

Not content with beating us on the field Kerry also held the biological upper hand, the likes of the Ó Sé's popping out footballing legends as a matter of course. But now it seemed that we were getting our act together with Bernard Brogan Senior, the man who drilled for oil against Kerry in '77, doing his bit. Alan was looking good and apparently there were two more to follow, Bernard and Paul. Bernard Senior even had the foresight to marry a Kerry woman and if that mix didn't produce a brood of natural footballers then nothing would. Seventy-eight thousand were expected at Croke Park on Leinster final day. With Meath already accounted for, it was no surprise to see that it was Kildare who were standing between Dublin and a return to the good times. It was a great day to be on the Hill as Dublin gained revenge for 2000 with a two-goals in a minute barrage of their own. It proved to be the defining moment. Once again Brogan and Cosgrove were at the heart of the Dublin revival, scoring 1-2 and 1-4 respectively as Dublin squeezed home by 2-13 to 2-11. John McNally chipped in with three invaluable points. The drought was finally over as Tommy Lyons and his players took the plaudits in front of a delighted Hill. For the likes of Darren Homan, Paddy Christie and Senan Connell this success was long overdue. Along with Ciarán Whelan they deserved their day in the sun more than most. The only time when the result looked in doubt was when two goals from Tadgh Fennin had put Kildare in the driving seat. The second was Duff's fault as we had to endure another of his 1993 specials. As a Dublin player caught the ball in front of his own square Duff shouted "Great Take." The ball was duly dropped to a grateful Fennin who rifled it home. It was up there with the "Keep Him Out There" against Derry. This Leinster title tasted all the sweeter as it included the slaying of the two sides that had caused us so much pain over the last seven years. And for now, we were happier than we had been for a long time. As we drifted out from the Hill, the usual refrain: "You're hardly going to believe us. You're hardly going to believe us. You're hardly going to believe us. We're Going To Win The Sam!" had a more realistic ring to it. But, in reality, we knew anything else from now on would be a bonus.

We basked in the glory of our Leinster triumph as we contemplated an All-Ireland quarter-final against our 1992 conquerors Donegal on the August bank holiday Monday, laughing at the commentators who kept saying that a provincial title didn't matter anymore. It mattered to us.

The darkness of Carlow was forgotten as the sun came out for the third day in a row. We'd forgotten what days like this could be like. I like Donegal. They have always played good football and they bring a sense of fun to Croke Park. Also, you never quite know what to expect from them: when they are good they are very good but when they are bad they are awfully bad. They are a unique people. Different in a good way; their free spirit has an infectious quality. You know from their otherworldly demeanour that they live beside the calming effect of the Atlantic Ocean and yet there is a wildness to them that comes with the winter storms. The last thing I wanted was a draw as I was off on holiday to South Africa the following day for two weeks before I embarked on a year studying guidance counselling in Maynooth. I had booked the holiday to fall in between the quarters and the semis.

The Hill was throbbing with colour and noise and the rest of the stadium looked wonderful as the Donegal people welcomed their team back onto the hallowed turf. It was one of those days on the Hill when you had to be careful not to get burnt on one side of your face. It can look ridiculous for days afterwards, definitely not what I wanted heading off to South Africa. I was standing next to a massive skinhead in his late thirties, and despite his tough demeanour, I got the feeling that this man knew his football. Maurice, P.O., Duff and my brother John and his girlfriend Suzanne were to my right, I knew I could count on them. Duff dug his fists into my back as the National Anthem came to its usual end with a shuddering roar. We were ready to rumble.

Then news reached the Hill that Tommy Lyons had fallen ill and had been taken to hospital. P.O. didn't think it would make any difference but I wasn't convinced. Pillar Caffrey took up the reins. I was beginning to usurp Maurice's job as chief critic of referees. Incensed by some poor decisions during a tense start, I lost the run of myself, launching myself down through a packed Hill to I don't know where, screaming as I went. I'd really lost the plot. As I lunged forward, I felt a hand on my shoulder pulling me back. It was the skinhead. He picked me up and planted me back down with a thump to where I had been standing just a few seconds before. "Calm down bud. Everything will be okay." It was very sweet. Just then Maurice piped up "and you're doing a counselling course next year" to much hilarity all around.

Two stunning goals from Ray Cosgrove put Dublin in the driving seat but Adrian Sweeney led a late Donegal fight back to earn the inevitable replay. The only consolation was that it was better than losing; the show would have to go on without me. The weather, combined with a cracking game played in an incredible atmosphere, made this another one of my most memorable days in Croke Park. It was still in my system as I boarded the plane the next day. I couldn't get Ray Cosgrove's two goals out of my head, he had struck both with a sweetness that marked him down as a born goal scorer. The Hill's newest hero had now scored five goals in an amazing debut season.

A week later, I was on the phone to my father to find out the result of the replay. Dublin had won by 10 points, it was a crushing victory. Tommy was back at the helm as Cosgrove bagged another stunning goal, perhaps the best of the lot. Somehow he managed to guide the ball into the top corner with the minimum of back lift, an instinctive execution on the biggest of stages and the sign of a player at the height of his confidence. It seemed that Ray just couldn't miss. For some reason some of the Dublin players saw fit to do a lap of honour at the end which was just asking for trouble as they must have known that Armagh would have been taking note...

The omens weren't good in the run-in to the semi with the media wittering on about Armagh's failure to win a match in Croke Park. It didn't make me feel anything but nervous. After all, like Donegal in 1992, there always has to be a first time.

Dublin were in with a real chance of making their first All-Ireland final in seven years, and I was back to see it. The Hill was packed to capacity on a boiling hot day with little pockets of orange dotted through a huge bank of blue. But it was all good-humoured as the Hill serenaded the Armagh fans with a moving rendition of "What's it like to have a Queen?" We might have been on the one road but all thoughts of a united Ireland were put aside for the afternoon. On the pitch there seemed very little to separate the teams, Dublin had started the better but Armagh had levelled the game up by half-time. 0-6 to 0-6. The second-half was just as tight and Armagh seemed to have stolen Dublin's thunder with Paddy McKeever's crucial goal five minutes in, but Dublin were having none of it. Almost immediately, Ciarán Whelan seized possession and drove at the heart of the Armagh defence before driving a spectacular effort in off the bar from twenty-five yards out – 1-7 to 1-7 – typical Whelan, thankfully he hadn't even given us enough time to fully absorb the importance of the Armagh goal.

The teams matched each other score for score as mistakes, frees and wides cut the natural flow. Dublin seemed to have regained their earlier ascendancy when fine play from Cosgrove put them in the driving seat: 1-13 to 1-11. But with only minutes remaining, Armagh hit back to draw level again and when Oisín McConville fisted Armagh ahead, we feared the worst: Armagh 1-14 Dublin 1-13.

For the first time that afternoon, Dublin flinched as panic set in. The clock was their greatest enemy now. Time and again, possession was squandered and better-placed colleagues ignored as speculative shots were taken on. We prayed to the heavens for some divine intervention and it arrived deep into injury time. For once, the Dublin players managed to retain possession allowing Ray Cosgrove to draw a foul. The resultant free looked kickable but it certainly wasn't going to be easy. Cosgrove picked up the ball 25 metres out and prepared to take his most important kick of the summer. He was slightly to the right of the posts from where we were. The weight of the capital was on his shoulders. Dublin's most prolific scorer already had six points to his name, he owed us nothing. It seemed strange that Declan Darcy, a recognised free taker, had just come on but wasn't asked to take the kick. So it was up to Ray. He looked confident. Time stood still as the sun decided whether it would go down on Dublin's season. The Hill was still and hushed in communal prayer as Ray stepped back, took two steps forward and released the ball from his hands before hitting it with his right foot. It arched upwards. I immediately got an ill feeling. It was going too far to the left. Duff had sensed as much. But he hadn't given up hope. "It's curling" he whispered more in hope than real belief as the ball began to drift back towards the right. "But not enough" I replied. As if to confirm my fears, the ball smacked against the upright and bounced down into the arms of a grateful Armagh. Time and again, I have replayed that moment in my mind. When the ball comes down in my improved version it is Jason Sherlock who grabs it and drills it into the Armagh goal to put Dublin into the final in the most dramatic of circumstances. But it wasn't to be. The whistle went immediately and Dublin were down and out in Croke Park again, blue shirts dejectedly dropping to the ground. Armagh had finally won at headquarters. A few weeks later, they went on to win their first All-Ireland by beating Kerry in the final. Not for the first time, Dublin had been the doormat for the realisation of another county's dreams. We were the shadow boxers of the footballing world.

We stood in stunned silence as the orange shirts away to our right hugged each other. It felt like a massive kick to the gut. We stood for what seemed like hours but must have been only a few short minutes. It felt like forever. It was hard to take but the team had come a long way in a short time. Tommy Lyons seemed to have the players playing with a great confidence. We had forgotten what days like this could be like, but having tasted them again we wanted more. Next year couldn't come quickly enough as we made our way towards Hedigans.

Chapter Twenty-five

To Yorkshire And Back Again

Saturday 14 August 2004

All-Ireland Senior Football Championship Quarter-Final
Dublin versus Kerry

The 2003 championship season began well with an easy win over Louth in Croker. Dublin were everything that we expected them to be: fitter, stronger, more direct. Ray Cosgrove picked up where he had left off the previous summer by setting up a goal for Alan Brogan. Our attack looked bright and vibrant, with points flying over from all angles. Bryan Cullen and David Henry made their championship debuts; fresh blood to add to an impressive mix of new and old. I spent the day high up in the Cusack Stand. Lately I seemed to be doing this more often, but I knew that I needed to get back to the Hill even if it meant standing on my own. Meath and Westmeath took to the pitch for the second part of an attractive double header but we didn't wait around. Within minutes most Dubs were gone.

The next day I have to listen to the usual shite about Dublin supporters being tribal, out of sync with the wider spectacle that is the land of the Gael. We'll put up with a lot but watching Meath? We heard later that the usually reliable Dessie Dolan had a kick from in front of the posts to win it for Westmeath right at the death. But he missed it. Perhaps it was just as well that we didn't stay after all.

Optimism is sky high with The Tommy Lyons bandwagon showing little sign of grinding to a halt anytime soon. Laois are next up, and not just any old Laois, Mick O'Dwyer's Laois. On the day, the Hill is empty due to ongoing preparations for the Special Olympics and we are sitting in the Hogan Stand surrounded by Laois heads. Interestingly, I am almost in exactly the same place I was for the 1985 Leinster final between the same two sides: that unforgettable day when the rain poured from the heavens and I got lost on the way to the ground with my brother.

It seemed that nothing could stop this Dublin team marching into another

Leinster final, certainly not a Laois team that was lacking in the physical stakes. But what they lacked in physique they made up for with pace and skill. Mick O'Dwyer had seen enough in them to leave Kildare and not for the first time he had the Dubs locked firmly in his sights. Micko has been a constant thorn in our side, following us around with monotonous regularity, as if beating us back in the seventies and eighties wasn't enough. Winning against the Dubs had become a drug for Micko. The mere sight of a tracksuited O'Dwyer was all it took to get a Dub shaking in his boots. Laois have been written off by the press who gave them no chance.

Tommy Lyons wandered out onto the pitch, strutting his stuff, a picture of noisy confidence. Micko looked like he was enjoying himself, he always does, like he's having a day at the seaside. That's the trouble with Micko, he enjoys a good game of football. His carefree attitude transmits itself to his players and when the tide starts to turn in their favour, they embrace it with open arms as if they didn't have a care in the world. Unfortunately today was one of days. As Micko slipped off his sandals and rolled up his trousers and prepared for a paddle, Tommy was having an altogether different kind of afternoon. It looked as if someone might well have stolen his candyfloss as he paced up and down wondering what to do. Any spare time was used scratching his head.

It is always dangerous to underestimate any Micko team. Laois had the forwards to damage Dublin and it wasn't long before they began to make their mark. In contrast, the Dublin forwards couldn't hit a barn door. In midfield, the Laois version of the ginger man, Padraig Clancy, was dictating the flow of the game. All around me, the Laois voices were growing in volume as I slunk down in my seat trying to pretend it wasn't happening. They had just come for a day out but now they could smell blood. O'Dwyer was at it again, leading another culchie uprising. There is nothing worse than sitting amongst the opposition support and listening to the whooping and hollering as hope turns to expectancy and finally celebration. I couldn't begrudge any of the Laois fans a bit of it; I just didn't want to be there when it happened. Once again, I looked at the empty Hill and wished I was there: all alone and out of reach. I much rather drown in my own misery than the joy of others. It was one of those strange days when the minutes seemed to be racing by. Every time I looked at my watch another ten had disappeared.

I had watched in horror as Dublin missed chance after chance. We could feel the game inexorably slipping away and there was nothing we could do about it. More importantly, there seemed to be little Tommy could do either. The ship was headed for the rocks as the pressure built and built with every passing minute. Laois had won by 0-19 to 0-17. At the end, I couldn't get out of there quick enough. But it wasn't that easy. Smiling Laois faces were everywhere.

The inevitable shit hit the inevitable fan the next day as the media picked over the wreckage. *The Herald* had a particular bone to pick with Tommy as he had aligned himself with the fledgling – and soon flown – *Dublin Daily* that year. In an instant, Lyon's aura of invincibility was dashed as rumours of player unrest began to surface. Tommy's honeymoon with the Dublin fans was over. I struggled to understand how it had all gone so wrong so quickly. One off day didn't make this Dublin team a bad one and we would be getting a second chance after all. But things were spinning out of control and there was no stopping the outbreak of media-led hysteria that engulfed the capital. By Monday evening a full-blown crisis had been declared; from the sublime to the ridiculous in seventy short minutes.

The qualifier draw could have been kinder, Derry in Clones, not the type of team you want to be playing against when your confidence is low. We piled into P.O.'s car the following Saturday and headed north with fear in our hearts. As Duff, P.O. and I settled into our seats in the ground, I noticed a couple of old codgers with strong Derry accents behind us. I wanted a quiet afternoon but I could tell they were itching to talk to us. There would be no escape: before long, we were being asked which club we were affiliated to. This is dangerous ground in GAA-dom, I couldn't very well say Arsenal; so I muttered something about Lucan Sarsfields. At least I knew where their ground was, but I was worried that they might know somebody there. These guys seemed to know everyone who played GAA in Ireland and I reckon they had us sussed – soft Dublin dilettantes, not the real thing at all, at all – but they let matters lie as the players emerged.

Despite all the despair in the week leading up to the game, Dublin had brought an impressive travelling support. The final score of 3-9 to 1-9 in our favour may have seemed comfortable enough but in truth it was a little flattering, the result of a disjointed performance that left a lot of questions unanswered as to whether the team had really recovered fully from its nightmare against Laois. But the three goals arrived at the right time. An early Dessie Farrell strike settled the nerves, before Senan Connell hit a second and Jason Sherlock wrapped it up with a goal of pure class to make it a great day out for the Na Fianna boys. But still doubts remained, Derry had lacked the necessary ammunition to put us away. Anyway, Derry in Clones was nothing compared to what was now awaiting us: Armagh, the reigning All-Ireland champions.

Having failed to retain their Ulster title that year, Armagh were in need of a boost too. What better tonic than a run out against Dublin at headquarters then? Crossmaglen might well have been a better option for the Dubs. I made the mistake of having a few too many pints before the game. Usually I leave my drinking until later in the day, but with P.O. meeting up with a Canadian friend of his in The Findlater pub on Dorset Street, I got carried away. By the time I got to Croker, I was a little the worse for wear, not exactly three sheets to the wind, but tipsy and grumpy at the touch of a button as the effect of the drink wore off. I either needed more or else I needed to go home. In these circumstances, the Hill would have been fine, but we were back in the Hogan Stand. Thankfully, I had my brother John to keep me company; it was twenty years since he had taken me to my first All-Ireland final. I was wearing a crazy looking Dubs hat that made me look even more dangerous than I was: a cross between Jamiroquai and Boy George. And I was well aware that I probably looked a little demented as we took our seats amidst the Armagh fans. I knew I was already out of my depth and the match hadn't even started.

The tension built throughout the first-half. It was nip and tuck as Armagh stuck to the same tactics that had brought them such success a year earlier: crowding their defence and cynically stopping Dublin further out the field. My hackles were up and I was letting my feelings be known to the referee and those around me. Armagh's upper body strength was telling as time and again, they turned over possession. The game was stuttering along with neither side gaining the upper hand where it mattered. It was an ugly type of game really, a day for the type of hand to hand combat that Armagh revelled in. Dublin just couldn't get going, with the rhythm they usually thrive on lost in the stop-start nature of the game. I was losing the run of myself as half-time approached, giving as good as I got to the Armagh folk around me.

When an experienced-looking Garda came up and stood behind our section for the second-half, I wasn't particularly surprised. He didn't need to say anything, his presence was enough. I pulled my hat down and hid from view. Things settled down in the stand after that but on the pitch, the fires were still burning. Armagh were already down to 14 men when Stephen Cluxton got himself sent-off – no need to burn the referee this time Maurice – this one was self-inflicted. Lyons reacted by removing centre half-back Johnny McGee and Dublin duly lost their shape and the match by four points: Armagh 0-15 Dublin 0-11. For much of the second-half Armagh had looked like their old selves, a team on a mission, and by the end, the gulf between the two sides was alarming as Armagh killed the game, picking off point after point. A year earlier, Dublin had matched Armagh stride for stride, but not this time.

The wheels were clearly coming off when Lyons criticised Cluxton in public afterwards, a move that wasn't going to do anything to repair the already frosty atmosphere between players and management. Cluxton was young and inexperienced, what he needed was an arm around his shoulders. Instead he was hung out to dry. All of the good work of 2002 was thrown overboard into a sea of indignation and anger. But still Tommy had one more year left to run. It already felt like a wasted 12 months. It's a hell of a long time to be a dead man walking. If Tommy had any doubts all he had to do was talk to Tommy Carr or Mickey Whelan.

Unfortunately, 2004 was to be more of the same, with another Kerry warrior from the seventies coming back to haunt us. Páidí Ó Sé had upped sticks and led Westmeath to an historic Leinster title. He had done for one Tommy and now he had another one in his sights. Páidí hadn't changed, his straight fringe still competed for attention with his flared slacks and dodgy runners. He was clearly having none of this Celtic Tiger shite.

Losing to Westmeath was a new level of humiliation, one of our worst ever performances. Duff had to be led to his seat by a Sherpa as he experienced a touch of vertigo on his way up the top tier of the Hogan Stand. The atmosphere at the end was venomous as some Dublin supporters vented their fury as only they know how. It is one thing being disappointed and angry but spitting at members of the coaching and backroom staff was unacceptable. The Dublin County Board had some soul-searching to do; they seemed to have learnt nothing from the Mickey Whelan saga. By allowing the situation to build up such a head of steam they were clearly doing nobody any favours.

It was just as well that we had the qualifiers to look forward to and we were getting used to them by now. London, at home, was the ultimate soft landing. It would have been nice to head off to good old London town but we were drawn at home. Home this time meant Parnell Park. The clash of two of the biggest cities in GAA must have pissed Cork off. As expected, Dublin ran out easy winners. We were up and running with Leitrim away to follow.

On the day, I set off to pick up Maurice and pretty soon I was lost in the maze of Dublin's north side. If reaching Glasnevin defeated me, then getting to Carrick-on-Shannon looked a tall order, but with Maurice navigating, the chances of us getting there were dramatically improved. Strangely enough for a Geography teacher, a sense of direction has never been one of my strong points. To tell you the truth, I was sick of the job I was doing. I had never felt that I belonged in the school, either as a pupil or a teacher. I had always felt like an outsider. It was everything that the Hill was not. I lived for June, July and August and although I was giving teaching everything I had, I was feeling bored and unfulfilled. Something about my situation just didn't seem to add up and after mulling it over for weeks, I realised that I wanted out. I opened up to Maurice on the way down, for over three hours he had to listen to my confused ramblings about what my life had become. The only interruption to my flow came when we spotted a big boat sticking out of a hedge on the side of the road which, with no sign of a river or a sea nearby left us totally bemused. Later on we found out that we had stumbled upon the aftermath of an accident, the locals treating it as if it was nothing out of the ordinary. We just nodded and let it go. It still didn't make much sense.

I told Maurice I was determined to leave, even if it meant giving up the holidays and the pension, the holy grail of the public service worker. Some of us like to fool ourselves that everything will be okay when we retire, that all the pain will have been worth it when the pension kicks in, but I wanted to live now. I wanted to do something that I enjoyed doing with people that I enjoyed being with. As we met a Garda checkpoint on the way into Carrick-on-Shannon, I decided that I would make an appointment with the Headmaster the next week and do the necessary.

After all my deliberations en route, the game itself proved fairly straightforward. With the hot air draining out of what was left of the Tommy Lyon's balloon this was one for the committed, a long way to come for a game we were expected to win, and not many had made the trip this time. Páirc Seán Mac Diarmada was picturesque and quaint. It felt like the Leitrim folk had come to see what a dying animal looked like. In the opening fifteen minutes, the Connacht men put it up to their more illustrious opponents but the longer the afternoon went on, the more comfortable Dublin and their supporters became. By the end we were well on top. One of the biggest cheers of the day greeted the return of Dessie Farrell: Dublin 1-13 Leitrim 0-4. Things were beginning to look up. But still there was a sense of unease, we had looked uncomfortable in the early exchanges and the suspicion remained that a better side would have exposed the lack of belief that seemed to be infiltrating every part of the team.

We didn't hang around afterwards. I pointed the car eastwards and hoped for the best. It was Maurice's turn to open up on the way back. As it turned out he wasn't all that happy in his job either – maybe that was what lay at the bottom of his need to burn so many referees over the years – he also had a deep-seated longing for something better. I listened and reiterated my determination to jump off the cliff of life the following week. As I dropped Maurice off in front of his house, I got the feeling we both felt a lot better about ourselves and the direction our lives were taking. We were bound for pastures new. Now all I had to do was find my way back to Lucan.

I woke up the next morning and promptly changed my mind. I told myself I needed the money and I needed the holidays and most of all I needed that bloody pension. What was I thinking of? So I backed down and any plans to see the Headmaster were shelved indefinitely. That Tuesday night, Maurice rang to say that he had felt so inspired by my talk on Saturday that he had handed in his notice: "You've gone and done what?", I roared back down the phone. I felt like a fraud as I told him that I had stepped back from the precipice but he didn't seem to mind. It proved to be the right decision for Maurice as he took some time out and moved jobs. He's been a lot happier ever since. There was a valuable lesson there, but I couldn't see it at the time and it would be four long years before I felt ready to follow in his footsteps. By then, it was almost too late.

Back in the land of Gaelic football, the draw had thrown up a third L in a row: Longford in Portlaoise, another winnable game, but a step-up from the canter in Carrick-on-Shannon. I travelled down to the midlands with Duff and his brother Vivian who knows Ireland like the back of his hand so I could lie back, relax and enjoy the scenery. On the way down, Vivian entertained us with stories of matches and characters from Dublin's past. He talked about one of his friends who he hadn't seen it for years and surprise, surprise the first pub we walked into, there he was, his long lost pal standing at the bar enjoying a pint of Guinness as only an Irishman can. His face lit up as his cream covered lips broke into a welcoming smile. That's Ireland for you: full of synchronicity and ghosts from the past everywhere you turn. People come and go but when you meet them again it's as if you just pick up the conversation where you left off all those years ago. Maurice, still basking in his new-found freedom, hadn't felt up to the journey. He was pencilled in to return for the next outing, provided we won of course.

As expected, Longford stuck with the pace of the game for a good deal longer than Leitrim had managed and the final score of 1-17 to 0-11 flattered Dublin. Like the previous game it masked many faults and Dublin's lack of cohesion was becoming worrying. There seemed to be no consistency to selection, especially up front. Ray Cosgrove came off the bench in Portlaoise but like so many of his team-mates, his confidence seemed to be ebbing away.

Next up was Roscommon in Croker and, for the first time since the Westmeath game, we were at full strength, we meaning Maurice, Margaret, myself, P.O. and Duff. Still suffering from our collective midlife crisis, we had seats in the Hogan Stand, and yet again, I was reduced to gazing at the Hill from afar. A Dub smoking in a designated zone in front of us was annoying P.O., and we noticed that the sweet aroma drifting our way suggested that he was breaking two rules rather than just the one. It was probably the only high he got that day as Dublin made very heavy weather of putting a very ordinary Roscommon side away. Jason Sherlock notched up 1-4 and Alan Brogan continued to do the business. Brogan was looking the most consistent of the Dublin forwards as the summer progressed. Unfortunately, Dessie Farrell's season ended that afternoon as he suffered a nasty looking injury. Would this be the last time we would see Dessie in the shirt he loved so much? A sad end for a player who had given his all to the cause and had become a firm favourite with the Dublin fans. We would miss his little forays into the corner as he took defenders to parts of the pitch they hoped they would never see. Nobody deserved that All-Ireland medal in 1995 more than Dessie.

On the plus side, Dublin were now into the All-Ireland quarter-final following a dodgy detour. But there had been nothing remotely convincing about their progress and with Kerry up next, there would have to be a massive improvement all round.

But hope springs eternal. I felt deep down there was one big game in this Dublin team. If they could put all of the issues that were clouding their view to one side and recapture the form of two years ago then they might just have a chance. I was going to be on holiday in Yorkshire with Jane. The more the papers hyped up the game, regaling us with stories of past clashes, the more I realised that I couldn't miss it. What if Dublin finally beat the Kingdom for the first time in the championship since 1977 and I wasn't there to witness it? So in true Baldrick style, I hatched a cunning plan. I would fly back from the holiday on the Saturday morning and go to the game before jumping on a return flight back to Middlesbrough that evening. Problem solved. Jane's twin sister, Lyn and her friend would be arriving over for the weekend on the Friday evening so Jane would not be left all alone. It seemed that I had all bases covered.

Everything was going to plan when we pulled into an eccentric little Yorkshire village on the Thursday morning. Jane suggested that this would be a good place to stay the following Saturday night as we parked outside a bed and breakfast on the edge of town. I had dozed off when Jane got back into the car. She had booked us in. Without any further delay, we headed off across the beautiful Yorkshire Dales.

The match day drew nearer and more in hope than confidence, I felt a big Dublin performance was in the offing. Saturday morning came and the three girls dropped me off at the airport. I managed to make it back to Ireland in one piece and in doing so, I got a feeling of what it must be like for those Irish wanderers who travel back from Britain year in-year out to watch their county take to the field in search of championship glory. In Dublin airport I noticed a number of men and women proudly wearing their colours. The news from the first two semi-finals the week before had thrown the cat amongst the pigeons. I couldn't believe it when P.O. told me the results over the phone. Two of the red hot favourites had crashed out to teams that many felt weren't fit to tie the laces of their more illustrious opponents. Fermanagh went and beat Armagh and before anyone could catch their breath, Mayo put an end to Tyrone's defence of their All-Ireland title. Shockwaves spread throughout the land. The tremors even made it as far as Yorkshire as I put down the phone and shook my head with incredulity at the sheer unpredictable nature of it all. Having stumbled through the back door, Dubliners went to bed that Saturday night knowing that a win over Kerry the following weekend, would see the door to the final swinging wide open.

It was good to be back in Dublin for the day and I felt like a tourist as I got the bus from the airport to Croke Park; on holiday from my holidays. I made my way into the ground and found P.O. sitting in the first row of seats back from the pitch in the Hogan Stand. Minutes later, we had delighted Derry supporters climbing all over us in their enthusiasm to get onto the pitch to celebrate their win over Westmeath. With Mayo, Fermanagh and Derry through, attention now turned to the last of the quarter-finals.

Dublin began well, but luck deserted them as they struck the woodwork three times in the first-half. A side like Kerry doesn't need a second invitation, never mind a third one. Having survived the Dublin onslaught, they stepped on the gas to cruise through a one-sided second-half to run out easy winners by 1-15 to 1-8. I consoled myself with the fact that we had made it to the last five teams left in the championship. As I said goodbye to P.O., I was glad that I was heading back across the Irish Sea, glad that the season was finally over. We should have been put out of our misery a lot earlier; in reality we had been on a downward spiral ever since 2002. The Kerry defeat heralded the end of the Tommy Lyons era. Perhaps now we could finally move on. Unfortunately, the taxi driver who took me back to the airport didn't feel that way. He had every right to be angry of course, the last two years felt like wasted ones.

Back at Middlesbrough airport, I was met by Shay Given and Gary Breen heading the other way for international duty; they looked a little surprised to see a sheepish-looking Dublin supporter wandering around Teesside. I hadn't travelled all that way to witness a massacre, but that's sport, no fairytales. I felt miserable as I caught sight of Lyn who had kindly turned up with her friend Dee to collect me and, after the forty minute drive back to the little village, we felt that a couple of pints were well deserved. I was determined to put Dublin out of my mind and let the pints of bitter do the rest. I should explain at this stage that Jane was safely tucked up in bed after feeling a little off colour earlier in the day.

As the pub closed, I said goodnight to the girls who were staying in another B & B and headed for home – I always call wherever I am staying for the night home – and as I approached the B & B I could see that everybody was asleep inside. Not a soul was stirring as I turned the door handle and entered. They had obviously left it open for me. But now what would I do? I had no idea of our room number and there seemed to be nobody around to ask. The fact that there were very few lights left on only added to my confusion. I looked to see if Jane had left a note for me. Eventually I crept quietly up the stairs, maybe she had left a note on the door to our room. Again there was no sign of any clues. I was getting a little worried, even beginning to think about sleeping on the landing when I spotted a door ajar. I pushed the door open and whispered my arrival only to find the faces of a shocked couple staring back at me. I mumbled my apologies and withdrew with as much decorum as I could manage in such a delicate situation, which wasn't much to be honest. It was only then that a cross looking landlady arrived on the scene. I tried to explain my predicament but she only seemed to grow grumpier. It was then that she pointed me in the direction of next door. I was in the wrong bed and breakfast. The first one Jane had tried had been full and I hadn't noticed her going next door. Minutes later I was tucked up in bed with my wife. As we sat at breakfast the next morning the phone rang and I heard landlady one saying to landlady two "Yes, he's here and he's very apologetic." I was getting redder by the minute as I encouraged Jane to eat up. It was time to get the hell out of this one horse town. I couldn't help feeling that Tommy Lyons was probably thinking exactly the same thing as he tucked into his cornflakes back in Dublin.

Chapter Twenty-six

There Is A Light That Never Goes Out

Saturday 31 July 2010

All-Ireland Senior Football Championship Quarter-Final
Dublin versus Tyrone

Saturday 31 July 2010 is the day when it all falls into place. We have just beaten Tyrone, finally we've taken out one of the big guns. I keep waiting for someone to tap me on the shoulder and tell me that it has all been just a cruel dream. It's the perfect end to a perfect day. In the end, life's not solely about getting by and paying the bills. It's as much about standing in a field watching your favourite band or standing on a terrace cheering on your favourite football team, tingles making their way down your spine, hair standing on the back of your neck, the sense of knowing that this is it, the moment that you have been waiting for. For years. It doesn't get much better than this. Elbow are correct. One day like this a year would see me right.

Understandably, we had feared the worst when we came out of the hat with Tyrone. I just wanted us to be competitive, to be in touch at half-time. Our last two quarter-final appearances had ended in disaster and the scars still ran deep. We couldn't afford another drubbing. Our trepidation mirrored the mood of the country as gloom and doom stalked the land. Ireland was on the verge of shutting down, and the exact date depended on whichever newspaper you chose to believe. At this rate there wouldn't even be any lights left to turn off when the last person left.

But all was not lost. At least the sporting heart of the land was still beating as the end of July came into view, so there were a few things still worth living for even amongst all the talk of bailouts and devaluation. The boys in blue and their merry band of followers had bigger fish to fry. Happiness has never been about the sort of things that have come to dominate our lives over the last couple of years; it just seemed that way for a while. Now that those in the know have decided that the economy is all we should think about, the chatter on the radio is about little else. Even the supposedly upbeat mid-morning shows are peddling the talk of recession: toxic banks, the IMF and negative equity are the terms that have come to define us it seems. But they mean nothing to me on a day like this. Dublin have beaten Tyrone therefore I am in heaven and nothing else matters. Kerry are gone as well, taken apart by a wonderful exhibition of football from Down when it was least expected. Down are like a sleeper agent who lies undercover for years before exploding onto the scene and taking out one of the top teams. Today was one of those days.

In a few short hours, the football world has been turned upside down. It's a pity the real world doesn't work that way. I am jumping for joy, hugging strangers, doing high fives and texting Duff. That's right; Duff missed out again. The legend of the jinx is growing, at this rate the committee will have to meet to adjudicate on his request to attend the semi-final. We are within touching distance of our first All-Ireland final for fifteen years so Duff needs to do what is best for Dublin, it would be a pity to ruin it now. P.O. is off the hook; he was here today so we know it's not him. "Hill 16 La La La. Hill 16 La La La." I'd forgotten what it is to feel like this. Two years earlier Ronnie Drew had gone to the great porterhouse in the sky on the same day that Tyrone delivered the mother of all hammerings to a fancied Dublin team. It was a God-awful day with an end-of-the-world feeling about it, a day when the darkness of the sky matched the pain we felt in our hearts: Dublin and Ronnie gone in the one day. We wondered who the hell had written that script.

But today is very different. The road to redemption looked a long way off twelve months ago but somehow Pat Gilroy has gotten us there in double-quick time; his startled earwigs morphing into a thing of beauty almost overnight. There had been casualties along the way, Shane Ryan was lost to hurling, and Jason Sherlock lost his place. But sporting transition is rarely painless. I must admit that I had given up bothering to think that a day like this was a realistic possibility. Somewhere during the last two years I stopped hoping, stopped feeling. Being surrounded by a recession-numbed populace made it easier to blend in. I had even stopped praying. We'd also given up on superstition; it never seemed to work anyway.

As the winter of our discontent consumed us we retreated into ourselves.

But today the summer is back with a bang, I have shed my winter clothes; hope has returned and it feels good to be alive again. Right now, nothing exists outside of this bubble of joy, nothing else matters. It was almost as if the Hill didn't know what to do for a few seconds after the final whistle. We just needed a little time to realise what had just happened. And then we exploded: we danced and we grinned but still we wondered if it had actually happened, was it real? So many times we have stood in terrible silence trying desperately to make immediate sense of another devastating defeat. Defeat is what we have become used to. Our summers always end in August but this year might just be different, might just be the one. As long as Duff stays away that is.

It starts to sink in. Tyrone and Kerry gone in one day. A glorious day for football; there will be new All-Ireland champions, a changing of the guard. Cork will be the favourites now: they have been the great pretenders of the last few years, but now they will feel that their time has come. Only Dublin stand between them and a shot at Sam, but Dublin have changed in the last few hours too. The Jacks are well and truly back.

With only six minutes left on the clock, the sides are level. Dublin have lasted the pace well, have hung in there, earning the right to be in with a chance. But Tyrone are turning the screw as the game moves towards a resolution. Time and again, they move in for the kill but each time the ball drifts wide of the Dublin posts and each miss lifts our spirits.

This isn't the Tyrone we had come to know and fear. Sean Cavanagh's radar is off kilter for once, two years ago he destroyed Ross McConnell, but not today. It is left to Owen Mulligan to keep them in the hunt. We know all about Mulligan; his goal of the season destroyed us in 2004. He is threatening to do the same again but he needs some support but it doesn't come. Tyrone have kicked seventeen wides, but still the game is tied at 13 points apiece. As if to celebrate their good fortune, Dublin break up field, Paul Flynn picks up possession and shoots for the point that will put Dublin back in front. The ball hits the far post before it drops into the welcoming arms of Eoghan O'Gara. Time stands still. O'Gara is yards from goal; he has time to think about what he is going to do next. Always dangerous. Better to follow your heart, to do what comes naturally. I imagine this moment to be like a car crash. The slow motion, the feeling of being lost in time. Dublin's fate rests on the next few seconds. O'Gara steadies himself as a couple of Tyrone defenders throw themselves towards him, trying to put him off. But O'Gara does what it says on the tin. Doesn't think, doesn't blink; he lets the ball fall from hand to foot. Minimal back lift. Bang. The ball rifles past a helpless Pascal McConnell before crashing against the back of Tyrone net. For a split second there is silence. Followed by an explosion of joy. And disbelief. We're ahead by three points against Tyrone with five minutes left. We'll never hold on. They'll come back, they always do.

Dublin started well. Within six minutes, we are three points to the good. We are pinching ourselves; for the first time in three years we find ourselves going into the game as the underdogs. No hype, no false expectations, unlike the previous two years when the mantle of favourites had hung heavy. After twenty minutes, Dublin lead by 0-5 to 0-2. Bernard Brogan's four frees mean Dublin are in control. All around the field, Dublin players are throwing themselves into tackles, chasing their illustrious opponents down. With each passing minute we believe just a little bit more. But not for long. In the second quarter Tyrone hit five unanswered points to leave Dublin looking increasingly desperate as they search for the answer to what's happening. Typical of Tyrone, they refuse to cave in and by half-time they are leading by eight points to seven.

The Hill is feeling the players' pain. Their pain is our pain. We wondered what lay ahead, feared the worst. Dublin don't do fairytales, not since the seventies anyway. Our dominant start has been dampened down, the fire almost out. We need to start the second-half well. But whatever Pat Gilroy says at the break clearly works and the arrival of Cian O'Sullivan in defence tightens things up, but even he can't stop Tyrone stretching their lead to two. It looks as if the Dublin goose is cooked. I can't see Tyrone losing it from here. But instead of killing Dublin off, they waste a number of opportunities to stretch their lead. Aware of this unexpected reprieve Dublin react by rattling off a lightening succession of points that turn the game on its head and put the doubt back into Tyrone minds. Bernard Brogan scores two beauties from play before his brother Alan puts us ahead. As Dublin's temporary supremacy draws to a close, it's Tyrone's turn to seize the initiative but something's not right with them today. For all their possession, they seem incapable of registering on the scoreboard. As chance after chance slips by, in the end it is left to Mulligan to nail an equaliser.

But all to no avail. A minute later the ball hits the back of the Tyrone net. And only seconds after that Conal Keaney is knocking over a simple free as Tyrone's decision to use the short kick out all day long results in the inevitable loss of possession in front of their own goal. It must have made sweet viewing for those Dublin fans watching on TV as coverage switched back to real time, following multiple replays of O'Gara's goal, to reveal Keaney getting ready to extend the lead to four points. In a matter of seconds, the game has turned upside-down. These things just don't happen to Dublin. After all these years, lady luck had finally decided to give us a break. The last five minutes are tense but deep in our hearts we know that Tyrone are gone. The final score of the day comes from Michael Dara MacAuley who has given another top class display. As he punches the ball over the bar, he raises his fist to a disbelieving Hill. We are home and dry. I still expect something to go wrong. Even after the final whistle.

It's never easy to do a post mortem on a win. We sit in Hedigans and stare at each other. Dublin had started the day as nine to four outsiders. Earlier, as we wandered along the canal, P.O. had predicted the end of the GAA world when he forecasted the demise of Kerry and Tyrone. We had looked at him and laughed. But there's something about Kerry and northern teams, they have some serious history with Down, going right back to the sixties. And history rattles Kerry, sows the seeds of doubt. Apart from when they're playing Dublin that is. Today they were missing two of their best players through suspension: Paul Galvin and Tomás Ó Sé. Injustice, the enemy within, was weighing them down and two hours later they were gone, well-beaten, swept aside by as fine a display of attacking football as we have seen in a long time.

As the second game begins, we hang onto P.O.'s prediction for dear life. And all through the game he repeats his mantra – "Dublin will win this" – but we are too frightened to pay him any heed. Even when we are two points down early in the second-half he refuses to budge, maybe he knows something we don't.

The absence of Duff is significant. Three games in a row now. Three wins. Niall sees it as a major boost to our hopes and now that we have a psychic in our midst the possibilities for the rest of the season are limitless. It's not like P.O. to be so positive, usually he is the one running this Dublin team down, raining on our parade when we are doing our best to walk on the bright side of the road. When it comes to the Dublin football team P.O. prefers the dark and lonely street. For some reason, today he is full of hope. By the end of the day he has predicted two of the biggest shocks in Gaelic football since Armagh and Tyrone tumbled out at the same stage in 2004. It's a pity he's not a betting man. And his smile says it all, he is like a man possessed as he heads home, and his parting words to us are: "Kildare and Cork to win tomorrow." Twenty-four hours later he is be luxuriating in the delights of a 100% record. The even better news is that he is predicting that Dublin will go on to beat Cork in the semi-final.

Over 62,000 turned up today for what was an attractive double-header. It seems that a lot of Dublin supporters are waiting for a sure thing. But this win changes everything and the throng will definitely return the next match day. There is always a greener hill farther away. And talking of Hills, the one at the Railway End is starting to look a little like its old self. It was fuller today. The left hand side has been empty and brooding. Redundant, cut off from the action as the stewards pushed people towards the middle ground. But today it returned to almost full employment as the faithless returned. But still it seems that not everyone realises the significance of what we have just witnessed.

As we head across in front of the traffic on Drumcondra road, I hear two Dublin supporters having a discussion about Dublin's style of play, "It's not the Dublin way", one of them pipes up. I can't believe it. Here we are, making our way home following our most significant win in years and some of our brethren are still unhappy. Maybe it's a Dublin thing; enjoying the good times doesn't come naturally. What Pay Gilroy has achieved this season is astonishing. Only seven of the side that started against Kerry a year ago were on the team sheet today – personnel, psychology, tactics – everything has been changed. They might not be quite the finished article yet but they are making huge strides. Today I got the feeling that some of the younger players expected to win; they were fearless, pulling the older players along with them. No startled earwigs today. Inevitably, we will be told that we were lucky, that Tyrone lost the game rather than Dublin winning it. But Dublin made their own luck with their ferocious tackling and defensive work. And despite the impressive performances all over the pitch one man stood head and shoulders above all the others. Bernard Brogan lit up Croke Park with a nine point salvo. No wides. Four points from play. Simply breathtaking.

I mention the two lads bemoaning Dublin's perceived break from swashbuckling tradition to the guys. To some fans, the very idea of getting bodies behind the ball, suffocating the space is heresy: puke football. But all that swashbuckling has left us nowhere over the last two years except battered and bruised and out. But today was very different. Today Dublin played with their head as well as their heart.

Gaelic football has always been fascinating in that individual counties have their own brand of football, the principles that they have remained loyal to over the years. Managers and players might come and go but the style remains the same, even if it fails to succeed. If you come back in one hundred years time, Kildare will probably still be hand-passing the ball from one end of the field to the other without much to show for it, and chances are, the ageless Johnny Doyle will be at the centre of it. Meath will always be physical with a never-say-die attitude that is part of their DNA. Born of the eighties. Down are a perfect example of a side sticking to their footballing faith, for them patience is the key, knowing that when they get it right they will get their reward. It happened in the golden age of the sixties, it happened in the nineties and there is no reason why it can't happen again. Armagh are as tough as nails, dogged. Cork are a bit harder to pin down, I always get the feeling that they are really a bunch of hurlers looking for something to do to pass the time, as if they don't care. And still they win more often than they lose. Kerry have the best footballers in the land but they do what it takes to win. They are and will always be, skilful, ruthless and efficient – no room for egos or showboating – the team is everything. At the moment that involves the uncomplicated plan of bombing the ball into Kieran Donaghy at every opportunity and letting the likes of the brilliant Colm Cooper pick up the leftovers. The Gooch is the type of player who can turn a few scraps into a three course meal. Tyrone are similar. Everything and everyone is geared towards the collective, no prima donnas. The likes of Mayo, Roscommon and Galway try to play football and when they get it right they play some great stuff. It's less rigid. They play like they don't give a fuck and if Mayo's performances in their last two All-Ireland final appearances are anything to go by it just might be true. But Galway's two recent All-Ireland triumphs show that doing what you do best can work. In the end it's about the players. Good players win matches and tactics just back them up.

That's not to say that good coaching can't make an ordinary team difficult to beat, and that is where this Dublin team find themselves right now: battening down the hatches, trying to compete, trying to make life difficult for their opponents. It's nothing to be ashamed of as teams that put defence before attack have dominated the last few years. Apart from Kerry that is. But even Kerry are learning new tricks. Kerry have always had good footballers all over the pitch. They do the job they are supposed to do. Individuals dictate the system in the Kingdom. What Gilroy is doing with this Dublin team is a quiet revolution in itself. He may have lost his nerve at the beginning of the championship, but today shows that he is back on track. For too many years, Dublin had relied on swagger to see them home, even when it was blatantly clear that it wasn't working. Nobody has tried anything different until Pat Gilroy that is. The legacy of the seventies has finally been consigned to the backburner as Pat set out to emulate the likes of Tyrone; dwindling crowds meant nothing to him as he tore up the Dublin script and got down to basics. Dublin would defend from the front, they would work hard to close teams down and dispossess them by swarming all over them. Strength in the tackle would be the key, turning over ball and turning defence into attack with bodies pouring forward in support of the player in possession. Pat's new plan has taken us this far. I was beginning to wonder whether it might just take us all the way.

As we get over the shock that there will be another match, another day out, our conversation turns to the semi-final – most likely against Cork – after all P.O. has spoken. After everyone has thrown in their two cents worth a consensus is reached. Maybe it's the drink or maybe it's the euphoria or maybe we've just lost the run of ourselves, but we feel that we can win. Of course there are doubts and we know that they'll grow to become giants over the next two weeks. After all it's taking us time to come to terms with the new style of play. It's clear that there is still some fine tuning to be done. Vivian wonders if a couple of weeks will be enough to bring even greater cohesion to the Dublin system. Too often, the full-forward line seems to be cut off and outnumbered, bodies aren't always flooding forward in support. Early in games, the need to protect the backline is dominant in the players' minds and later on, tired minds and exhausted limbs curtail attacking instincts. Without Bernard Brogan we would be sunk, he has carried the attack, kept the scoreboard ticking over, and kept our noses in front. Against Cork, it will be crucial to keep the supply lines open or the scores will dry up.

Pat Gilroy appears on the telly in the corner of the snug, he does his usual dance, playing it down and describing Dublin as a work in progress. "Still a lot of work to be done. Cork will be favourites but sure we'll give it our best shot." At one stage he almost smiles; beneath that reserved exterior must be satisfaction at a job well-done. Even Pat seems a little surprised by the outcome as he tries to make sense of a win that he never saw coming. I hope he hasn't made any plans for the rest of the summer. He talks about luck falling on Dublin's side today: about Tyrone under-performing and about Cork being favourites for the semi-final. Keeping his cards close to his chest, he turns and walks away. But there is no getting away from the significance of the victory, for Pat, for his players and for us too. They've been written off for months now, by the press and by their own supporters. Through all the grief they've held their council. Until today that is. Today they did their talking on the pitch.

More opinions are thrown into the pot. The pieces are falling into place. The full-back line is growing in stature with every game, the leaks have been plugged. Rory O'Carroll continued on from where he had left off in the Armagh game by keeping an out-of-sorts Sean Cavanagh scoreless. Dublin completely dominated the middle of the field with both Ross McConnell and Michael Dara MacAuley continuing their excellent form of recent weeks. From early on, Tyrone decided that their best bet was to build from deep inside their own half, a tactic that allowed Dublin to get men behind the ball and to suffocate their opponents far away from their own goal. Only in the minutes before half-time did Tyrone look like their old selves, perhaps this was the day when all the miles on the clock caught up with them.

Dublin looked weary as they surrendered the initiative in the last few minutes of the first-half but whatever Gilroy put in the tea at half-time certainly worked. More of the same will be needed against Cork. It won't be easy, Cork are a physically imposing side with hunger in their bellies. But Dublin will not be frightened. Right now, they should be more worried by the news that Duff will definitely be at the semi-final, I know I am. Niall looks less than pleased but Duff is not taking no for an answer. If we lose this one, he will have a lot to answer for.

In the RTÉ studio, you can almost see the winds of change sweeping through Michael Lyster's hair as the three musketeers warm to this Dublin team. Joe Brolly is waxing lyrical about Dublin's work-rate, at last, the lads have something different to talk about as Tyrone and Kerry are no more. Right now, it's almost impossible to pick a winner. Even Colm O'Rourke has a few kind words to say about the Dubs. Pat Spillane rabbits on as only Pat Spillane can do.

As I prepare to leave I look at the happy smiling faces of Niall, Tom, Vivian, Donal, Brian and their offspring, the Dublin torch being passed from one generation to the next. Unfortunately, I'm on the water as I am homeward bound in a few minutes, I have just called in to say hello. It would have been rude not to on a day like this. It turns out that Brian had almost caused a dust-up in the stand. Vivian and Tom had arrived early and were giving Down their full backing much to the annoyance of two Kerry fans who voiced their displeasure: "Support your own team"; seems that Jack O'Connor isn't the only one suffering from a siege mentality. Have they never heard of the rivalry between Dublin and Kerry? It doesn't take a genius to work out that Kerry getting knocked out of the championship might be good for us. If we end up playing them later on, there is every chance that they would beat the pants off us again. Things had calmed down when Brian ambled in to watch the Dublin match, oblivious to what had gone on before. So when the Kerry folk began to shout for Tyrone, he took umbrage and told them that they should concentrate on supporting their own team.

As I drive home, the recession is on my mind. Nobody is thinking outside the box. It's time for solutions. I begin to think of ways that our beleaguered government can find new streams of tax revenue. They've nearly taxed the country to a standstill at this stage. Soon we will have to pay to get out of bed in the morning. My imagination goes to town as I head towards Kildare. Moving in the opposite direction to where I was going. That's the sort of thinking that is needed now. I ignore the obvious such as water charges and property tax. They're already coming down the line. One possibility is that people could be taxed on the amount of sleep they have each night; special machines could be sold in local supermarkets, which would measure our sleep patterns. If we had to buy them ourselves it would save the taxpayer millions. Taxing meaningless conversations would target women and farmers, freeing up supermarket aisles for people who actually wanted to shop, making it easier to get into a rural bank. Fashion styles would be another area with great potential for pulling in extra revenue. The cap and culchie tax would again hit hardest in rural areas, the idea being to hammer the same sections of society again and again until they are forced to emigrate out of sheer frustration. The likes of the Healey-Rae clan from Kerry would be a rich source of income in this case. Widening the smoking ban to outside would force smokers to leave the country to have a smoke increasing the amount taken in tax revenue at points of entry and exit. Smokers would head off for a smoke and come back a few days later. Taxing joy would be another good idea, although it probably wouldn't bring in all that much at the moment.

And then it dawns on me. We could wipe out our whole debt in one afternoon; we could tax moaning on Hill 16, a whine tax. It'd be sure to get the backing of the majority of the country. And it would probably bring in about 80 billion in a couple of hours.

Chapter Twenty-seven

Rebirth

Sunday 17 July 2005

Leinster Senior Football Championship final
Dublin versus Laois

Following an extended period of procrastination from the County Board Pillar Caffrey replaced Tommy Lyons as Dublin manager after the 2004 championship season. The familiar old name of Mick O'Dwyer resurfaced as the media played their usual guessing games. When rumours of Micko's arrival in the capital started doing the rounds, we didn't know whether to laugh or cry at the thought of a Kerry man leading the Dubs. For many, it didn't bear thinking about. The whole saga didn't exactly make Caffrey look like an inspired choice. To many supporters, Pillar was already damaged goods having played an integral role in the Lyons' regime, even taking control against Donegal when Tommy was rushed to hospital. But you only had to look back to the elevation of Pat O'Neill to realise that success can come from failure. O'Neill had been Paddy Cullen's right hand man, but once he took the reins, he was able to stamp his own authority on the role and duly delivered Sam three years later.

Like so many of Dublin's recent managers, Pillar had an uneasy relationship with the press. It was hard to blame him; they built his side up only to knock them down again when another campaign ended in disappointment. So from day one, Caffrey circled the wagons. Unusually for a member of the Garda Síochána he also saw the energy of the Hill as something he could harness. If he could get it running through the veins of his players then it could only add to their performance. During Pillar's reign, the team would march down to the Hill, chests out, intensity stretched across their faces, ready to do it for us. And the Hill would respond in kind, as the decibel level went through the roof. We loved it. We felt important. We felt wanted.

Pillar's first championship season began promisingly. Dublin looked efficient and reinvigorated as they destroyed Longford in Croke Park. The hesitancy and doubt that had symbolised the last two years was gone, we looked like a team again. Next up was Meath, the yardstick by which every Dublin manager is measured, beat the old enemy and he is instantly guaranteed a special place in our hearts. Pillar's Dublin did the business, but only just, beating a weak Meath side by 1-12 to 1-10 in a very poor game. I had to spend the next half hour trying to explain to P.O. that any win over the Royals was to be savoured, no matter how shite the game was. I had finally managed to convince Duff and P.O. that the Hill was the only place to be and we left Maurice behind as we returned to our natural habitat. It was certainly good to be back.

And that was that for me for the time being. I was off to Australia and New Zealand on honeymoon meaning that Dublin would have to brave the rest of their Leinster campaign without me. At least things had improved on the communications front, texting had taken over the world and now I could get instant updates even though I was on the other side of the planet. The only minor problem was that it would be the middle of the night in Australia when Dublin were taking on Wexford in the semi-final. So I set my alarm clock for three o'clock in the morning and switched the light off. I woke up at six o'clock, slid out of bed, grabbed my phone and headed for the bathroom. Sixteen missed messages, Maurice, Duff and my brother John all vying for my attention. I went through the messages one by one, starting at the beginning. Why ruin the suspense? I sat on the loo seat and let the story unfold. It was just as well. Dublin had started well but two Wexford goals either side of half-time left us tottering on the brink. The messages were nervous, uncertain. I prayed and clicked on Duff's fifth message. It read simply "Jason Sherlock goal." After that things began to look up. Maurice brought matters to a close: "Dublin 1-17 Wexford 2-10". I was a relieved man as I climbed back into bed beside a sleeping Jane. My mind was racing. We had dodged a bullet but a win is a win and now Dublin were back in the Leinster final for only the second time in ten years.

I was in New Zealand for the final. Laois had been deemed favourites as they had been causing a lot of damage in Leinster since their breakthrough win over Dublin in 2003. This time I was determined to wake up on time and I spent the evening pacing up and down the hotel room waiting for the time to pass. When the flood of texts started, it was clear this one was going to be tight. With only minutes remaining, it looked like Laois had it in the bag as they nosed in front by 0-13 to 0-11. But this Dublin side was made of sterner stuff, and for the second game in a row, they refused to panic. The messages came hot and fast as Collie Moran cut the lead to one, then Mossy Quinn levelled matters with a 45 before scoring the winning point from another placed ball: Dublin 0-14 Laois 0-13.

Waiting for the final whistle to go via text is even more excruciating than being at the game. Minutes later the phone rang. It was Maurice and the sound of the boys celebrating after hotfooting it up to Hedigans; one of the sweetest sounds I have ever heard. I struggled to go back to sleep as my imagination played out the final two points into the Railway End. The Hill must have been a blue heaven as the winning point sailed over the bar. Sweet dreams are made of this.

I was back on the Hill for the quarter-final against Tyrone. Another match we weren't expected to win, but anything after our Leinster title would be a bonus, so I settled in to watch with a relatively untroubled mind. Pillar's no-nonsense attitude seemed to be going down well with the players. His appointment was looking even more inspired as an undaunted Dublin tore into Tyrone. Mossy Quinn's early goal set the tone and Dublin were looking comfortable until one moment of brilliance changed the course of the game midway through the second-half. Owen Mulligan beat one Dublin player after another, a final outrageous dummy sending the Hill the wrong way, before planting an unstoppable shot past a helpless Stephen Cluxton at the Canal End. In one fell swoop, the whole mood of the afternoon changed, red and white shirts were suddenly everywhere as the Dublin players tried desperately to hold back the tide. We had given up hope by the time the ref started looking at his watch, but Dublin had one more push left in them, their reward was a slightly fortunate free in front of the Hill. In a repeat of the Leinster final, it fell to Mossy Quinn to rescue the day. We held our breaths and did what we always do in these situations: we talked to God. "Please, please don't let him miss." He didn't. The ball sailed safely over the bar and Dublin had sneaked a draw: Dublin 1-14 Tyrone 1-14.

A ticket mix-up meant that we were left standing in that area beside the Hill that used to house the Nally Stand for the replay, the one place I don't want to be. The only advantage of not being on the Hill is being able to see the colour and the excitement that it generates but you can't even see that from the Nally. So here we were in no-man's land, near a huge bank of Tyrone fans sitting at the end of the Hogan Stand. If they started winning, it wouldn't be long before we would hear all about it, and sadly, we had a lot of listening to do as Tyrone picked up where they had left off two weeks earlier. Dublin struggled to hang onto the coat tails of Mulligan and company and it looked bleak at half-time. Somehow, Dublin managed to drag themselves back into contention with five glorious unanswered second-half points. The atmosphere was building with every point until the whole ground was in a frenzy as the fifth went over. Now Dublin needed to keep the momentum going, but cutting a commanding lead point by point is hard work. What we needed was a goal. Unfortunately, the goal came at the other end. Stephen Cluxton's short kick out was intercepted by Mulligan and a player of his quality wasn't going to look such a gift horse in the mouth. Game over. Tyrone 2-18 Dublin 1-14.

But we weren't too disheartened. Pillar had every right be content. Dublin had come a long way in a short time, and they were beginning to look like the team that started the 2003 season before everything went belly-up. The two games against Tyrone would prove invaluable in bringing them on. Some of the football Dublin played in that second-half when they clawed their way back into a game that seemed lost showed a spirit and a determination that could only bode well for the future.

Dublin headed to Pearse Park in Longford to begin their 2006 campaign. Having beaten Longford easily a year earlier, no one expected anything other than an easy Dublin win. No such luck. If it hadn't been for Mark Vaughan's first-half goal, Dublin might well have been heading for the qualifiers on what turned out to be an extremely frustrating afternoon. Three weeks later, it was clear that Pillar had cracked the whip, as a very disappointing Laois were crushed in Croke Park. With Dublin momentum building Offaly were not expected to cause us too much trouble in the Leinster final. And they didn't: having weathered the traditional first-half storm, Dublin's fitness and physicality began to tell. Jason Sherlock's goal in front of an expectant Hill did the rest as Dublin ran out easy winners by 1-15 to 0-9.

The next target was a place in the All-Ireland final. That would be seen as progress. And for once the quarter-final draw was kind: Westmeath in Croker. The pundits were now chattering about Dublin needing a test before they got to meet the big boys. Not if it meant them getting beaten, I thought, I was quite happy to take the easy route. Of course, we hadn't forgotten that

Westmeath had dumped us out of Leinster two years earlier, another score to settle. Dublin were always comfortable but as ever, they tried to make it as hard for themselves as they could. The 1-12 to 0-8 final score hid a multitude of sins with sloppy, disjointed, and careless play amongst them. Do this against the likes of Kerry and we'd be gobbled up. But at least they had gotten the job done. We would have taken this result two years earlier. I was desperately trying to keep some degree of perspective at the game as one of the doomsayers standing near me trotted out his pessimistic mantra. Doctor Doom was no novice in the art of moaning, he never stopped all afternoon, howling at every misplaced pass, every fumble. The pessimism proved catching as my pal Darran was drawn in, but I felt compelled to take Doctor Doom on, to argue the case for the team. "Better not to use too much energy before the semi" I cautioned. "Westmeath are just dragging us down to their level." But nothing I said was getting through and he remained defiant: "We'll pay for this in the semis."

How right he was. Darran's perspective is always interesting as he only attends the odd game and doesn't get dragged into the general malaise that affects our thinking on the Hill. He was clearly frustrated by some of Dublin's play and so he should have been, but I was coming from a different place. After all these years of hurt, a win is a win any day of the week. Duff keeps out of the argument; meditating. Afterwards, a couple of Duff's friends join us in the pub. Mark and Rachel have been meeting up with us after the game for years. They have no great interest in football, but they still come along and put up with the analysis before we drain ourselves dry and move on to other topics. It's good to have people like that around, someone to give you a sense of perspective. I get to realise that life goes on when Dublin are playing, that a lot of the capital's population couldn't care less whether the Dubs win or lose. Rugby heads and Sunday shoppers: people with other lives. It's kind of refreshing to meet someone who lives outside the bubble; just as long as they're not from Meath.

Chapter Twenty-eight

The Walls Come Tumbling Down

Sunday 25 August 2006

All-Ireland Senior Football Championship Semi-Final
Dublin versus Mayo

And so we come to that fateful day, Sunday 25 August 2006: Mayo in the semi-final. My brother's wife Suzanne is from Mayo. She gave her ticket to her brother Peter who followed us to the Hill even though we tried to shake him off. Peter was confident, a bit too confident for my liking. Where was this coming from? Did he know something we didn't? This Mayo team was nothing special if their performances in this year's championship were anything to go by but here they were in a semi-final. Now they had nothing to lose.

As ever, the media had Dublin as hot favourites. As usual, I wasn't so sure. In 2004 Mayo had beaten a fancied Tyrone side. What if they could find another performance like that? Anything is possible against Dublin. Dublin and Croke Park have a strange affect on teams, lifting them to places they have never been. Opponents who have struggled to do the simplest things suddenly start doing the impossible. Dublin have to play well and then some more if they are to prevail, just being better never seems to be enough, we have to be five or six points better to win by one.

There are too many Mayo people in my life to contemplate defeat. This one is personal. To add to the sense of trepidation we know that the following year, Leinster and Munster will be on the same side of the draw meaning a potential semi-final against Kerry. We shouldn't really look that far ahead, but we do. On the Hill fatalism knows no bounds. It's just the way we are. It is now or never for this Dublin team.

Mayo are first out of the tunnel and instead of turning towards the Canal End they are running towards us; the psychological battle is already on. The Hill is a sea of righteous indignation as the Mayo players go through their paces. The last team to try this was Tyrone in 1984. Dublin emerge next to pepper Mayo with a barrage of footballs, incoming missiles aimed with intent, no backing down. The boys in blue gather themselves together after the obligatory photograph before marching down through the Mayo players towards Hill 16. The place is hopping. The management teams are squaring up to each other. One of the Mayo backroom staff is hit by a flying ball and collapses to the ground. The whole episode seems unnecessary and by the time the National Anthem ends, the dust seems to have settled. Peter manages to squeeze a "C'mon Mayo" into that little window of opportunity that comes at the end of the anthem. He is told in no uncertain terms to quieten down. Emotions were running high. Better if he doesn't draw attention to himself.

Just as I had feared, Mayo play like a team possessed in the early minutes to race into a four point lead. Perhaps distracted by the pre-match shenanigans, Dublin are looking hot and bothered. Mossy Quinn has the chance to settle the capital nerves but hits the post before missing two more chances. This isn't going to plan. Jason Sherlock receives a yellow card for a high challenge on Ger Brady as Dublin's frustrations begin to show. After 18 long minutes, Dublin register their first point of the afternoon when Conal Keaney fires over. Ciarán Whelan is lucky not to see yellow after a clash that injures the impressive Ronan McGarrity. Ten minutes later, the shaken McGarrity is replaced but Mayo maintain their impressive rhythm, Ger Brady hitting a fifth point for Mayo before Ray Cosgrove gets Dublin's second. It is good to see Cosgrove back in the team, he was never the same after Armagh, a one season wonder. But Pillar is doing his best to find the Ray Cosgrove of old.

Minutes later all Mayo's good work is undone, an Alan Brogan shot is parried by Mayo keeper David Clarke but the ball falls into the path of Keaney who tucks away the rebound. Dublin 1-2 Mayo 0-5.

The goal wakes Dublin from their slumber and a driving run from Shane Ryan sets up Cosgrove to give Dublin the lead for the first time. The Hill is a lot happier now but Mayo refuse to lie down and are level again when Alan Higgins points. Conal Keaney restores the Dublin lead with a fisted point but his refusal to go for goal when one-on-one with Clarke draws some exasperated sighs from the blue masses. Seconds later, Jason Sherlock is in on goal but his shot rockets off the crossbar and away to safety. As if inspired by such a narrow escape, Mayo break up field and Mortimer levels matters again.

But this time it is the Mayo faithful who are shaking their heads as Mortimer ignores Dillon who would have had an open goal. Mossy Quinn puts Dublin back into the lead with a well-struck 45 after Keaney has a goal-bound shot blocked. But Mayo hit back to lead at the break with further points by substitute Kevin O'Neill and another by Mortimer. Mortimer is playing like a man possessed. At half-time the score stands at Mayo 0-9 Dublin 1-5.

We do our best to digest everything that has happened in a topsy-turvy first-half, but 15 minutes isn't enough time to get through it all. Mayo are playing way above their normal level. There is no pattern to the game. Dublin need to take it by the scruff of the neck. Hopefully Pillar's half-time talk will do the business.

Dublin respond well with the first point of the second-half, courtesy of Alan Brogan. Then along comes Dublin's second goal, Jason Sherlock finishing off an incisive move by flicking the ball into an empty net. Suddenly Dublin are flying, attacking in waves, the Hill losing the run of itself. Brogan adds two more quick points.

Mayo boss Mickey Moran sends on the experienced David Brady to try and stem the tide. But Mossy Quinn stretches the lead from a free after he was taken down by Alan Higgins when through on goal in what could well have been the defining moment of the game; another goal then would have buried Mayo.

The Hill is buzzing now and Peter is looking thoughtful as Keaney adds another point to put us seven ahead. Some idiots even begin singing "We're going to win the Sam and now you're going to believe us" before they are drowned out by those of a more nervous disposition. Never count your chickens chaps – still a long way to go – the fatalism of the true Dub is coming out to play. All we have to do is keep this tempo up for a few more minutes and Mayo will be gone. One little push and they will be history.

But for some reason the push never comes. As points by Ger Brady and Dillon cut the lead to five we begin to worry. Then, with crushing inevitability, the Mayo goal arrives. Kevin O'Neill's superb pass finds Andy Moran who exposes Shane Ryan to turn the game upside down. The lead is suddenly down to two. Dublin are reeling. A few minutes earlier they had the game won, their suits measured for the final, but now they have to go and win it all over again.

Peter is getting louder by the minute and I fear a little for his safety as I look at the suffering faces all around me. Duff has retreated into himself. Niall is urging the lads to lift it again, clenching his fists in defiance at the natural order that has screwed us so many times in the past. My brother John is shaking his head at the sheer predictability of it all. "Please God. Not today." P.O. reckons Dublin are fucked, the game as good as over, and he says so. Not what we want to hear right now. The worst thing is that we know he's right, we're still two points to the good, but suddenly we are the ones teetering on the brink. The Hill is helpless, our lack of influence hangs heavy at times like this and there's nothing we can do. A sporting tsunami is coming our way and we're already on the higher ground, all we can do is wait for the destruction to come. And it does as Mayo push on. O'Neill cuts the gap to one, then Dillon levels, then Mortimer puts them ahead with fourteen minutes left to play. Amazingly, there is still plenty of time for us to save the day.

The next 10 minutes are pure agony as both sides fail to add to their tally. I've had better days getting teeth taken out. But with three minutes to go, the excellent Alan Brogan levels matters. The Hill breathes a huge sigh of relief. Mark Vaughan comes on in place of Quinn and goes close to giving Dublin the lead but his shot strikes the post. Then Mayo go ahead again when Ciarán McDonald scores from an almost impossible angle in front of a stunned Hill 16. But still the pain goes on as Dublin fight for their lives. Vaughan has another chance to be a hero but his 45 is punched away by Clarke from above his crossbar. Dublin win another free but again Vaughan's effort is unsuccessful. We hit the wall when the final whistle brings an end to our agony. We know that much worse is yet to come: sleepless nights, flashbacks, panic attacks, counselling. Mayo are back in another All-Ireland final and Kerry will trash them. Again. As for us, there's nothing for it but to think of what might have been.

It still feels like yesterday to me. I have never felt as forlorn after a Dublin game as I did that day: angry, sad, frustrated, hormonal, ready to explode as I wondered how the fuck that happened. This is the one match I have never managed to come to terms with. It has lived in my head for years now, tormenting me, eating away inside, like a recurring nightmare that just won't stop. I have never watched the game on television, I was there and that was enough, the minute I got home that evening, I deleted the recording.

Mayo showed incredible character and no little skill to come back when all seemed lost, but from a Dublin point of view so much of the damage that day was self-inflicted. The slow start, the failure to take our goal chances in the first-half, the failure to land the knockout punch when Mayo were there for the taking, the failure to regroup when Mayo started to regain a foothold in the game. A couple of points in those scoreless ten minutes after Mayo had regained the lead would have been enough. But time and again, Dublin players chose the wrong options. Not for the first or last time colleagues in better positions were ignored as panic set in. Fear became their only friend; Armagh in 2002 all over again.

I was just too disappointed to talk. Peter was on top of the world and Suzanne rang John to ask him to get her a Mayo flag for the final. We had to tell him to put it away in the pub. We'd have to listen to all the shite about Mayo taking the Hill in the warm up for years now.

This one hurt more than most. Returning to school the next day was even harder than usual. Growing increasingly disillusioned with school life, I thought back to the conversation I had had with Maurice on the way to Carrick-on-Shannon. The previous day's defeat didn't do anything to better my mood as I re-entered the staffroom. To make matters worse nobody cared. This was rugby country.

That day still comes back to haunt me from time to time. Country people don't like us. Everything is Dublin's fault: pot holes, the weather, the drug problem, whatever. Some hate us even more when they beat us, it upsets their natural equilibrium. I met one such creature in a Maynooth pub, a couple of hours after Dublin had made hard work of beating Westmeath in 2008. He came from Mayo but he spoke for the rest of Ireland, beyond the Pale, bitter that his team had won the never-to-be forgotten semi-final a couple of years earlier, a defeat that is tattooed across every Dublin supporters heart, the day when the lights went out on the Pillar Caffrey story. He was a big angry motherfucker frustrated that Dublin had been lucky enough to win earlier that day. He locked my scarf in his sights and let fly with a torrent of abuse. I agreed with him about the Westmeath game, hoping to defuse him before he built up a head of steam, but all to no avail, he was on a roll. I could tell he'd been waiting for this day all his life, the day he got close enough to a Dub to tell him how much he hated us. I was patient, waiting for the rant to end, but it showed no signs of abating. So I changed tact, asked him what part of Westmeath he came from, I've never been good at accents. He spit the word Mayo out as if he'd left it behind him years ago, emigration forcing him eastwards in search of a job. I spied a chink of light and before he could utter another word I brought up Mayo's semi-final heroics, asked him how happy it had made him. Bad move, it hadn't, if anything it seemed to make him even more irritable, as he spat out a fresh diatribe with a venomous blast that tells you when a man has carried something around with him for years, better out than in, but why me? Brick shithouse or not I'd had enough, attack is the best form of defence, and l let him have it, both barrels, we were the ones who had thrown the seven point lead away. What the fuck was his problem? I had more than enough stored up my locker, it was a day I haven't been able to leave behind. Now it was my turn to empty the tanks. I told him he was prejudiced and we agreed to leave it at that. He didn't say another word to me all night.

Chapter Twenty-nine

We'll Meet Again

Sunday 26 August 2007

All-Ireland Senior Football Championship Semi-Final
Dublin versus Kerry

Dublin had a lot to prove in 2007. The fallout from the Mayo debacle was fresh in our minds as we faced into a Leinster quarter-final with Meath. The regret had stayed with us all winter, never abated even for a day. As for the team, I wondered if they would have the hunger to go again. The game against Meath would tell us everything we needed to know.

Dublin and Meath no longer play each other with the same intensity these days and the games seem more about football than physical domination. I guess we are all that little bit older and that little bit more relaxed. This was the closest we have come to the blood and thunder of earlier years with another replay needed to separate the sides, with familiarity breeding the usual contempt. The first game ended in a draw – Dublin 1-11 Meath 0-14 – with Dublin always in control. But, in typically dogged fashion, Meath rescued a replay with a late point.

I wasn't about to miss this one. As I have grown older, days out in Croke Park have become more precious and I rarely miss a game now. That's one of the perks that come with greying hair, you tend to do what makes you happy rather than doing what you think other people want you to do. I had been invited to a christening in Carlow that day, and Jane told me later that the men folk had stood around the television roaring Meath on. Even a man of the cloth was heard to say how nice it was to see Dublin being beaten. I wasn't shocked, I have come to expect as much. I just took out my black book and jotted the names down. It made the win in the replay all the sweeter. The second game was exactly what Dublin needed as they proved their nerve by pulling away to win by 16 points to 12 with a late scoring burst. Coming into the final seven minutes, only a solitary point stood between the teams but unlike the previous year against Mayo, Dublin handled the pressure to record an impressive victory and a happy Hill went home for tea.

The relief that greeted Conal Keaney's crucial free brought the brooding intensity of past encounters flooding back. Despite the thaw in relations on the field, that underlying feeling of mistrust between the supporters is still there. We eye each other suspiciously on the way to the ground. I still don't buy petrol in Meath. In fact, I try not to spend any money there if I can possibly avoid it. Of course, that's become a little more difficult since my brother moved there and I have to plead guilty to frequenting the local Centra on the odd occasion as well as the local pub. I have always had a feeling that any money spent there goes to a charity that hands out footballs to the next generation so that they can learn the Meath way. I have always reckoned that the people there live by barter alone. It's that kind of place.

A week later, Dublin diced with death against a spirited Offaly side. They were still blowing hot and cold, their only consistency was their inconsistency. Laois awaited in a repeat of the 2005 Leinster final. Dublin were chasing three in a row but it was Laois who burst out of the traps to seize the initiative with an early Ross Munnelly goal, before a slightly fortuitous goal – Bryan Cullen took too many steps in the build-up but got away with it – from Mark Vaughan put us level. Straight from the kick out, Dublin struck again when Jason Sherlock and Conal Keaney combined to put Bernard Brogan in for a quick fire second Dublin goal. Nothing like two goals in quick succession to set pulses racing just like Kerry 1977 and Kildare 2002. Now we had Laois 2007 to put alongside them.

After that, Dublin remained in control to run out easy enough winners by 3-14 to 1-14 with Alan Brogan's goal the icing on the cake in a controlled performance. As we left the ground, there was a sense that this team had unfinished business, that another Delaney Cup was no longer enough. It still didn't stop us celebrating as "C'mon you boys in blue" erupted from the throats of the fans spilling out of Hill 16. The next step meant getting to an All-Ireland final, nothing else would suffice.

With Kerry lurking menacingly in the other half of the draw, there was still a lot of work to be done, not least the small matter of a quarter-final against Derry. I waited anxiously for the date to be announced. I was heading away on holiday with Jane to Dubrovnik and we were due back on the Saturday afternoon. Sunday would do just fine, but not Saturday, anything but Saturday.

So Saturday it was. And in a nice twist of fate, our plane would be touching down in Dublin airport just as the final whistle was blowing at Croke Park. I was left hoping for good news on two fronts: a soft landing and a Dublin win. I was in the hands of Duff who had promised to text me the minute the game was over.

I had made my mind up in Dubrovnik, I was leaving the school. Here I was sitting in a beautiful city having a lovely meal with my incredible wife and still something wasn't quite right. I was restless and unhappy. As I sipped my beer I tried to make sense of it all: I had a good job, long holidays and a pension but on the inside I was dying a little bit every day. I wanted to live in the now, not in the future. I felt like somebody I wasn't, doing things to please other people, acting out a role. Teaching has the ability to turn you into someone you never wanted to be. I had tried everything to find contentment and satisfaction in the job but nothing had worked. It was beginning to wear me down. This time I would go through with it. No backing down. Next summer I would be gone. I needed to let the real me out, the one that appeared on Hill 16 every summer. He was the person I wanted to be day in, day out.

The news was good; Dublin had come through by 18 points to 15. At first I thought Dublin had won a lot more comfortably as Duff's text read "Dublin by 3-18 to 15". I took this to mean Dublin had won by 12 points – 3 goals in such a big game. I was excitedly telling anyone who would listen on the plane. It was only later that I found out the margin was a measly three points but that was fine by me, more than enough.

As usual, Dublin had made hard work of putting Derry away. We were back in the semi-final courtesy of an injury-time match winning block from Barry Cahill that stopped an almost certain Paddy Bradley goal. The reigning All-Ireland champions Kerry had also made it through safely. If Dublin were going to realise their dream of making the final then they were going to have to do it the hard way.

The semi-final began as we feared it would, with a Kerry point after only 14 seconds. After three minutes Paul Galvin hits a second and a minute later he adds another. Kerry are up to their usual tricks, exploding out of the traps. But Barry Cahill's first point in championship football ignites the Dublin challenge. Conal Keaney slots over a second, before Alan Brogan levels up matters. The Hill is in dreamland when Mark Vaughan puts us ahead. Kerry's mood worsens as Darragh Ó Sé goes off and the tension is all too apparent as players from each side clash for the third time, skirmishes breaking out every few minutes. But Brian Sheehan lifts the Kingdom's spirits with a typically inspirational point, only for Dublin's latest golden boy Vaughan to restore Dublin's lead. It's nip and tuck from thereon in, at half-time Dublin are ahead by eight points to seven, the game tense and fractious.

Now that Dublin have a foothold in the game, they need a good start to the second-half to build their momentum. The Hill knows it, Kerry know it, and that's why they go and score a goal right here, right now. In front of the Hill – a dagger through our hearts – the killer blow two minutes into the second-half. Kerry know when to hurt you most. It might be the first minute or the last. They just know. A famous old GAA proverb says that 'goals win games'. It was never truer than today as Declan O'Sullivan's strike off the bottom left hand corner of Stephen Cluxton's left hand post proves to be the difference between the two sides.

Despite shipping such a body blow Dublin continue to play without the fear that has characterised so many of their displays in recent years. At one point we trail by six points, an Everest against Kerry. But we drag ourselves back point by point. With five minutes to go the gap is down to one and Darragh Ó Sé has returned in a desperate attempt to halt the Dublin advance. That was until the defining moment of the game came along and bit us on the arse with time running out. There seems to be little danger when Stephen Cluxton receives the ball in space. He has all the time in the world. For the first time that day, I was beginning to believe that if we could get the next point, Kerry's wobble might develop into a full-blown crisis. The force was with the Dublin. As Stephen looked up, he must have spotted an unmarked Ciarán Whelan doing a very convincing impression of a windmill, but inexplicably he decided to ignore one of Dublin's best players of the last ten years. Instead Dublin's goalkeeper advanced up the pitch, with the Hill suffering a collective seizure as he moved towards the 45-metre line. He had gone far enough for Kerry's liking and way too far for ours. He was now deep into no man's land without a gas mask. As the green and gold jerseys gathered round, he panicked and hoofed the ball up field into space: Anywhere but here. His kick dropped into the waiting arms of Donaghy who set in train a Kerry attack that ended up with the ball sailing over Cluxton's crossbar. Game, set and match. Luckily for Stephen, the Hill was speechless. We still loved him. Stephen was the final piece in an astonishing goalkeeping jigsaw that has seen three superb Dublin keepers spanning over forty years. Our chance was gone: Kerry 1-15 Dublin 0-16.

Our underdog status seemed to suit us as Dublin produced probably their best performance under Pillar Caffrey: full of guts, character and skill. Sadly, it wasn't good enough against an excellent Kerry team, but it was everything that the previous year's semi-final display was not. Kerry were put to the pin of their collar, so much so they enjoyed it. That's another problem with Kerry; they love a challenge. Except against the northerners that is. It's different against the Dubs though, they haven't forgotten about 1977, the Greatest Game, they never will, it still hurts. Against us they dive in head first, immerse themselves in the atmosphere. Beating the Dubs in Croke Park is a rite of passage for every Kerryman; even better than sex.

Chapter Thirty

The Day The Music Died

Saturday 16 August 2008

All-Ireland Senior Football Championship Quarter-Final
Dublin versus Tyrone

2008 was Pillar's last season in charge and my last in school. I had finally done what I had told Maurice I would do four years earlier. Louth went the way that they always do against Dublin, losing in a one-sided Leinster quarter-final. But the other side of Dublin's split personality surfaced as they struggled past a limited Westmeath side in the semi-final with only two points to spare. In contrast, the Leinster final was a demolition job as we destroyed a shell shocked Wexford by 3-23 to 0-9 and the press duly went crazy on the back of it. This was the year, they said. Sam was coming home. We had the momentum. Now all we needed was a good draw but instead we got Tyrone.

If there was one team that could rain on our parade, it was this Tyrone side. Written off by everyone except themselves, deserted by their own fans following defeat in the Ulster championship, they had been waiting in the long grass for a day like this.

The skies opened on the morning of the game and they stayed open all day, a bad omen. We had tickets for the same section from which we had watched Tyrone defeat Dublin in the 2005 quarter-final replay. Bad karma. I knew that we were finished when I saw a Tyrone supporter doing a rain dance in the middle of a puddle outside the ground crying: "They'll never beat us in this." Vivian looked as down as I have ever seen him as he headed off to his seat in the stand. We hoped against hope, but each and every one of us seemed to know what was coming down the line that day. When captain Alan Brogan went off with a hamstring problem in the first few minutes, it only seemed to add to the gloom that was settling in on the city. Dublin owned the ball in those early minutes but time and again, they failed to nail the scores that would have given them a foothold in the game. In fact it took them fully 14 minutes to register their first score. Two minutes later, Dublin missed a golden chance when a careless pass by Mossy Quinn evaded the clutches of Diarmuid Connolly with the goal at his mercy. By the twenty-fourth minute, Dublin had hit six wides and none of their forwards had scored from play.

Having survived Dublin's initial assault, Brian Dooher and Tyrone started to take control. Sean Cavanagh began to get the better of Ross McConnell and that was that, all over in the blink of an eye. Cavanagh's first goal set the ball rolling and when Joe McMahon buried another right on the stroke of half-time there was no way back. Tyrone 2-05 Dublin 1-03. The score line didn't reflect the true story of the game. After surviving our initial onslaught Tyrone were walking all over us. The only bright spot had been Conal Keaney's goal which had given us a little bit of false hope prior to Tyrone's second. But we stayed and watched, Pillar and his players deserved that much, they had given us so much to be proud of in the last four years. Davy Harte's superb strike with twenty minutes left sealed the deal and after an hour, Tyrone had stretched their lead to 14 points. It was sad that it had to end this way. As Dublin's players trooped off a chorus of "C'mon you boys in blue" rang out across the ground – a moment to remember – even in the darkest hour many of the Dublin fans had stood by their team.

Tyrone gathered in a huddle, their job done. The ground was emptying now. As I looked back at the famous old stadium at the end of another season, I got the feeling that Tyrone knew exactly where they would be come September. It turned out the Tyrone boys weren't the only ones who knew where they were headed. Ronnie Drew had called time and headed off to the great pub in the sky. Underneath the stands, another proud Dubliner was preparing to say his own goodbyes. Pillar Caffrey's last words to RTÉ said a lot about the man. They wanted to know his plans for the future. He might as well have been leaving on a jet plane for all they cared and Pillar was having none of it. He took them at their word: "I'm off to have a pint". As a parting shot it was pure class. We were off to do the same. And that was the last we heard of Pillar. Apparently, he went off on holiday the next day. I don't know if he ever came back.

Chapter Thirty-one

Rebel Hell
(The Langers' Revenge)

Sunday 15 August 2010

All-Ireland Senior Football Championship Semi-Final
Dublin versus Cork

With only a minute on the clock, Dublin are a goal to the good as Niall Corkery's long ball falls beautifully for Bernard Brogan. Dublin's man-of-the-moment leaves Ray Carey for dead before drilling the ball low to Alan Quirke's left in the Cork goal and the Hill erupts in an outpouring of joy. We think back to Colm Cooper's early goal for Kerry in 2009 and dream of an avalanche of scores to come. We're on our way now, only 69 minutes to go.

Far too early to be worrying just yet, but that's the strange thing about an early Dublin goal, it only serves to make us more anxious as we wrestle with the infinite possibilities of what fate will throw at us. Semi-finals have been our graveyard in recent times. Heartbreak Hotel. The game recovers quickly from the shock of Brogan's interruption, but Dublin remain on top and any worries about Cork's physicality prove to be unfounded as Dublin continue their recent improvement in the contact area, turning over their fair share of ball as their intensity unsettles the rebel players. The blue shirts are chasing their opposite numbers down at every opportunity, giving them no time to think. But there will come a time when their level drops, it's unavoidable in this heat, and how they cope with that when it happens will go a long way to deciding the outcome. Right now, the Dublin players are wrapped up in the present, battling for whatever tiny advantage they can gain in the opening exchanges.

The game is proving to be every bit as intense as the build-up. Matches between Dublin and Cork have a character all of their own as the capital trash takes on the home of the langer, no love lost. But somehow different to when we play Kerry or Meath, those battles are personal. Dublin and Cork eye each other up like untrustworthy strangers on either side of a city street. "What the fuck are you looking at?" It feels like they've never met before, like there is no history to them, making each game between the sides a blank canvas. "Not much." We know Cork like to see themselves as an independent republic, separate from the capital, better, more sophisticated. None of this bothers us of course because we beat them too often to care. For some reason, Dublin have held an Indian sign over Cork in recent years with some crucial semi-final wins that have paved the way to All-Ireland success. Nineteen eighty-nine was the only year that Cork managed to reverse the trend. And on two of the other three occasions, Dublin have come from nowhere to win the All-Ireland. With Kerry and Tyrone gone, the door is wide open again this year. All we have to do is beat Cork and Dublin will be in their first final since 1995, the year when a Jason Sherlock goal turned another tight semi-final against the Leesiders in Dublin's favour, the year that saw the return of Sam. Beating Cork has always been a step on the way to greater glory, never an end in itself.

There are plenty of reasons to feel optimistic as we head towards Croker. Even P.O. thinks Dublin will win and, given his success rate in the quarter-finals this can only be good news. He thinks that Cork are shite but that doesn't mean that they will be easy to beat. In Gaelic football, being shite can be a definite advantage, often it is enough to land the ultimate prize. It's a game that continues to reward qualities that have been consigned to the sands of time in other sports. Doggedness is Cork's greatest trait. That, along with their size and fitness, means they will run all day. But to what purpose? Well, to tell you the truth I'm not even sure that they know themselves at times. They also have some good players who are capable of making the difference when they can be bothered to do so, but so far, Cork have sleepwalked their way through this year's championship. Getting beaten by Kerry in Munster was a masterstroke. They have been installed as hot favourites to lift the title, more as a result of what has been going on around them than anything they have done themselves. It seems that Dublin have nothing to fear but fear itself.

Countering the feel-good factor is the news that Duff is back, today will tell us all we need to know about the sway he holds over our fortunes. But as ever, it'll be good to see him. Match days aren't the same with nobody to punch me on the back prior to the throw-in. But winning is everything and

I'm prepared to do what needs to be done. And if that means locking Duff in a darkened room for the duration, then so be it. But fair is fair, P.O. had been given the opportunity to step out of the darkness against Tyrone and today it is Duff's turn. On the plus side, I am guaranteed Sunday lunch.

Over lunch in Duff's place, his mum is nervous, Pauline knows what lies at the end of the rainbow if Dublin can win. Duff is quiet, contemplative, worrying about the jinx. "Cork will be too strong." I try my best to counter his pessimism with a show of confidence built on the feel-good factor of the last three games that surprises me. I felt the momentum on the Hill, watching on TV wouldn't have conveyed that to Duff. But Duff is having none of it as he stabs at a stubborn piece of broccoli. He states the case for Cork: six semi-finals in a row and two final defeats against Kerry, all money in the bank. They too will feel that their time has come. They have beaten Kerry too many times in recent years to be that bad a team. He rests his case as his mother plonks two bowls of ice cream down in front of us.

Croker looks magnificent with 82,225 packed in. It feels as if we have returned to the heady days of the Celtic Tiger as the teams parade. The place is rocking, anything seems possible, even a Dublin victory. Rebel red mingles with sky blue, great swathes of colour bisecting the stadium. The Hill is at fever pitch as the teams march past. Tingles run down my spine. Some of the younger members of our clan show their humorous and fun-loving side with a banner that reads 'Langers-welcome to the capital'. It is masterful in its simplicity, poking right at the heart of Cork's superiority complex.

The National Anthem brings a brief respite before our angst begins in earnest. Duff's fists pound my back. Win or lose, seventy minutes of gut-wrenching hell lies ahead. Win, and we will instantly forget the pain we went through to get there, lose and we will carry it with us forever. One minute in, all our fears are blown away: Cork look shell-shocked. But over the next few minutes they use all of their experience to hang on in there, doing what this Cork team has always done. Toughing it out, pretending it's not happening. After weeks of intrigue, the Cork captain Graham Canty has been passed fit. I have spent the last two weeks looking up Aertel every day to see if he has been ruled out. Instead Cork toyed with us: one day he was in and the next he was out. And now here he is shaking it all about. I shouldn't really have cared, better to concentrate on your own team, and if

Dublin are good enough they will beat Cork with or without Canty.

Aertel has never been a place for the faint-hearted GAA supporter. Following the course of a game on RTÉ's supposedly up-to-date information service can lead to a heart attack. One minute your team is leading by eight points to four. But the fact that they end up leading by the same score for over a half-an-hour should arouse some degree of suspicion, but no matter how hard you try, it lures you in, gives you a false sense of well being. You search for other explanations: the defences must be on top or maybe both teams are playing into the teeth of a howling gale. Not impossible in Ireland, especially in Connacht. And you look at your watch – surely time must be up? – it will become a result any second now. Then the final score flashes up but it bears no relation to what has gone before. Your team has been hammered, their four point lead washed away and they end up losing by thirteen points. The shock is sudden; a bit like watching Dublin in the flesh. You never saw it coming. And how could you be expected to? Instead of the slow drip of disappointment that a score for score update would bring, your system is hit by a power surge that would shut down the national grid. The curse of Aertel strikes again.

Not for the first time, Michael Dara MacAuley is burning down the house – he is everywhere as Dublin dominate – everywhere except the scoreboard. Cork stay in touch, even managing to hit nine first-half wides as well as creating two goal chances. No matter what Dublin do, they can't seem to create a significant gap in scoring terms. Donncha O'Connor opens the Cork account in the 3rd minute. Alan Brogan hits back with the first of his two points. Goulding replies. 1-1 to 0-2 after eight minutes. Philly McMahon hits another inspirational point from half-back to stretch the Dublin lead to three again. After 12 minutes, Stephen Cluxton is forced to save from Alan O'Connor – goal chance number one has passed Cork by – Bernard Brogan adds a point to his earlier goal but Cork refuse to go away as Daniel Goulding's free keeps them in the hunt. It's tit-for-tat until Dublin score two quick fire points, O'Gara doing well to get out in front of his man to win a free which Bernard Brogan knocks over, before his brother Alan punishes Aidan Walsh's error with another fine point. Suddenly, Dublin are in control 1-5 to 0-3. But Cork hang on as Walsh redeems himself with a crucial point. Dublin get lucky when a Michael Dara MacAuley point is allowed to stand despite the fact that he had lofted it over the bar with an open hand. Patrick

Kelly replies with one of the scores of the game after some slick interplay with John Miskella. Another great point follows at the other end as Bernard Brogan shows huge hunger to win the ball before flashing it over the bar: 1-7 to 0-5. Now it's Cork's turn to score two in a row courtesy of O'Connor and Paul Kerrigan: 1-7 to 0-7. Just before half-time, we breathe a huge sigh of relief as Kerrigan's dipping shot hits the Dublin post with Cluxton stranded. Dublin race up-field and we see O'Gara at his most effective as he seizes possession before releasing Bernard Brogan for another crucial point.

But, rather than luxuriate in the glow of a job well done, Eoghan shows us his ugly side less than a minute later. Once more, he does well to win the ball but for the second time he fails to take the opportunity to test Canty's hamstrings and fires a poor shot wide of the posts. Dublin's number 14 needs to keep it simple. Bernard Brogan seems to be telling him as much as they leave the field. At half-time Dublin lead by 1-8 to 0-7. Despite their superiority, Brogan's early goal is all Dublin have to separate the sides. Their decision to put only one man on Dublin's danger-man seems a strange one and right from the off, Ray Carey is out of his depth. Cork look lost, hanging on by a thread, devoid of ideas. It's Dublin's game to lose and that's what frightens us.

Up in the RTÉ studio, Michael Lyster starts off by wondering how Dublin aren't further ahead, Colm O'Rourke waxes lyrical about Bernard Brogan, calling his first-half display one of the best he has ever seen in Croke Park. High praise indeed from a Meath man. Lyster alludes to the sound of the fire brigade being heard in the rebel defence every time the younger Brogan gets the ball. But Pat Spillane brings us all back down to earth by telling us that it's not a great game of football. But even he has been won over by Dublin's sense of purpose and the fact that they seem to have a plan. This is good news; it's always good to have a plan. Having heaped praise on Dublin, Pat goes to town on Cork, "Innocence, naivety, stupidity, cluelessness". It's just as well he doesn't hold back. I just wasn't sure whether he was talking about today or the last 15 years in general. It gets better: "If these Cork fellas invented the satnav they'd take you all over the country: backwards, sideways and then you'd end up back where you started." It could well be that Cork are taking the scenic route in an attempt to avoid the dangers of motorway monotony. Arrive alive. No falling asleep at the wheel. The bendy back roads have the added advantage of allowing one to slip past any Dublin rush hour traffic that may be coming your way. I expect them to quietly appear at Newland's Cross as we reach a critical junction with only minutes left on the clock. For all the weeping and wailing in the studio, the rebels are still only four points adrift and they haven't even put their foot on the gas yet. Joe Brolly compares Pat Gilroy to José Mourinho – the good side of Mourinho, the coaching element – not the bullshit that goes with the Special One. "The Dublin players know what they have to do, Cork do not".

The crowd on the Hill is quiet, pensive, reflecting on missed opportunities, knowing that we should be further ahead. Most of all, it is readying itself for the Cork backlash that is sure to come. Logic says that Dublin will win. But logic rarely wins games where Dublin are concerned. I just want half-time to pass as quickly as possible, to get the whole thing over and done with. I can't enjoy this, the outcome is just too important. P.O. remains convinced, Dublin will win.

Both sides miss opportunities at the beginning of the second-half before a Ross McConnell point stretches the Dublin lead in the forty-second minute. Five ahead. Twenty-three to go. We have Cork by the throat, it's time to move in for the kill. It takes Cork thirteen minutes to register their first point and whatever solace they gain is swiftly cancelled out as O'Gara feeds Bernard Brogan for yet another impressive score: 1-10 to 0-8. I turn to Duff and whisper quietly that Cork will need a goal; no need for the gods to hear me. All we have to do is stop them raising the green flag, hold our nerve, knock over a few points and we'll be home and dry.

Cork's commander-in-chief Connor Counihan sends on Eoin Cadigan and Nicholas Murphy as he empties his bench in one last desperate throw of the dice. They may be in trouble all over the pitch but they haven't given up just yet. The fifty-second minute proves pivotal. Paul Kerrigan drives at the heart of the Dublin defence and draws a foul from Ross McConnell who is booked for his sins. Goulding points the free and Cork are hanging on – 1-10 to 0-9 – seconds later, Colm O'Neill comes on and makes an immediate impact. A long ball into Nicholas Murphy is punched away by Ross McConnell who suddenly finds himself in his old full-back role. The ball falls to O'Neill who advances towards the Dublin goal. Only McConnell stands between him and Stephen Cluxton, so Ross needs to stand tall and delay O'Neill so that Dublin can get numbers back. Instead, he lunges forward and brings him to the ground. With outstretched arms, Maurice Deegan signals a penalty. Even from the other end of the ground, it's hard to argue with the decision but that doesn't stop us. I can see Maurice sitting in the stand turning the pages of his programme, doing that Hannibal Lector thing with his mouth. It takes ages for the injured McConnell to be treated and after what seems like a lifetime, Donncha O'Connor places the ball on the spot before he shoots in off the post as Stephen Cluxton goes in the opposite direction. Goal for Cork. Exactly what we didn't want to happen. But it could have been worse; McConnell is lucky to stay on the field having just been booked and we still lead – 1-10 to 1-9 – with 15 minutes left. The whole complexion of the game has changed in the last two minutes.

Somewhat amazingly, Dublin take it on the chin, and go back up field to post two points of their own, a surprisingly swift riposte. We look knowingly at each other with quiet confidence, but nobody wants to say what we are thinking. Nearly there now. It seems that Dublin have weathered the briefest of Cork storms. It doesn't stop us screaming for Pat Gilroy to make a substitution. O'Gara looks dead on his feet, Bernard Brogan is also tiring and with Dublin's half-forwards falling back to protect the lead, our attacking threat is receding. As if to confirm our worst fears, Cork hit two points to cut the deficit to the minimum with 8 minutes left. The second from Paddy Kelly could easily have ended up in the back of the net but thankfully his shot went high and wide. Nevertheless, it was signalled as a point, making up for the Michael Dara MacAuley effort that should have been disallowed earlier. Dublin manage to get the ball back up the Cork end but fail to take advantage as both Ger Brennan and Bernard Brogan shoot wide. Brogan's effort is that of a tired man. At the third time of asking, substitute Conal Keaney nails the point that Dublin so badly need from a free that he had won himself. His impact is immediate having just replaced O'Gara. With four minutes left Dublin are two points to the good again: 1-13 to 1-11.

Time seems to taking for ever to pass, each minute an eternity and Cork keep coming. Colm O'Neill wins what appears to be a soft free when he runs into Rory O'Carroll and Donncha O'Connor does the necessary to reduce the gap to one with three minutes to go: 1-13 to 1-12. From the kick-out, another controversial decision goes the way of the Cork men as a line ball is flagged against Dublin. From the kick, the ball is fed into O'Neill who is adjudged to have been pulled back by Philly McMahon. O'Connor takes full advantage to kick Cork level. It has taken them 69 minutes to regain parity: 1-13 to 1-13. Rory O'Carroll limps off to be replaced by Denis Bastick. It's all Cork now. Dublin have lost their shape, their composure and their discipline as wave after wave of red shirts pour forward.

Again, we lose out in the battle for possession following another Cluxton kick out. Noel O'Leary races forward and is taken out by a high tackle resulting in a red card for Ross McConnell. We're down to fourteen and more importantly behind as O'Connor kicks yet another free. Cork lead for the first time as the game enters injury-time: 1-14 to 1-13. It feels like Dublin haven't been out of their half for years. The last few minutes have passed by in a blur of Cork frees. When we finally do get the ball up the other end, Conal Keaney's shot is blocked down allowing Cork to put their best move of the game together. Another point. Incredibly, they now find themselves two ahead and it is us who need a goal. But, unlike 1983, it doesn't come. Denis Bastick kicks a long free wide and Bernard Brogan's last gasp point proves to be too little too late as the final whistle heralds yet another heartbreaking semi-final defeat for Dublin. Cork 1-15 Dublin 1-14. Amazingly, Cork added four unanswered points in the final six minutes before Brogan's effort right at the death. We are lost for words.

Michael Lyster begins the post mortem by asking a simple question: "How did Dublin lose that?" Have you got all night Michael? Colm O'Rourke and Joe Brolly look as shocked as Michael sounds and it is left to Pat to pick up the pieces. No better man. We know we're not going to like what he is about to say: "In a sense, naivety, stupidity." Pat doesn't hold back. Now it's Dublin's turn to feel his wrath. I sense a level of anger and frustration amongst the panel at the manner of Dublin's defeat. Especially from Pat who has the most to lose. The thought of a Cork All-Ireland coming over the horizon with all the rebel fanfare that will entail is enough to unsettle even the most laid back of Kerry men. He bristles with an intensity that makes you wonder how he makes it through a day when there is no GAA game; weekdays must be hell in the Spillane household. Colm puts it down to indiscipline: 1-7 of Cork's total came from frees and, of course, the penalty. It all goes to show how Dublin lost their shape and discipline and with it the match. Joe feels that Cork will be as bewildered as anyone about how they won. Michael Lyster says: "The Dubs will be in shock this evening after that. Fans, team, everybody." How right he was.

I only get to watch this on TV later on – about four months later to be exact – and it seems even more surreal then. By then, Cork are All-Ireland champions.

It's clear that Cork mugged Dublin in the last five minutes. For long periods of the game, Dublin had looked the stronger, better-organised side but it all counted for nothing as we lost our cool in the sweltering heat and with it went a place in the All-Ireland final. All of Dublin's earlier intensity had left the tank empty as the Cork engine began to purr. Some of the decisions that went against Dublin may have been questionable but the players gave the referee the opportunity by throwing themselves into the tackle. All afternoon Cork had struggled to score from play, so gifting O'Connor chance after chance from the placed ball was alarmingly self-destructive to put it mildly. In the end, Cork's experience and hunger was enough to see them into the final. As we make our way down towards the exit on the Hill, it feels like we are leaving a scene of devastation. Supporters stand and stare into the distance, lost souls, silent, broken. Some are crying. Others just shake their heads and move slowly down the terrace. The dream is over; snatched from right under our noses. Stolen. The haunting Special Olympics music that the GAA play as the crowd disperses connects with the hurt in our hearts. The walk to Hedigans passes by in a daze. There's nothing we can say to Duff to make him feel any better. Niall can't resist a told you so as we pass a car full of smiling Corkmen but Duff ignores him. P.O.'s days as a soothsayer have come to an abrupt end. As if to prove that the magic is gone, he tips Kildare to beat Down the following week. For some reason, I don't feel as bad as I thought I would. This one felt different.

This Dublin team can take a lot of pride from the strides that they have taken. They have come a long way since they leaked those five goals to Meath. Boys have turned into men. This is a young team that is prepared to work hard for one another with a definite purpose. But Gilroy will know that he needs to unearth a few more players before next summer rolls around; Cork's bench proved to be difference in the end. Pat has work to do: O'Gara needs to be fine tuned. The balance between attack and defence needs to be bridged. Diarmuid Connolly needs to beg forgiveness, having exited the squad earlier in the summer. Today was a painful lesson but experience like this can't be bought. It can only be earned in the heat of battle. As we sit around the table wondering what to say, I take advantage of the awful silence to listen to far-off conversations. O'Gara is to blame. Gilroy is to blame, the usual suspects, the same old shite being talked as the beer goes to our heads. I try my best to be positive, Gilroy deserves more credit, he is a hostage of recent history, of all those failures that weren't his fault. Thankfully, Pat has the brains and the balls to understand that. He will know that we missed a great chance today. Not just in the context of the game itself but in the bigger picture too; it's not every year that Kerry and Tyrone get shot down in the quarter-finals after all. It makes today all the harder to stomach. Because so much rested on it. That's why there's anger and recrimination in the air tonight. But Pat doesn't seem to be bothered by what other people think; he knows where he is going and I get the feeling that he knows what it will take to get there.

Today was too early. Dublin are still over-reliant on the defensive side of their game but we are no longer the whipping-boys, our pride has been restored. A new full-back line is bedded in, the half-back line has undergone major redevelopment and there is a new midfield pairing. Bryan Cullen is adapting to a new role in the half-forward line. The likes of Paul Flynn and Niall Corkery will reap the benefits of a year in the sun. Alan Brogan may not have had his best year but he too is a changed man, prepared to look up now, more willing to pass. And what can we say about Bernard? Out of this world. He carried the attacking threat for most of the season. Alongside him Eoghan O'Gara remains an enigma; his unpredictable nature may well turn out to be his greatest asset, that and his strength of purpose. But he needs to learn to do the simple things well, to win the ball, to lay it off to the runners. With another All-Ireland Under-21 title in the bag, there is much room for optimism.

A lot depends on the referee – the careless and needless ones need to be eliminated – before you get excited Maurice, I'm talking about Dublin conceding unnecessary frees. Easier said than done, it's all very fine roaring about it up on the Hill, it's entirely another thing putting it into practice down on the pitch. Dublin's hunger, harrying, chasing and closing down has been a joy to behold. The startled earwigs have been consigned to history. Only to be replaced by tired ones.

I still don't know what to make of this Cork team. They are a sporting psychologists worst nightmare. The way they go about things makes no sense. It doesn't add up. They wander through matches as if they don't care only to come out on the right side of the result at the end. Apart from the times that they face Kerry in Croke Park, that is. But that's taken as a given, another unwritten rule of the qualifying system, Cork aren't allowed to beat Kerry twice in a championship season, it goes against the natural order. Cork games are beginning to take on a remarkable likeness to the tortoise and the hare; they know there is only one time when you need to be ahead. There's a bit of the Muhammad Ali rope-a-dope about them today too, soaking up our frenzied blows like we were George Foreman that night in Zaire. In contrast, Dublin landed their haymaker too early, at a time when Cork had the energy to absorb it, as well as the time to recover.

A year ago, Kerry had followed up Cooper's early goal with a series of jabs and uppercuts to a fragile Dublin chin. Brogan's goal had set the stage; this was Dublin's big chance. But in the end, Cork's bloody mindedness won the day. It's a pity really: the other three sides left in the race all had a bit of romanticism about them. Dublin with their big extended family that can be relied to turn up on a good day. Virginal white Kildare who are keeping their football pure as they wait for their big day to come. And Down: the dangerous ones with a glint in their eye, always up for a one night stand. And yet Cork are the ones most parents would choose for their daughter: reliable, steady, never getting ahead of themselves, the equivalent of a safe civil service job.

For all the regrets they must be feeling, Dublin have come a long way and when the dust settles, they will realise as much. But tonight is a night for drowning our sorrows. The crowds came flooding back to Croke Park today, in their thousands, as many finally realised the error of their ways. Now that they're back, they're laying down the law, telling us what's what. They left after Meath and came back for Cork, two defeats. They missed the in-between, missed the climb back up the rock face. But maybe they've learnt a valuable lesson. Never ever lose the faith.

Chapter Thirty-two

Capital Trash
(The Langers' Revenge II)

Sunday 24 April 2011

National Football League Division 1 Senior Football Final
Dublin versus Cork

Sunday May 1 2011 was very different from a lot of days that had gone before. It was sunny for a start, something that always makes any day stand out in Ireland. It was even more unusual than that though – in Gaelic terms a cow might as well have jumped over the moon – as Dublin went and won their first national senior title since 1995.

It wasn't as big a surprise as it might sound; things had been looking promising since winter had turned to spring. But not only did they go and win a trophy, they did it pulling away from one of giants of the game. Dublin pulling away. Unheard of, heady stuff. A sense of giddy euphoria gripped the capital as the impossible became probable and Dublin ran out deserved National League Division One champions by a massive margin of 12 points. The last 10 minutes were glorious as Dublin sailed off into the sunset on a sea of unanswered points. It will live long in my memory. Successive Dublin teams have had a habit of looking over their shoulder as the winning line comes into view, but all that changed today. The Hill could hardly believe it as they danced and sang their way to heaven as their victorious team made its way over to them with the National League trophy. At long last it was time to rejoice. There was only one problem – or not so much a problem as a peculiar conundrum – it was the hurlers who had finally seen the light.

Only a couple of weeks earlier, it had been the footballers that looked best placed to lift the elusive silverware. Despite a bright opening to their league campaign, it had looked as if a final place was beyond the hurlers following a last gasp defeat to Galway. In contrast, Pat Gilroy's men had guaranteed a place in the football decider with a late goal against Down in their penultimate game. They could rest easy as they headed to Galway for their final outing, knowing that their next game would see them take part in their first national final since 1999. The hurlers headed to Cork knowing that they needed a win to have any hope. Not only that but they also needed Waterford to beat Galway.

I was in a West Ham pub in London when the news came through. I was expecting some smart comment from my friend Ger as his team Liverpool frustrated championship chasing Arsenal on the big screen just a few yards away, but no, the text was short and to the point: "Dublin hurlers beat Cork. In National League final against Kilkenny". I quickly passed on the good news to my brother, Irish news in a London pub, the gold dust that we pass around.

I was pleased. But, of course, I gave them no chance against Kilkenny. A few weeks earlier, they had drawn with the Cats on a horrible Saturday afternoon and although a draw was a superb result it seemed to end any chance of Dublin making it through to the final. Two weeks later, the whole picture had changed. It seemed that it was up to the footballers to bring a trophy back to the capital but I wasn't too worried in the days leading up to the final. Sure, it would be nice to win a National League title and get that monkey off our back, more importantly, it would allow us to gauge how far the team had come since their defeat to Cork in the All-Ireland semi-final only nine months earlier. It would be great for the confidence of the players to go out and beat the team that ended last year's dream. Pat Gilroy had used the league to blood more new faces. In doing so, he managed to maintain the momentum that had been building for well over a year now. We have been banging in goals for fun and wins over Cork and Kerry had sent out a significant message.

The Dublin Spring series saw Croke Park opened up for Dublin's home league campaign. With the Dubs in good form too there was plenty to cheer, but still doubts remained about the defence with the squandering of a massive fourteen point lead against Mayo standing out. Thankfully Dublin pulled themselves together to win in the end. Amazingly P.O. had predicted that we would throw away the lead in the minutes before half-time. We shook our heads at his lack of faith and shook our heads even more when it came to pass. The psychic was back in our midst. Diarmiud Connolly had starred with a hat-trick against Mayo. Having left the squad of his own volition the previous summer, Connolly was back and the league had been good to him.

After a difficult start to his Dublin career he was finally beginning to look like the real deal. It said a lot that Gilroy had wanted him back at all, if he could repeat his impressive form in the championship it would take a lot of pressure off Bernard Brogan. Another success story has been the impressive form of Kevin McManamon with his bustling style bringing an aggressive edge to Dublin's forward play. In contrast, the league had proved to be a huge disappointment for Eoghan O'Gara as an eight week ban meant that he had missed out on a massive opportunity to cement a starting place in the team. All told though, Gilroy's options up front were growing. I get the feeling that he really knows what he wants now. The final pieces of the jigsaw are slipping into place. Form is everything with Pat, form in training, form in matches, drop below the standards expected and you're out.

On the morning of the game, I was beginning to realise the importance of winning. We needed to beat the likes of Cork to finally sweep away the painful memories of the previous August. It was only at Christmas that I finally felt ready to watch that awful day again, I had kept a copy of it because I felt that it was a beginning rather than an end for this team, if they could learn from those last sapping ten minutes when the game drifted inexorably away from them they would go places. Today would tell us a lot. Seven minutes in, Bernard Brogan sets up Mossy Quinn who scores the early goal that Dublin craved. Cork are their old selves: hanging in there, looking out of sorts, appearing disinterested and keeping the scoreboard ticking over. The game is coming nicely to the boil and, in the minutes before half-time, Dublin take control to lead by 1-10 to 0-10 at the break.

Dublin make a storming start to the second 35 minutes. Kevin Nolan pops a point over from 45 yards after ignoring my advice to pass the ball and 2 minutes later, Bernard Brogan bangs in a second Dublin goal to stretch the lead to 7 points. Diarmuid Connolly increases the rebel's pain with another point. It's Dublin's game to lose now.

The first signs of nerves begin to permeate the Hill as we realise that we have the game on the bag. And still I couldn't rid myself of the feeling that the next point was crucial. I get a lot of slagging about this, apparently I say it a lot. Today it looked particularly hilarious. Surely even Dublin couldn't lose this one. But nothing surprises us anymore, our fatalism knows no bounds; we carry a history of missed opportunities with us everywhere they go.

Cork hit back with three unanswered points. Suddenly we are not so sure. Why won't the bastards just give in and let us have our day in the sun. But these guys never give up. They are not All-Ireland champions for nothing. It's up to us to put them away.

Out of the corner of my eye, I notice Bernard Brogan lying on the ground in front of the Hogan Stand stretching his hamstring. Get him off. Now. Not in five minutes. Now. The last thing we need is our best player suffering a serious tear that ends up haunting his summer, but he stays on.

What happens next is as predictable as it gets, 49 minutes in a high ball is lofted over Brogan's head, the type of ball that destroys hamstrings. He turns and chases it. After only a few yards, he pulls up sharply, grasps the back of his leg and heads for the sidelines. With him go Dublin's hopes. With sixteen minutes left, Dublin remain in control but Cork refuse to give up the ghost, trailing by 2-14 to 0-15. Dublin don't score again, and with a frightening sense of déjà-vu, Cork reel off six unanswered points to take the title.

The final minutes pass by in a familiar blur as Dublin blow chance after chance. Pat empties the bench but there's nothing there. I try to be positive as the lead disappears, but P.O. is having none of it. He doesn't stop talking for the last fifteen minutes, barking out his words of doom. Inexplicably, Mossy Quinn misses a simple free to put Dublin back in front. All I could hear as he stepped up to take it was P.O: "He's going to miss this." To confound our sense of desperation Cork go straight up the field to score the winning point. The familiar sight of Dublin players running around like headless chickens had us scratching our heads again. I thought we had left all of this behind, that this was the new Dublin: Cork 0-21 Dublin 2-14.

I was feeling sick. This was only the league; we shouldn't have to do this until at least August. Feeling deflated in April is a new sensation. But each year I grow a little stronger, a little bit older, and better able to handle the end; and after a couple of days I was beginning to see the light. The whole summer still lies ahead of us. In some ways it's better that this has happened now, no room now for the early summer bullshit about All-Ireland success.

A week later I was doing a spot of parenting, spending most of the afternoon of the hurling final flicking channels, afraid to watch. The first time I switched over to check the score, Kilkenny scored a goal. In my mind, I was jinxing whatever slim chance Dublin had, so after that, I kept my distance. About 20 minutes later, I changed channels again, expecting Kilkenny to be over the hill and far away, I was shocked to find that Dublin had regained the lead and were 0-10 to 1-1 ahead. Kilkenny hadn't scored since. Better not to take any chances; I switched back to Coronation Street. Surely it was only a matter of time. Cody would tear strips off his Cats at half-time. A flurry of Kilkenny goals was sure to follow.

With this in mind, I continued to dip in and dip out of TG4's coverage. It helped that I couldn't understand a word they were saying. And it was working; each time I dared to turn over, Dublin remained ahead. The expected Kilkenny avalanche had failed to materialise as the game entered its last ten minutes. Maybe now Kilkenny would shake themselves from their slumber. But nothing happened. They were gone. Dublin saw the signs and stepped on the gas to rip Kilkenny apart. There's no other way to describe what happened in those last few minutes as Dublin started scoring points from every angle. Apparently viewing figures rocketed as people realised what was happening, just for today, our country cousins were cheering on the Dubs. At the end, Anthony Daly looked like the happiest man in Ireland. He probably was. I cried as the Dublin team lifted the trophy and I am sure I wasn't the only one. The Jacks were finally back. It just wasn't the Jacks we had expected.

Chapter Thirty-three

Rip It Up And Start Again

Sunday 5 June 2011

Leinster Senior Football Championship Quarter-Final
Dublin versus Laois

Duff is under pressure as the 2011 Championship season gets underway. The jinx theory is still our best explanation for our big match failure, and our capitulation in the National League final only seems to add to our suspicions. This is going to be a big season for Duff. He needs to be there when Dublin slay one of the big guns. But that's the least of his problems with his beloved Fianna Fáil no more; crushed in the general election. Right now, Duff has more cats than there are Fianna Fáil TDs in the capital and he's not taking it well.

As for me, I've been out of the teaching game for three years now and I am slowly beginning to find the person that I lost nineteen years ago. The Friday night before Dublin's opening encounter of the summer against Laois, I get together with my old teaching friends and colleagues. It's a little strange to be amongst them again. They have just finished another year and are now facing into three months of holidays. The lucky bastards. I always loved this day, I used to meet up with my colleagues Ciaran, Amy and Susan early in the afternoon and sit outside The Bailey off Grafton Street and watch the world go by. It had to be outside, a summer evening watching Dublin going about its business, just the four of us drinking in the realisation that we were free. Other years, we would go to O'Donoghues to mix with the eclectic crowd that frequent The Dubliners' old stomping ground, the business folk, politicians, tourists and bowsies like us who had nothing better to be doing. People who want to forget who they are and what they have become. In places like this, they can be themselves. Like the Hill, it's a place of refuge. These nights were all the more satisfying because the following Sunday brought with it Dublin's opening championship game. But as the years went by, I found myself wishing that it could be summer all the time, I would struggle towards the end of term like a Dublin team trying to defend a precious lead. I just didn't have it in me to go on with this anymore. It was finally time to listen to my heart.

So here I am, dipping my toe hesitantly back into the world of my former colleagues. The numbers who turn up for the end of term drinks has grown significantly, familiar faces mix with new ones as the younger staff throw themselves into the evening with the sort of abandon that only comes with youth. I used to be like that, full of hope and expectation as my life stretched out ahead of me, but somewhere along the line I slipped off track. I stay for most of the evening but the time comes when I know it is time to go, I say my goodbyes and head off back to the present.

The following afternoon, I wander around the city. Dublin is at its best on a Saturday afternoon: shoppers, tramps, laughing youngsters, the beautiful people on Grafton Street doing their thing. The Riptide Movement are brewing up a storm, the drummer full of love and life, in front of an angry bookshop. They tell us to keep on keeping on. In Ireland, that's what we do. It's the same on Hill 16. We never give up, year after year we keep on turning up with an air of defiance, a feeling that things will get better. Starting with a win against Laois tomorrow.

I head over to Duff's about five o'clock. He has only just arrived, having made the usual pilgrimage from Ennis. I wonder what shirt he will wear this year. It turns out he's going retro this time, taking a step back to the seventies. It's as if we have come full circle. His mother Pauline greets me with her usual refrain: "So how will the Dubs do this year Paul?" I wish I had the answer to that one. It would make it easier on all of us. After a lovely dinner, we watch the first-half of Ireland against Macedonia before heading over to see Mark and Rachel. Climbing out of Duff's car I notice a sign down the road telling people to pay some tax or other. It shows how times have changed, a couple of years ago it would have been selling us a dream, a new car, a holiday, now it's taking our money and dreams away.

I wake up with a clear head the next morning. The skies are overcast and threatening. Nothing new there then. I wonder what today will bring. Laois are an unknown quantity, they've been quiet these last few years but they are coming off the back of a promising league campaign. After 2003, Dublin won't be taking anything for granted. It's a big day for Maurice, bringing his son Matthew to his first Dublin game. He will soon be teaching Matthew his refereeing ways. Like father like son. A whole new world of refereeing incompetence will soon open up to Maurice when he goes to watch the beginning of his son's football career. We spend the morning drinking tea, reading the previews. Not surprisingly, Dublin's League final collapse against Cork hangs in the air like a bad smell.

Eventually the time comes to head down to meet Niall in Phibsborough and as usual he is late. Finally arriving, he scuttles around the corner and goes to the bank machine before buying his usual bottle of water and heading across the road to meet up with us. We are creatures of habit, doing this for so long now that we know each other's every move. Strolling towards the canal, I take in the changes since I first walked along here over twenty-eight years ago. We have progressed so much but in doing so we have lost so much of ourselves along the way. We are almost unrecognisable from the ghosts of the seventies. No longer Irish, we are now European, our heritage torn away. As a city, Dublin has lost a lot of its craziness and the characters that used to enrich the lives of those who lived there. J.P. Donleavy's *The Ginger Man* must be turning in his grave. It was always a multicultural city with culchie mixing happily with jackeen for years without any problem. The Dublin-Kerry clashes of the seventies were classics of their kind because they brought country and city into direct sporting conflict. Now, we are told we are multicultural as if it is something new.

Sixteen long years now since Dublin lifted the Sam Maguire, the noughties proved to be the first decade ever where Dublin failed to win an All-Ireland title. For years now it's been all or nothing with this Dublin team, either ripping our opponents apart or falling apart ourselves. No in-between, just like the economy. And that's where Pat Gilroy finds himself now as he tries to find a happy medium. In that respect, very little has changed in Dublin football over the last thirty years. Hope always springs eternal. At the beginning of every summer, we hope beyond hope that this will be the year. 2011 is no different to 1974. No matter what happens the Dubs will live on. The seventies have made sure of that.

As we pass our first cider drinkers, my mind drifts onto Hill 16. A lot may have changed since the seventies – Duff has a man bag – never thought I'd see the day. I thought that was my department. Maybe we'll find out what's in there this year. In about twenty minutes, I will once more find myself standing on the most hallowed piece of ground in Dublin's north side. Despite everything, the Hill has managed to stay the same. Thousands of Dubs have grown up there, where they learned about life, learned the colourful language that permeates the very core of the Dublin character. The Hill is a bit like the Hill of Tara in County Meath. Where once it stood alone and untouched it is now surrounded by progress. But it has somehow managed to retain its sense of self, its separateness from the modern world. Three rejuvenated stands look down on it as if it is an insignificant brother, but it stares back with a pride that comes from having survived all of the changes that have engulfed the Gaelic Athletic Association. It has retained its integrity as a place of worship, a place where people congregate to feel ordinary in an extraordinarily annoying world of reality and celebrity. A lot of us want no part of the modern madness. We go to places like Hill 16 to forget, to step back in time. Memories seep out of the very ground that the terrace is built on. It has undergone a couple of face-lifts over the years but has managed to retain its soul. The position of the railway helped; lessened the options when it came to redeveloping that end of the ground. For all those bitter culchies who see the Hill as a symbol of everything that is wrong with the world that would have been the ultimate victory. To them, its blue shirted hordes are coke-snorting monsters, a beer-swilling eyesore, but most of all a reminder of something they would love to be a part of. Getting rid of the Hill might well have killed the GAA. But the blazers knew better than to slice off the hand that feeds. They too have a sense of past that drives and tempers their decision making.

If the Hill had been wiped from the Croke Park canvas, the descendants of Heffo's Army would have found themselves easing into regimented rows of blue seats, with higher ticket prices bringing a fresh middle class feel to the whole experience. But the Hill has always been a meeting place for all kinds of people, a confluence of class. And now that working class Dublin is all but dead and gone, what small bit is left can be found on the Hill. It is an archaeologist's dream, a place where the present meets the past and the mists of time roll into the future. A mystical place where the names of great warriors of whose likes we may never see again stalk the land: Heffernan, Hanahoe, Keaveney, Mullins and all the heroes of the seventies: Barney Rock and Ciaran Duff, my favourite ever player Mick Holden, John O'Leary, Charlie Redmond, Jason Sherlock, Keith Barr, Dessie Farrell, Ciarán Whelan, Alan and Bernard Brogan; an endless list of gods upon who we pinned our hopes and dreams. They're with us still. They live in our hearts and our minds and when we take that walk along the canal towards our football home on a championship Sunday they are by our side.

As we wonder down Clonliffe Road I look at P.O., Duff and Niall chatting amiably about this and that as they stroll along. They all look a little older now but it is days like this that brings out the little boy in them. I lay two bets with Niall for the coming months. Both revolve around Eoghan O'Gara. Niall doesn't believe that O'Gara has what it takes. Strong and direct, he is different to anything else we have got. But the jury is still out. He needs to begin to do the right thing at the right time, lay the ball off quickly to runners, get closer to goal, run at defenders and draw fouls. He needs to be patient and we need to be patient with him. He must be able to hear the Hill sighing with frustration every time he gets the ball. It can't be easy. They weren't sighing when he banged in that goal against Tyrone. Gilroy knows. Knows something we don't. A fiver on each bet then. Niall believes that Stephen Cluxton will score more than O'Gara in the championship. His second assertion is that Eoghan will score more goals than points in this year's championship. We shake on it. It'll add another bit of excitement to a season that promises much. We show our tickets to the stewards standing at the barriers outside Hill 16, wondering where the next few months will take us.

And, as I look up at the darkening sky overhead, there are a couple of things that I know for certain. One: I'll have to buy another bloody poncho and two: I'll be there every step of the way.

Chapter Thirty-four

Ronnie's Revenge

Saturday 6 August 2011

All-Ireland Senior Football Championship Quarter-Final
Dublin versus Tyrone – for the third time in four years

The omens didn't look good. It felt like 2008 all over again – the same opponents and the same weather – and the poncho sellers were the only people looking happy as the crowd ambled towards a game that held more questions than answers for both sets of supporters.

We didn't even bat an eyelid when the draw came out. Kerry got Limerick: the team that everyone wanted. For us it was Tyrone, for the third time in four years. Mickey Harte will be looking for revenge for what happened a year ago, the day when Eoghan O'Gara's fortuitous goal turned the tide and the day when we began to believe that anything was possible. A year on we're not so sure. We should be in a better place, but the collapse against Cork in the League final was followed hot on its heels by a lacklustre Leinster campaign.

Having done just enough against Laois, Bernard Brogan's last gasp free edged out a typically feisty Kildare. Dublin were back where they wanted to be, in their sixth Leinster final in seven years. But early in the second-half against Wexford, things were not looking good until a harmless Mossy Quinn pass resulted in an unlucky own goal from Wexford full-back Graeme Molly. Minutes later a superb run and finish by James McCarthy, son of seventies hero John, completed the comeback. It didn't feel like a victory on Hill 16. Dublin's forward play had been abysmal, with Diarmuid Connolly, Eoghan O'Gara and Bernard Brogan all substituted as their manager's patience wore thin. Gilroy even saw fit to sub the sub when he took Mossy Quinn off as things went from bad to worse. In the end Dublin just about managed to get out of gaol. Bernard Brogan had one of his poorest days for a long time. It was back to the bad old days with Dublin's forwards choosing the wrong options, going it alone, looking like they'd never met each other. The withdrawal of the Dublin's star player sent out a clear message. Mess with the team philosophy and you will be hauled ashore. Bryan Cullen's acceptance speech was short and to the point. The serious business started now. We couldn't agree more and as we grumbled our way home we tried to make ourselves feel a little bit better with the thought that after this display nobody would be losing the run of themselves. First Cork and now this. It was as if Dublin were doing their very best to stay under the radar.

In contrast Tyrone seemed to finding their feet. Sean Cavanagh had looked more like his old in a second-half master class against Roscommon. All week the media had been hyping up the Tyrone renaissance and shredding our nerves in the process.

About an hour before throw-in the heavens opened. The phone rang as Duff and I squelched our way towards Croke Park. It was P.O. to say he was thinking about giving it a miss. Bad karma, he had missed 2008 for the same reason: the pouring rain. I did my best to convince him that the consequences of such a decision were too dark to contemplate. We needed him now more than ever. Even then it probably wouldn't be enough. Having missed the Wexford game Duff was back. More bad karma. If we lost today the jinx would take on a fresh impetus. The time since Dublin's last outing had stretched to five weeks, courtesy of that perennial thorn in our side Mick O'Dwyer. Wicklow's draw with Armagh had slowed up the qualifiers, leaving Dublin twiddling their thumbs for an extra week. The usual words were swilling around our head, rusty and undercooked. Everything pointed to a Tyrone win.

Before the match, we had huddled under the terrace with thousands of others as the rain beat down until it was time to take our place. We had agreed to meet Niall and P.O. on the Hill, but as we settled into our usual spot to the left of the goal there was no sign of them. Not for the first time I was glad of my poncho; Duff had been kind enough to buy me a slightly more upmarket version earlier that day.

Up in the RTÉ studio the boys were finding it hard to predict a winner, too many variables to be considered. Joe Brolly, the bubbly Derry man, plumps for Tyrone "with their pedigree, with their slightly better all round football." Joe spends most of his time laughing at Pat Spillane. He seems to find Pat funny, but annoying, rails against the perfection that the former *Sunday Game* presenter demands. Joe is a jack-in-the-box, he speaks about the game the way he played it, dancing around issues with a slight of tongue that matches his magical feet, his lyrical efficiency often leaves Pat gasping for air before he launches forth with another burst of Kerrydom.

Despite his move to daytime Pat is still fighting the world, raging against the defensive systems that now litter the game and lessen the chance of Kerry winning the All-Ireland year-after-year. However it's not all bad news as he points to the changes on the Dublin team and goes for "Dublin to edge it." Michael Dara MacAuley is back in midfield, following a compound fracture of his finger against Kildare, Barry Cahill is in on the 40 with Cian O'Sullivan in at left half-back. We have been crying out for Barry Cahill for the last few weeks.

And then Colm O'Rourke puts us back in our box. Colm is every inch the headmaster he is in everyday life, choosing his words carefully before he delivers his verdict in as slow a manner as he can muster, as if handing down a particularly harsh detention. Colm doesn't suffer fools gladly, but he too manages to see the funny side of Pat. I suppose it's hard not to. "As a fully fledged Meath man I hope Dublin win the All-Ireland and that's what I'd really like, it would be great for football, but in this case I think Tyrone are a better team and I take Tyrone to win." So that's Tyrone to win tonight and Dublin to win the All-Ireland.

All three seem to like the Dubs for different reasons. Spillane because the sight of a sky blue jersey takes him instantly back to his own glory days, which let's face it are never very far from his mind, much to the amusement of Joe. We also remind him on a yearly basis of Kerry's undoubted superiority, even if he was a member of the last Kerry team to lose a championship match to Dublin, one of the guilty few. Time and again Pat luxuriates in our latest failure, telling us that Kerry are simply better footballers. It's not like we don't know already.

Joe has the memory of Derry's famous 1993 semi-final win over the boys in blue to fall back on when the going gets tough in the here and now. Joe has a definite fondness for the Dubs and what they bring to the table, and yet we frustrate the hell out of him. He's like one of us, left scratching his head time and again trying to work out what went wrong.

Colm, because we remind him of his greatest days, we take him back to 1991. He has to fight his Meathness every time he enters the studio, he knows he should hate us but he can't. We've been too good to him. It was in the games against Dublin that O'Rourke was at his most brilliant, his ability to find time and space magnified by the intensity of the battle raging around him.

Tyrone are immediately into their stride as Mark Donnelly breaks off Rory O'Carroll to fire over the first point of the evening after only 33 seconds, just the start we didn't want. There is still no sign of P.O. or Niall. We need to settle down and get some scores on the board, to stop Tyrone building up momentum. And that's what happens a minute later when Dublin strip Tyrone of possession and Paul Flynn puts Bernard Brogan clear, but his fierce shot is superbly beaten away by the giant Paschal McConnell in the Tyrone goal. Stephen Cluxton soothes our nerves by banging over the resulting 45.

Before long Tyrone are back in front with a Sean Cavanagh free. Diarmuid Connolly scores his first point in the seventh minute, a lovely finish. The game is being played at a high tempo as both sides fight to gain the upper hand. Alan Brogan's sublime point gives Dublin the lead for the first time. After 11 minutes Connolly hits his second. Dublin's work rate is impressive with Bernard Brogan chasing and tackling with a hunger that was absent against Wexford. Kevin Nolan finds Connolly who turns and fires over another superb effort to put Dublin three points to the good. After 16 minutes he hits another beauty. Dublin are purring. We're scratching our heads as we try to come to terms with what we're seeing. Bernard Brogan takes advantage of another lovely delivery to stretch the lead to four points.

The Hill is warming to the Dublin display, shaking off its doubts with the rain. Things get even better when a bedraggled P.O. arrives. Bernard welcomes him with another point. Dublin's seventh from play. They are looking composed and assured. Qualities that have been in short supply over the last thirty years. But still we try not to get ahead of ourselves, we've been here before, no point in getting our hopes up. There's still a long way to go. But Dublin aren't listening. A lovely Bryan Cullen point puts six between the sides, before two quick fire Tyrone points bring back the doubts. The ghosts of 2008 still haunt our minds. Alan Brogan misses a good chance and our mood worsens before James McCarthy repeats his Wexford heroics with a driving run, to set up Diarmuid Connolly for another superlative point: 11-5. Another lovely move encapsulates everything that has been good about Dublin this evening. Cian O'Sullivan wins the race for possession deep in his own half and some slick inter passing releases Kevin Nolan into space, Dublin's left half-back transfers the ball to a resurgent Barry Cahill who drives through a challenge and heads for the heart of a congested Tyrone defence, his short pass into Bernard Brogan allows Dublin's number 15 to feed his brother Alan who engineers another clinical finish to stretch the Dublin lead to six. Niall texts from elsewhere on the Hill to say he will join us at half-time. I tell him to stay where he is. Better not to mess with gods.

At half-time we try to absorb what we had just seen. Even P.O. is stunned by the quality of the Dublin performance. The Hill waits quietly for the second-half to begin. We're not used to this. There was nothing to give out about, so we give out about what's to come.

Michael Lyster says what we are all thinking when he turns to Pat Spillane. "Can Dublin keep this up?" The million dollar question. Pat begins by praising the standard of play, especially the kick passing which he spends most of every summer lamenting. Having got off on a surprisingly positive note he turns his attentions to Dublin, "A younger fresher, fitter, hungrier Dublin team beating Tyrone at their own game." But – there's always 'a but' with Pat – Dublin should be further ahead. Michael puts the case for a Tyrone comeback pointing to their second-half recovery against Roscommon. Joe bats it back with disdain, "This isn't Roscommon." We'll take that as a definite compliment. Colm is expecting "the fifth cavalry to arrive in the form of Dooher and Cassidy... too late." "Talk about shutting the stable door after the horse has bolted", it's Joe again. It seems that they've forgotten that they're talking about Dublin. It's as if they've wiped our troubled past from their minds. I know we haven't.

I'm glad that I'm alone with my thoughts. Tyrone make us wait. And the more we wait the more we worry. Time is our enemy. That used to be our game; trying to psyche out the opposition. Pat Gilroy is having none of it, walking amongst his players, keeping them focussed, asking the referee where the hell Tyrone have got to. Maybe they've gone home. But no such luck as they trot out of the tunnel.

The second-half begins in a whirlwind as a rampant Dublin tear their illustrious opponents to shreds. Connolly, on his third marker of the evening, takes up where he had left off with another point. Denis Bastick adds another beauty and within three minutes the excellent Paul Flynn hits a third. The Hill is in dreamland. And still we worry; eight is a dangerous lead in Dubland. We grow even more anxious when Dublin squander three gilt-edged goal chances in a matter of minutes, with the best falling to Paul Flynn whose side footed finish slides inexplicably wide. Bernard Brogan begins the sequence by fizzing past a helpless Justin McMahon before blazing narrowly over and Alan finishes it by burning his marker before firing across the face of goal, but for once it doesn't matter. After 55 minutes Dublin lead by 0-18 to 0-10. The balance of power that had rested on a knife edge a year earlier has swung decisively in Dublin's favour.

With seven minutes to go, a final point from the excellent Alan Brogan puts us ten points clear. It might have been enough for many of the Tyrone support, but still we remained anxious. The exiting Tyrone supporters were sent on their way with a chorus of "Cheerio Cheerio" from a small minority on the Hill, who in turn were chastened by an outpouring of angst from the rest of us who had seen so many leads slip away in the most extraordinary circumstances over the years; arguments breaking out as we turned on the guilty fools. As if sensing our fear Tyrone lift themselves for one last hurrah with three unanswered points, but no matter how hard they try the goal that they need won't come. The final score: Dublin 0-22 Tyrone 0-15.

This was the evening when it all came together. Everything that Pat Gilroy had been working towards since that humiliation against Kerry: the perfect performance, decision making, execution and tactics all in perfect harmony. It was an exhibition of footballing brilliance against one of the heavyweights of the last decade. So often in the past Mickey Harte had won the tactical battle, well not this time. The naivety that had so often characterised the bad days gone, to be replaced with a realism and a focus that we thought we'd never see. Dublin had finally become a modern day team.

Joe Brolly is calling it "a mutilation", describing Dublin as "a proto-typical modern extremely well organised, fast, fit team. They've achieved a very good balance between defence and attack"– everything that had been lacking for the last sixteen years – "A massive psychological breakthrough for

Dublin in the quest for an All-Ireland." Colm O'Rourke sees it as "a humiliation" before Pat puts the boot into his colleagues by reminding them that they had tipped Tyrone, eliciting a giggling "O let me out of here" from Joe and a look towards the heavens from Colm. Our favourite Kerry man goes on to describe Dublin as "superb." He did, he said it. I listened to it four times to make sure.

In the pub we talk quietly, not knowing what to do. Nobody had seen this one coming. We were as happy as we had been for a long time but unsure of how to react. We could see the lights of home, a place in the All-Ireland for the first time in 16 years and yet we were only too aware that Donegal would present a whole new set of problems.

In the corner Niall was seriously questioning his timing, his decision to get married on the Friday before the third Sunday in September was having unexpected repercussions. Maurice had predicted as much a few months earlier. And we had all laughed at the thought of Dublin getting to the final. A couple of weeks prior to the Tyrone game I had received a text informing me of the stag party in Amsterdam. There was only one problem; it was on the same weekend as a possible Dublin All-Ireland semi-final. I mumbled an excuse as I didn't want to put a curse on our quarter-final chances. Finally I was able to tell him why I wouldn't be there. And if we won the semi-final his wedding would be on the Friday before the final, exactly seventeen years to the day that Maurice had married Margaret in the run up to the ill fated 1994 decider against Down. But for that to happen we had to beat Donegal.

Duff was looking relieved. For over the year he had carried the weight of the jinx on his shoulders. But all that was gone now; blown away in one magnificent evening.

As I headed for the first fatal piss of the night I received a text message from my brother who had watched the match in a Galway pub. "Where the hell did that performance come from?" I wasn't even sure myself.

One thing is certain. Pat Gilroy knows. But he isn't about to tell us. Pat doesn't do ego. Everything is low key, the hype being kept to a minimum. And his own absence of ego has translated itself into a cohesive squad where the team is everything, an excellent example of the effect that a wise head at the top can have with his principles and values filtering down through the system. Individuals no longer rule the roost. And behind him Mickey Whelan, David Hickey and Paddy O'Donoghue are working their magic; three former players with Hickey providing the almost compulsory link to the seventies. But it's Gilroy that is the front man, the one that takes the heat, allowing the other three to work in splendid isolation. It is clear that no stone is being left unturned in the pursuit of Sam. Dublin's training sessions are becoming the stuff of legend. Early mornings; training twice a day; getting stuck into each other in carefully staged practice matches. We are starting to sound like Kilkenny.

Chapter Thirty-five

It Took A Lost Weekend In A Hotel In Amsterdam

Sunday 28 August 2011

All-Ireland Senior Football Championship Semi-Final
Dublin versus Donegal

Donegal now stood between Dublin and a place in their first All-Ireland final in 16 years. Anything less would be seen as a step backwards. I had done a jig of joy when two late Donegal points did for Kildare in a wonderfully gripping quarter-final a few weeks earlier, more to do with the fact that I didn't want to have to face Kildare again. But now I wasn't so sure. The media were at it again, talking up the Donegal challenge. Their manager Jim McGuinness was causing bitter indignation in the world of GAA with his overly defensive tactics. Ever since their opening day victory over Antrim the knives had been out. We were told that this was even worse than puke football.

Pat Gilroy preached the gospel prior to the game: patience, composure, to have faith in what we're doing, to collectively work as a group and to stick to the game plan and if we did that we would eventually get the opportunities. So that's the Hill sorted. Now he can concentrate on the team. Pat expects a low scoring game with Dublin's substitutes playing a crucial role in eventual victory. It looks like our leader has a plan. For once I'm confident. At least we know what to expect.

It's just as well that I'm on the Hill so that I can't hear what's being said in the RTÉ studio. As another heavy bout of summer rain starts to fall Colm O'Rourke states the case for the defence. "A rainy day will be good for the backs, manna from heaven for Donegal". P.O. is too busy bemoaning the absence of his poncho which he has left at home to worry about who will benefit the most. Today I don't care about the rain, if Dublin win I don't mind getting wet. Semi-finals are all about winning. Nothing else matters.

Joe Brolly doesn't do much to lighten the mood when he describes Donegal as "remorseful, fanatical underdogs" before predicting "a cliff hanger... a battle to the bitter end". Not exactly what I had in mind but if Dublin can come out on top I'll take whatever's going. But wait, he's not finished yet. "Something the Dubs haven't been good at in the past, over the last thirty years". He's talking about battles again. Tell us about it. There's no need to remind us, we bloody well know. We're nervous enough as it is, especially with the Dublin minors struggling to put a resolute Galway away. I'm grumpy already as the pressure begins to tell. I think back to the four semi-finals we've lost since 2002 and pray that this will be different. "Please God not today." We have the better forwards and surely that will count for something. But not much it seems with the rest of the GAA fraternity readying itself for Armageddon.

Maybe Pat Spillane has some solace for us; it's not very often that we turn to Pat for a tonic. But today is like no other so needs must. It's not good news. Pat points out that Donegal have "damned good forwards" before he compares them to the Taliban. Next up is his favourite topic of conversation, the kick-pass. Last seen in Donegal a couple of years ago.

Back to Colm O'Rourke who's on the Gilroy wavelength as he preaches patience, a virtue that has been in short supply in the Dublin locker over the last thirty years. Panic: YES! Patience: NO! A good start is critical, we can't afford to get bogged down, dragged into a battle we want no part of. We have to play the game on our terms. With this in mind I've spent the last few sleepless nights visualising a flurry of early Dublin points.

As the parade begins Joe asks the question that has lived in our minds since time began. "The question remains about the Dubs..." Just the one, surely not. "Can you trust them?" to which the Hill would undoubtedly answer with a resounding no. But right now we're deep in communal prayer. Joe continues his worrying theme. "Thirty years, the last big test was '83 when they came through the All-Ireland final against Galway, since then no big test". He must have forgotten about Tyrone in '95. And what about all those wins against Meath? It seems that Mr Brolly is trying his best to educate the uninitiated as to the extent of the misery suffered by Dublin and their long suffering supporters. Fear of failure is in our DNA. He finishes by refusing to pick a winner, preferring instead to predict "a titanic battle".

Spillane thinks that "Dublin are in a better place than they were this time last year". Not if we lose we aren't Pat. Colm goes for Dublin in "a low scoring intensely fought game". Somewhat bizarrely the masochist that is in every Irish headmaster comes to the surface when he says that it might even be "enjoyable". If you like having teeth pulled that is.

Sensing that the viewing public need a breather from all this talk of gloom and doom the game begins. On the Hill we do our best to rise above our worries as we go all out to lift the team as they prepare to go to war. Maybe "Pack up your troubles" would be more in keeping with theme of the day. But we're creatures of habit. "C'MON YOU BOYS IN BLUE. C'MON YOU BOYS IN BLUE. C'MON YOU BOYS. C'MON YOU BOYS IN BLUE." Hands clap in time and reach for the sky as we give it everything we've got.

And then we go silent as Dublin take 12 minutes to register their first score, a free from the ever reliable Bernard Brogan. One point all. The younger Brogan already looks like he needs some leave from the front line such is the ferocity of the exchanges taking place in the Donegal half. Dublin can do what they want in their own territory but when they dare to cross the halfway line all hell breaks loose. It's not looking good. The Hill is agitated, already booing the Donegal tactics. Our nerves are shot as our worst nightmare threatens to come true. P.O. is talking incessantly, trying to make some sense of what's going on. It's just as well as we need whatever distraction we can get right now.

Over in Amsterdam Niall's Stag Party is taking time out. Having traipsed through the red light district they are holed up in the Molly Malone pub, hidden away on a lovely small canal close to the Central train station. His brother Art had found it on the internet before they left Ireland and now here they are. It's sunny and a number of the boys choose to stay outside and drink, except for Niall, Art, Darran and another Dub. Seats are not hard to come by. The game is being shown on the big screen. Over in the other corner sits a little telly, showing the other main event. Manchester United versus Arsenal. Just for today I don't care and neither does Niall. Today is all about Dublin. For once Arsenal will have to go it alone.

Back on the Hill our anxiety is growing as Donegal continue to hand pass the ball to death. After 24 minutes the score remains the same. It's Donegal's time wasting that is doing my head in. From the first minute they've been slowing the game down, conserving energy for the battle to come. We just can't get going. I try my best not to contemplate failure but it's beginning to creep into my thinking like an insidious disease. Losing is a real possibility now. My mind drifts back to Pat Gilroy: patience, composure and faith, as important on the Hill as down on the pitch. We can't afford to let our worries transmit themselves to the players. I'm sure the players believe in his mantra, but up here I'm not so sure.

Suddenly an avalanche of scoring erupts as one of the most painful halves in Gaelic footballing history draws to a close. After 24 minutes Ryan Bradley puts Donegal ahead with the first point from play. Dublin draw level immediately when Bernard Brogan gets in front of his men and draws a foul. He picks himself up and bangs the ball over the Donegal bar. A minute later Rory O'Carroll goes off as a result of an earlier injury. I don't even bat an eyelid. Usually losing such a pivotal player would be crucial but with Donegal's star man Michael Murphy having emigrated to midfield there wasn't much doing for Rory anyway. After 29 minutes Donegal have hand passed the ball 102 times to Dublin's paltry 38. Kevin Cassidy interrupts their flow with another point to put them ahead for the third time. On 31 minutes Colm McFadden doubles the Donegal advantage with another fine point from play, it's just as well they don't attack very often because they're actually pretty good at it when they give it a go. Four points in eleven crazy minutes. That's the good news. The bad news is that Dublin trail by two at the break. The pressure is getting to Dublin, their nervousness apparent as they resort to wayward attempts from far out, with Alan Brogan the main culprit. Just before half-time Stephen Cluxton kicks his second wide of the day. Our nerves are jangling. Donegal 0-4 Dublin 0-2. The Hill is a dark place to be right now.

In the Molly Malone the mood is lightened slightly by the arrival of a group of cosmopolitan hipsters who take their seats directly in front of the Dublin jury. Niall is taking it all in his stride. Even from so far away he can sense the anxiety on the Hill; at least he's spared our doom laden chatter. A few young Dubs trickle into the bar, followed by a Cork man who becomes increasingly frustrated by the Donegal tactics. He's not the only one. Cork man does his best to explain the intricacies of the game to a stray Dutch man. Another group of disinterested English and Dutch lads look around quizzically whenever a roar goes up in response to what is happening back in Dublin. The only other presence is a deep thinking Irish man sitting quietly at the bar, probably a Kerry man doing his homework.

Back in the world of RTÉ the plot thickens. Michael tells us that he has just met a Donegal woman in the corridor who had compared the game to watching paint dry. And that's being kind. I bet she didn't let him by all that easily. Nevertheless Joe thinks it's "fascinating" and it probably is if you're not directly affected. Michael advances the theory that Dublin knew that this was going to happen, exactly the kind of thoughts that have been filling my head for the last 35 minutes. Joe bites back with "Nothing can prepare you for this." Even the panel are showing signs of battle fatigue. Colm goes so far as to point a finger at us. "They (the Dublin team) have become completely frustrated and the Dublin crowd are frustrated which is only adding to the confidence of the Donegal team." Maybe we should all go home.

Pat is upset at the consequences for the wider game. He doesn't know whether "to laugh or cry". He goes on. "Heaven help us if this is the way the game of Gaelic football is going to go because I have seen the apocalypse there in the last 38 minutes." Michael can only utter "the horror, the horror" in response. But Pat isn't finished as he returns to the Arab world in an attempt to convey his pain. "Remember that tribe in Iraq, the Shi'ite tribe? Well, we've been watching Shi'ite football. You know, there are people who go to the Hague for war crimes, I tell you this, some of the coaches nowadays should be up for crimes against Gaelic football." It might even be funny if it wasn't so serious. "Is this the sort of game that you'd like your youngsters to aspire to play?" It's always the bloody youngsters that people worry about at times like this. What about us? Those adults whose very existence depends on the outcome of days like this. Do we not get a say? Joe keeps harping back to the word coming out of Letterkenny on Friday night that Donegal would be even more defensive than usual. They might as well have sent a big "FUCK YOU" by carrier pigeon. Dublin face a dilemma. Do they push on and leave holes at the back and fall into Donegal's trap? Colm and Pat go for the pushing on approach. Joe's not so sure.

Five minutes into the second-half Dublin do just that, but not before Donegal scare the bejaysus out of us. McFadden dummies his way past the Dublin defence and with the goal at his mercy, fires a rasping shot narrowly over Stephen Cluxton's cross bar. Still Donegal are sitting pretty, three to the good. The news from Old Trafford is equally distressing with Arsenal 3-1 down at half-time, but I am focussed on the here and now. And then the small things start to go Dublin's way. As another speculative effort from Paul Flynn drifts distressingly wide, I turn to P.O. to say that the tide is turning. Finally we're taking the game to Donegal, but we've yet to make it count where it really matters.

On 41 minutes Stephen Cluxton does just that when he nails a free to reduce the gap to 2. But any respite is short lived as McFadden kicks another great free.

The Hill is uptight as we try to lift the team. "C'MON YOU BOYS IN BLUE" rings out in defiance. It also drowns out P.O. who is undergoing a nervous breakdown. Whatever happens we need to stick together. We've been here before and we'll deal with the fallout if we have to. An angry Dub shouts out "You're not playing Tyrone now." Something I never thought I'd hear. P.O. receives a smug Kerry text "I'm really shaking in my boots watching this." The usual shite. I am finding it increasingly difficult to breathe. All I can hear is a thumping inside my head and P.O.'s voice. At one point I have to tell him to shut up.

In the Molly Malone Niall is feeling oddly calm. He's expecting Donegal to tire, that the game will open up in the last 20 minutes. He wonders if he would have thought that way on the Hill. Over there he finds himself cut off from the collective trauma that we are going through.

And then the pendulum begins to swing significantly as a high ball results in a free to Dublin which Bernard Brogan kicks to leave two between the sides. A minute later another long ball ends with a 45 which Cluxton deposits over the bar. Suddenly we are within touching distance. Donegal 0-6 Dublin 0-5 with 16 minutes left. Three minutes later Diarmuid Connolly wins another kickable free but in the pushing and shoving that ensues he pays the ultimate price. The red card seems harsh with the Hill baying for blood as the referee throws the ball in. For the next quarter of an hour injustice is our greatest ally with Dublin seizing the initiative. With 10 minutes to go Kevin McManamon, on since half-time, begins to weave his magic when he is set up by a clever flick from Bernard Brogan. He makes light of the three Donegal men bearing down on him to kick the equaliser, incredibly Dublin's first score from play. Eoghan O'Gara replaces James McCarthy as Gilroy goes for broke.

On 62 minutes a flowing move ends with O'Gara's shot being blocked but the ball falls to Bernard Brogan who fires a lovely pass across the face of goal to an unmarked Bryan Cullen and the Dublin captain shows great composure to fire Dublin into the lead for the first time. The Hill is in raptures, but we rein our sudden happiness in. Surely Donegal will go for it now? But strangely they don't. There's no plan B as Dublin dominate the closing stages. Bernard Brogan kicks another free to stretch the Dublin lead to two.

But still we fear a sting in the tail that a Donegal goal would bring. The last two minutes stretch into eternity. We try to sing the team home but we can't, we're too nervous. The added time goes up: three minutes. It might as well be three hours. We've waited for this moment for 16 years. To lose it now would be so cruel. I can hardly bear to watch as Dublin put together the move of the day. Kevin McManamon starts and almost finishes it as he bursts past two exhausted Donegal jerseys but with an insurance point at his mercy he tries to set up Michael Dara MacAuley for a goal. As Donegal come away with possession our fears grow.

In Amsterdam Niall's brother Art is losing the run of himself, talking about the final already. He's told to quieten down.

And then the whistle goes. Niall goes nuts but feels the über-cool stares of the Dutch drinkers and heads outside to let it all sink in. Dublin had reached the All-Ireland final and all because he had chosen that weekend to get married. Maurice had been right all along.

The Hill is an explosion of joy mixed with an overriding sense of relief. These are the days we live for. I turn to Duff and P.O. and we embrace. The Hill stands together for the next five minutes. *Molly Malone* and *Dublin in the Rare Auld Times* are being sung. Songs for special occasions. We're savouring the moment, doing our best to take it all in. Sixteen long years wiped away in an instant. And then we move on mass towards the exits with "C'MON YOU BOYS IN BLUE" sung with a throaty gusto that I haven't heard in years.

Niall's joy dissipates as the majority of his friends fail to understand the significance of what's just happened. Suddenly for the first time today he feels the urge to be with us, making his way down the steps of the terrace with delirious happiness swirling all around.

All of the Dublin players look absolutely knackered, none more so than Bernard Brogan who has been battered and bruised by three Donegal men all afternoon. He even seems to be looking forward to playing Kerry; he must be the first Dublin player in 34 years to do so. Anything is better after Donegal. He states as much when he says "Kerry always bring a bit of flair and a bit of football" (let's hope it's just a bit because if they bring the lot we're fucked). Pat Gilroy is his usual cool and calm self, but you can see that he's pleased. It turned out exactly as he told us it would, a point he reiterates as he makes light of a difficult afternoon. "We expected it, so we probably weren't as frustrated as the people watching were." There and then I recognised what I had known all along. We finally had a man of steel behind the steering wheel.

Pat Spillane is having none of it. "A Turkey of a game" he declares as he continues his attack on the Muslim world. Joe Brolly is still singing the praises of a "fascinating game", even if it "stank the place out." Colm O'Rourke is less forgiving. "This was the game from hell," he states, "Donegal reduced it to a shambles, in a cynical sort of way (he was certainly right there). They got what they deserved, which was nothing."

Not that we cared all that much in the end. As far as we were concerned it was a beautiful shambles. We were finally where we wanted to be. The same could not be said for Arsenal. Eight goals to two losers at Old Trafford.

It was only later in the pub that Duff revealed his secret weapon: he was wearing a pair of Baile Átha Cliath underpants. The jocks are back.

Chapter Thirty-six

The Boys Are Back In Town

Sunday 18 September 2011

All-Ireland Senior Football Championship Final
Dublin versus Kerry

Thirty-six seconds of injury time remains. The referee awards a free to Dublin. Thirty-five metres out. To the right. It's within range. The sides are level. Stephen Cluxton saunters forward with the slow jog of a condemned man, except he's nothing of the sort. He's done this before; he kicked one from exactly the same spot against Donegal. Calmly he takes the ball from Bernard Brogan and runs it through his hands. He knows it intimately, an old friend whom he has come into contact with several times during the last seventy-one minutes. Composing himself, he takes a last look at the posts before he places the ball down. Dublin's goalkeeper must feel the years of expectation on his shoulders, a city's mood resting on what happens next.

The Hill waits in prayer. One shot. One opportunity to win the All-Ireland. We've learnt the hard way. Our minds drift back to Thurles in 2001. Never the future. Always the past. Never give Kerry a second opportunity, they will make us pay.

Cluxton plants his left foot in front of the ball and takes five steps back, then two to the right. Eighty-two thousand three hundred pairs of eyes follow his every move. We expect him to pause, to look up once more, it's what the occasion demands, but there's no hesitation. Five steps forward, boot connects with ball – BANG – the ball takes off, heading into the welcoming arms of Hill 16...

Just eight minutes earlier Dublin had looked down and out. Four points down with Kerry in total control. The game had begun ominously with Darran O'Sullivan driving through the Dublin defence to set up Brian Sheehan for the first score of the game. Not for the first time that week our minds drifted back to 2009, to that Colm Cooper goal. Seventeen fucking points. Kerry are at it again, trying to put the game out of Dublin's reach in those early minutes. But this time is different. As O'Sullivan bears down on the Dublin goal blue shirted bodies throw themselves in front of him. This time Kerry have to be content with a point. No harm done.

I am sitting in the Canal End Lower with Duff. Understandably tickets have been unbelievably hard to come by. Dublin versus Kerry. City versus country. Past versus present. All year I have stood on the Hill but beggars can't be choosers. At least we're in, that's the main thing. And we have a good view of the Hill. I have been on the Hill for two of the five Dublin finals I have attended and lost both. I am better off out of it for today. High above us in the lap of the gods sit Niall and Maurice, reminiscing about the seventeen year gap between their wedding days. An even longer gap than the years since Dublin last won the All-Ireland. In the week leading up to today the roof had fallen in on Maurice, the result of a burst pipe. But he's still here hoping to see a Dublin captain lifting Sam for the first time in the flesh. Niall looks and smells a little the worse for wear; it's only two days since his wedding and the hipflask of Clavados that's passed to him at the throw in is gratefully received. P.O. is in the Cusack, talking to himself.

The day begins badly, with the Dublin minors losing out to an ecstatic Tipperary in a gripping minor final. I put it to the back of my mind. I just want the senior final to begin. I go to the loo twice, despite the fact that I have drank very little. Anything to pass the time. I know what Dublin have to do, weather the early storm, hang in there for as long as they can. If we're there with ten minutes to go then we might just be in with a chance. Kerry have cracked under the pressure before, just not against Dublin. The Kingdom have waltzed through to the final without any real pressure, whereas Dublin have spent most of the summer fighting for their lives. It's bound to stand to them if it comes down to the wire.

I get myself in trouble in the opening exchanges, blotting my copy book with a Kerry man sitting directly in front of us. I have forgotten that I'm not on the Hill. Stephen Cluxton's first kick at the posts drifts wide when Kieran Donaghy sees fit to have a word with the Dublin goalkeeper as he makes the long journey back home. Donaghy likes to get people going. Cluxton stops, looks him in the eye and responds. Pat Gilroy has noticed too. He misses nothing these days. And it's good to see Dublin's Messiah-in-waiting having a few quiet words with Kerry's number 14 from the sideline. We're in this together; there will be no backing down today. I let Donaghy know what I think of him, it's nice to get rid of the angst that has built up over the last two weeks. A Kerry man doesn't like my choice of words; his angry glance says it all. Only a few minutes gone and I'm already on a yellow.

I spend the first few minutes praying for a Dublin score, something to give us a foothold in the game. Alan Brogan duly obliges with two wonderful points to put us ahead for the first time. And then along comes the moment we had feared. Darran O'Sullivan does the initial damage with another scything run through the Dublin defence, forcing last man Michael Fitzsimons to abandon Colm Cooper. The Gooch takes full advantage to coolly fire the ball home: Kerry 1-01 Dublin 0-2. I'm too busy thinking about the present to think about the past this time. Especially with Kerry man doing a convincing impression of an angry Hannibal Lector as he screams into Duff's face. Thankfully the goal doesn't seem to rattle Dublin all that much as Barry Cahill drives through the Kerry defence to win a free that is tapped over the bar by a grateful Bernard Brogan. The scores may be coming slowly but a gripping game is sucking us in.

The drama continues when Alan Brogan fashions a great opportunity only to see his shot beaten away by Brendan Kealy in the Kerry goal. Two minutes later it's Kerry's turn to curse their luck as Donaghy's goal bound shot is brilliantly blocked by a diving Cian O'Sullivan. Dublin recover their composure to hit the next three points. The first comes from a long range free from Cluxton. No comment from Donaghy this time. The following point from Bernard Brogan puts Dublin ahead for the second time, a superb score following an angled ball from Michael Dara MacAuley. Dublin's talisman stretches the lead to two with another free, but nobody is getting carried away. And it's just as well as Kerry hit back with a tidy point from Paul Galvin, the Kingdom's *enfant terrible* having already been thrown into the mix, a sure sign that Jack O'Connor is taking the Dublin challenge seriously. Taking off a player so early in an All-Ireland final isn't a decision he would have taken lightly. Kerry are sufficiently worried to act now.

Just before half-time Brogan and Cooper trade misses, Duff is feeling the pressure. He buries his head in his hands as Bernard's attempt drifts wide. He watches every effort from then on. The half-time whistle blows with Dublin one point to the good. I am even more nervous now. We've survived the potential of an early Kerry blitz, now we're in with a real chance. I go to the loo again. The Kerry supporters are giving out about Galvin. Duff heads for a smoke.

Dublin begin the second-half with two quick fire points, one from Bernard Brogan and a lovely effort from Denis Bastick to increase the lead to three points, with all the energy and purpose that brings. I am feeling more confident. It's like the Tyrone game with Dublin quickest out of the blocks. Usually this is Kerry's territory, the time when they take control and begin to strangle the life out of their opponents.

And then the change begins. Three Dublin kick-outs, all won by Kerry, three points; it only takes five minutes. Effortlessly Kerry are level. It could have been even worse. Donaghy punching the ball over Cluxton's bar when we feared a goal was on the cards. The tide has well and truly turned. It's obvious that Jack O'Connor has done his homework on the Cluxton kick-out. Slowly but surely Dublin are being squeezed back into their shell. Kerry man is looking smug, stealing the odd glance to see how we are coping.

We need a score; anything to lift the siege but it's not forth coming. A Bernard Brogan effort drops wide of Kealy's far post, the intake of anxiety from the Hill palpable. On fifty minutes Brian Sheehan kicks Kerry into the lead: Kerry 1-6 Dublin 0-8. A minute later Kevin McManamon, Dublin's semi-final hero, replaces the injured Paul Flynn.

His impact is almost immediate. Alan Brogan finds Barry Cahill whose run sets up McManamon but his shot is blocked. But referee Joe McQuillan awards a controversial free to Dublin. Kerry argue that they didn't touch the ball on the ground. Dublin feel that it should have been a penalty. I'm just relieved that it's not as we've missed too many to go there. The last thing we need to do now is give Kerry a further shot in the arm. After all they seem to be doing just fine as it is. A free will do nicely, thank you very much. We are level again when Bernard Brogan knocks it over the bar. Despite Kerry's dominance we are hanging in there. Just about. Brian Sheehan, the Kerry number nine, continues his hot streak with a superlative 45. Two minutes later he repeats the dose when McManamon hauls down Galvin: 1-8 to 0-9. Two points behind now, Kerry's remorseless march towards fulfilling their destiny is becoming a tiresome reality.

The Dublin crowd are readying themselves for their latest disappointment, picking the meat that remains from another gut wrenching defeat. The Hill is suffocating as Kerry dictate the pace and direction of the game. I sit quietly next to Duff. We know each other so well now that we have nothing left to say.

Dublin are struggling to get their hands on the ball, Kerry's dominance at midfield continues as they add another two points courtesy of the Gooch, his second a typically languid score that gives Kerry the insurance of a four point lead: Kerry 1-10 Dublin 0-9. Eight of the last nine scores have gone to Kerry. With seven minutes left it's the same old story. I do the sums in my head. I'm proud of the Dublin players but today is a step too far. They have given it their all, lived with a great Kerry team for as long as they could, but Kerry's class and experience is telling. This Dublin side will be back, they'll learn from this. I look again at Duff, like me he seems resigned to our fate. I try not to think about afterwards, the long faces in the pub, images of Kerry's latest triumph taunting us, the Kerry folk acting as if it was just another day, business as usual.

I hardly notice Dublin winning the free. Kerry's possession game has me hypnotised. It doesn't seem to matter. Cian O'Sullivan chips the ball forward to Alan Brogan. Suddenly out of nowhere acres of space opens up. Blue shirts pouring forward in support. Two years ago Alan would have overplayed the ball, ignored the options to his right and left, but not today. No egos. He spots Kevin McManamon coming up like a steam train on his right shoulder, his pass perfect, allowing Dublin's substitute to receive the ball without breaking stride. McManamon jinks inside Kerry's Declan O'Sullivan, the man responsible for giving the ball away in midfield. He looks into the goalkeeper's eyes, steadies himself, picks his spot and lets fly.

The ball hits the back of the net, the Hill shaken by the earthquake. The whole stadium reverberating to the aftershock. I've never felt this alive in all my years, months, weeks, days, hours, minutes and seconds watching the Dubs. I punch the air again and again and scream. Scream at the top of my voice; all the angst that has built up over the last thirty years exiting my system. Duff is in danger of self-combusting. All around blue shirts are out of their seats in an orgy of pure delight. And when we are finished, Duff leans over and whispers into Kerry man's ear "GAME ON."

But still we are behind. It demonstrates the mountain we are climbing. We need a point quickly to prevent panic creeping in again. Kerry move the ball slowly across their backline, as they attempt to regain their shaken equilibrium. Instead they cough up possession when Michael Dara MacAuley throws himself between the ball and its intended target Declan O'Sullivan, who hauls the Dublin man to the ground. Free to Dublin. Alan Brogan has the ball in his hands. He'd love to be within scoring range, but it's too far out. Instead he's looking for someone to receive the ball, to take responsibility. Diarmuid Connolly answers the call, takes the ball and moves laterally across the field, buying some time as he looks for space. Dublin's number 14 spots Kevin Nolan coming up on his left. Connolly hand passes the ball. Nolan in one continuous fluid motion takes the ball high above his head, pulls it down and steps inside to score a wonderful point. Positive energy is sweeping through the Dublin crowd. People are losing it, crying, jumping for joy. The place in a frenzy. Unperturbed Kevin Nolan saunters back towards his defensive position. No high fiving, no false dawns, there's still work to be done.

The sides are level for the fifth time and suddenly this game is anybody's. Disbelief is written across the Kerry faces in the crowd. Disbelief too on the Dublin faces. Back on the field the blue shirts are everywhere. Hunting Kerry down. Possession of the ball is the difference between football life and death now. Croke Park is numbed, yet the decibel level threatens to go through the roof. I am struggling to hold it together, the first tears trickling down my face with the enormity of what is happening.

We have Kerry in our sights, even though the scores are level. Kerry hold possession for the next minute and a half, for 16 unbearable passes as they probe for an opening. But Dublin's defence is superb, forcing the Kerry shirts sideways and backwards. Finally the pressure tells as Diarmuid Connolly forces Barry John Keane to release the ball on the ground. Huge roars greet the turnover as Kevin McManamon comes away with the ball. Kerry man has his head in his hands. Duff is up out of his seat urging Dublin forward. But a promising move comes to an end when Bryan Cullen's pass to Bernard Brogan fails to find its target. It seems that Kerry are rattled as their keeper's rushed kick goes into touch. Dublin are poised.

Alan Brogan takes the sideline ball, finds a hungry Connolly who makes a probing run, asking questions of a tired Kerry defence, before turning back inside to find Michael Dara MacAuley who advances towards the Kerry goal. Bernard Brogan looks like a traffic policeman on a busy roundabout as he gestures towards his teammate. MacAuley follows Brogan's instructions perfectly, goes past him before he turns and feeds the ball back to Bernard who steps off his marker to fire his sixth point of the day, a superb effort into a delirious Hill. Craziness and blue bedlam is all around. Dublin ahead with less than two minutes left in normal time. But still I refuse to believe that Kerry are history. They'll come back. They always come back.

Kevin Nolan wins the next kick out. A tumultuous roar goes up as he feeds Kevin McManamon. The ball ends up with Alan Brogan who finds the marauding Nolan advancing deep into Kingdom territory. Nolan says everything about the Dublin attitude in those final minutes; here they are trying to win the game rather than trying not to lose it. His pass sets up MacAuley but his shot drifts wide. We know that we'll pay for it. The tension is unbearable.

Kerry move the ball purposefully up the field. Kieran Donaghy has it in the left corner. No danger, he's well marked but still I fear the worst as he connects with the ball. It spirals up into the sky, takes a breather as it hangs in the air before it drops over Stephen Cluxton's bar, an astonishing point; I am reminded of Maurice Fitzgerald's point in Semple Stadium ten years ago. Kerry man doesn't even bother to look at us. He has the dignity to know that we're hurting right now.

I can't feel my arms or my legs. It's as if the blood has stopped circulating. Everything is happening so fast. Time is almost up. The board indicates two minutes additional time to be played. It has come down to one kick out. I can't remember when Dublin last won a kick out as Stephen Cluxton sends the ball towards midfield. Crucially Ger Brennan wins possession for Dublin. I let out of a sigh of relief. At least we have the ball. And a free. Only for Brennan to undo all his good work with a silly push into the face of the obstructive Donaghy. It's the only error of judgement that Dublin have made since McManamon's goal. The referee decides to throw the ball in. What a time to take the bait.

Thankfully Dublin win possession when Eamon Fennell taps the ball down to Alan Brogan who hand-passes to McManamon, who moves the ball onto

Bryan Cullen. Dublin's captain switches the ball to Dara MacAuley who brings Diarmuid Connolly into play. Connolly, so often seen as a luxury the Dublin forward line couldn't afford, shows incredible composure to fight off Aidan O'Mahony's desperate attempts to dispossess him. It's just as well that Connolly's appeal against his sending off against Donegal worked out. He waits for his moment before he finds a marauding Kevin McManamon who draws a clumsy tackle from Barry John Keane. The referee awards a free to Dublin. Thirty-five metres out. To the right. It's within range.

Bernard Brogan grabs the ball. Is he thinking about winning it for Dublin or is he thinking about winning it with Dublin? No egos. He turns towards Stephen Cluxton and beckons him forward. Thirty-six seconds left.

Cluxton plants his left foot in front of the ball and takes five steps back, then two to the right. Eighty-two thousand three hundred pairs of eyes follow his every move. We expect him to pause, to look up once more, it's what the occasion demands, but there's no hesitation. Five steps forward, boot connects with ball – BANG – the ball takes off, heading into the welcoming arms of Hill 16...

But still I refuse to believe.

And then the Hill erupts.